Special II

Hippo Books
Scholastic Publications Limited
London

Scholastic Publications Ltd.,
10 Earlham Street, London WC2H 9RX, UK

Scholastic Inc.,
730 Broadway, New York, NY 10003, USA

Scholastic Tab Publications Ltd.,
123 Newkirk Road, Richmond Hill,
Ontario L4C 3G5, Canada

Ashton Scholastic Pty. Ltd.,
P O Box 579, Gosford, New South Wales,
Australia

Ashton Scholastic Ltd.,
165 Marua Road, Panmure, Auckland 6,
New Zealand

First published in the UK in this edition by
Scholastic Publications Ltd., 1989
First published by Scholastic Inc., USA

ISBN 0 590 76186 2

Made and printed by Cox & Wyman Ltd., Reading

Lisa Norby

Feuding

CHAPTER

"*DEE*-fense! *DEE*-fense!*"

Mary Ellen Kirkwood jabbed the air with her fist in time to the pounding rhythm of the cheer. The temperature in the overheated gym was above ninety degrees and her feet and ankles ached from doing cheer routines on the concrete apron that ran along the sidelines of the Muskeagtown High School's basketball floor.

In spite of her discomfort, she looked like the ideal cheerleader: blonde and blue-eyed with a perfect figure.

True, she hadn't particularly noticed the heat as long as it looked like a sure win for Tarenton High. Now with the Tarenton Wolves' star center, Hank Vreewright, out with an injury, 'the Wolves' game plan was starting to fall apart. And Mary Ellen felt as if she might disintegrate along with it.

As the cheer ended, Mary Ellen turned to the

3

members of the squad standing nearby. Her face still glued into a smile that could be seen all the way up to the top row of the bleachers, she wailed through her clenched teeth, "What a disaster!"

Olivia Evans and Nancy Goldstein regarded her calmly. Sometimes Mary Ellen wondered how much those two really knew about sports anyway. Fine cheerleaders they were!

The whole of Tarenton had been holding its breath, hoping that Hank's famous glass knee, the veteran of several operations last year, would last through the season. Unfortunately, those hopes had been in vain. Hank was out of commission for the foreseeable future. And within minutes of his departure, the Muskeagtown Maulers had narrowed Tarenton's lead to a scant five points. Jimmy Hilbert was put in in Hank Vreewright's place. But Jimmy wasn't Hank.

"Who *is* this Jimmy Hilbert, anyway?" Mary Ellen screeched in frustration. "I mean, I've seen him around school. But I didn't even know he *played* basketball. Where did he come from, all of a sudden?"

"Well *I* knew he played," Olivia said evenly.

"So did I." Nancy, at least, couldn't resist grinning openly at this unexpected chance to top Mary Ellen in sports savvy. "He's pretty good, they say. He can't help it that he's had to sit on the bench all season while Hank hogged the spotlight."

Mary Ellen was stunned. Only a few weeks ago, she'd had to explain to Nancy what a full court press was. Since when had *she* become such

4

an expert? And what was all this about Hank Vreewright hogging the spotlight? At six-foot-ten, he was Tarenton's only hope for state All-American.

Mary Ellen shot a supplicating glance in Angie Poletti's direction, looking for help in defending Hank's reputation. But Angie, the squad's most enthusiastic and knowledgeable basketball fan, was momentarily distracted. Mary Ellen noticed that she was trying to catch the eye of a darkly handsome young man with a mustache who happened to be sitting about twenty rows back in the section reserved for visiting Tarenton adults. Suddenly the young man noticed Angie looking his way and grinned, flashing a set of movie-star perfect teeth.

Angie's reaction to the greeting was cut short by Pres Tilford and Walt Manners, the male contingent of the squad, who were calling for the girls to join them in the "Growl, Wolves, Growl" cheer. Mary Ellen ran down the sidelines a few steps ahead of Angie and the others, relieved that someone still seemed to have some enthusiasm left.

Part of her mind, however, was occupied with the scene she had just witnessed. For all her wholesome image, Angie had dated older guys before. In fact, she was still semiofficially going out with Marc Filanno, a Tarenton grad who was now away at the state university. This new mystery man of Angie's was definitely older than Marc by a few years. Mary Ellen guessed that he might even be in his thirties. If so, no wonder

Angie hadn't mentioned him to any of her friends from school!

Out on the court, the last minute substitute, Jimmy Hilbert, was more than living up to Nancy's review of his abilities. Snatching the ball in midair, he robbed the Muskeagtown center of a sure basket and bounded downcourt toward the Tarenton basket. There, ignoring the signals of his teammates, who were calling for passes in their direction, he lobbed in a shot from outside and watched with obvious satisfaction as it circled the rim three times before dropping in for a score.

Pres hoisted Nancy onto his shoulders so that she could be seen in the far reaches of the bleachers, and Walt followed suit with Olivia. Once again, this time more hopefully, the squad launched into the growl cheer.

> "We've got the bite!
> We can't be beat!
> Come on, Wolves,
> Let's bare our teeth!"

"Grrr . . . rrr" began the response from the visiting Tarenton cheering section, the low growl gradually building into a menacing crescendo and ending in a full-voiced roar.

Mary Ellen grinned to herself at the response, recalling that when she had first proposed adding this new verse to the cheer, Olivia had objected. "But beat and teeth don't *rhyme . . .*" she'd said plaintively.

6

It had taken a ruling from coach Ardith Engborg to override Olivia's objection. "I don't think the English faculty is grading cheers for literary merit," Ardith had said. "At least, so far, none of them has suggested it."

Tonight Olivia appeared to have set aside her problems with the bad rhyme. "Are we sharp?" she bellowed through the megaphone.

"*Yesss...!*" roared the Tarenton fans.

"Then let's do it again," Olivia commanded. "Come on!"

On the court, as if on cue, Jimmy Hilbert repeated his earlier maneuver, snatching the ball from the hands of one of the Maulers and bounding downcourt for another solo basket. Mary Ellen held her breath, sure that he had committed a foul, but apparently the referee had missed the beginning of Jimmy's move. The basket counted, lifting Tarenton to a comfortable seven-point lead.

"Not exactly what I'd call team play," Walt said dryly, referring to Jimmy's single-handed scores.

"Maybe not," Pres said. "You can't argue with success, though. I'm sure I never do."

Olivia had heard that little exchange between Walt and Pres, but she'd decided to keep her opinion to herself. Later, in the section of the girls' locker room that had been assigned to the visiting cheerleaders, she hurriedly claimed one of the few private shower cubicles for herself and began to undress.

She always felt a wave of relief when the away

game facilities turned out to offer her a chance to change out of sight of the other girls. She was the only girl on the squad who hated being seen nude. She had a small, compact body that made her a dazzling gymnast.

But comparing her own body to Angie's and Mary Ellen's well-endowed figures was enough to throw her into a depression for days, if she let it.

Olivia had another reason for not wanting to change in front of them. Her secret consisted of three vertical scars running up the center of her chest, reminders of the open heart surgery she had survived as a child. Plastic surgery had made the scars much less noticeable than they once were. Her mother kept telling her fhey could hardly be seen at all, but Olivia didn't believe it. She felt sure the scars were so disfiguring that her world would end if anyone discovered their existence.

Tonight, however, she was not about to let anything happen to bring out her feelings of inferiority. Olivia had promised herself just last Sunday that she was going to change her image. And so far, her plan was working out beyond her wildest dreams. Only yesterday she had accepted a date for next Saturday's school dance with Jimmy Hilbert. And now, after warming the bench for an entire season, Jimmy had suddenly emerged as the hero of tonight's game.

Olivia could hardly believe it. Even though she'd been on the crack Tarenton cheerleading squad for months now, she still felt like an impostor most of the time. Most of the rest of the squad had earned their places, not just through skill but by being among the best-looking and most popular students at school. Olivia, though a good athlete who could do amazing routines, was not in their league socially. She had told herself for months that she didn't mind. Popularity was not really important in the long run anyway. So all the advice columns in the magazines said, anyway. From the outsider's point of view it sure looked like fun, though. And for once, Olivia was determined to grab some of that fun for herself.

"Eat your heart out, Michael," Olivia muttered under her breath. Then she did her best to ignore the wave of pain that flowed through her at the thought of Michael Baines.

In her more reflective moments, Olivia felt that she and Michael belonged together. But so far, the relationship had been more headaches than it was worth. Michael was even more competitive than she was, if that was possible, and like her, he put in long hours to achieve perfection in sports, schoolwork — anything he set his mind to. As a result, he and Olivia did not see enough of each other to make her feel they were a real couple. And when they did manage to find time to spend together, more often than not their moments alone were ruined by some pointless misunderstanding.

No more! Olivia promised herself. From now on she was going to stick with guys who knew how to enjoy themselves.

Jimmy Hilbert and Olivia Evans. . . . Olivia rehearsed the combination of names in her head, as she toweled herself dry and struggled into her clothes in the tiny cubicle next to the shower. Tall, happy-go-lucky Jimmy and petite, high-strung Olivia. The rest of the world might consider the two of them an unlikely couple, but Olivia was well on her way to convincing herself that the match was destined for success.

Before heading for the parking lot, Olivia waited outside the boys' locker room to catch Jimmy alone to deliver congratulations in private. Then she headed outside to the yellow mini-bus that was waiting to take the Tarenton cheerleaders and their gear home.

As usual, the players' bus had completely loaded and pulled out of the parking lot ahead of them. Mary Ellen and Nancy straggled out to join the rest of the cheerleaders, looking surprised that once again their fussing over makeup had kept the others waiting.

For once, even Coach Engborg didn't show any sign of impatience. "Well, squad," she said contentedly as the driver got under way, "I'm very pleased. Not only did our team win, but tonight you looked like a team yourselves. I think we are finally transforming ourselves from a bunch of individualists into a true squad."

Mary Ellen, seated a few rows behind Ardith on the other side of the aisle, looked up in surprise. Only this evening she'd been feeling like she wanted to strangle Olivia. And she still had to fight down pangs of jealousy every time she

10

looked at Nancy Goldstein, with her perfect little gold earrings and those fawn-colored calfskin boots. Fortunately, no one else on the squad seemed aware that Nancy spent more on a single pair of boots than Mary Ellen's mother earned in a week.

Mary Ellen decided that Ardith was basically right. Except for herself, the rest of the squad fit together. Mary Ellen was grateful that no one else was aware of the ringer in their midst.

Seated beside Mary Ellen, Angie Poletti was smiling and nodding in agreement with Ardith's little speech. Nancy and Olivia looked contented as well. And Walt, always a dynamo of energy, was already out of his seat, demonstrating his latest version of a Michael Jackson dance step. Ardith, usually a stickler for using seat belts, let him finish his routine before motioning him back into his seat.

Pres, from the row behind Mary Ellen and Angie, led the appreciative laughter that greeted Walt's performance.

Unknown to Mary Ellen, Pres had noticed her moodiness and found himself liking her better for it. Pres had always admired Mary Ellen's cool, blonde good looks. Physically, he and Mary Ellen were similar, his dark blond hair and blue eyes complementing hers. But he'd also assumed that they had nothing in common when it came to their personalities. Behind Mary Ellen's sweet face and baby-blue eyes, she was a bundle of ambition. Mary Ellen dreamed of leaving Tarenton behind on the day after high school graduation and going on to a successful career in the world of high fashion modeling. Her chances were good, too. Pres, for his part, wanted to leave Tarenton to *escape* success, not to find it.

Pres had been in sixth grade when he first came to realize that his family's house on the peninsula overlooking Narrow Brook Lake was known locally as the Tilford mansion. At first, he'd thought the name was a joke. By now he knew better. It wasn't just that the Tilfords lived in a fancy house and drove fancy cars. No one in Tarenton was likely to forget that the Tilford family had founded Tarenton Fabricators, the only major industry in town.

Pres did his best to forget how different his family was, but last night he'd been reminded once again that the Tilfords were hardly your average Tarenton residents. His dad had insisted that he hurry home from squad practice to make an appearance at a dinner party. On his way up the walk, he had caught a glimpse of his parents, waiting for their guests in the living room. Both of them were wearing evening clothes. And Martha the maid, who usually wore slacks and an old sweater to work in, had changed into a long-sleeved gray uniform. Pres couldn't help thinking that the gathering looked like something from a *Masterpiece Theater* production. Not what most Tarenton kids came home to — not by a long shot.

Pres had gone up the back staircase to change, and when he came back down into the foyer, his parents still didn't realize that he'd arrived home.

12

"I've put up with it long enough," he heard his mother saying as he neared the living room door.

"I wasn't aware that you'd been suffering, Felicia. It seems to me that you have a very pleasant life." Mr. Tilford was using the aggrieved tone of voice that he usually reserved for father-son arguments.

Sensing that something was up, Pres had stopped short in his tracks and eavesdropped.

"I'm not without resources," his mother had said then. "I can always live with Hildy until I get a job."

Bit by bit, Pres figured out that his parents were discussing a separation. He'd been bowled over. Not that he'd ever thought of his parents' marriage as especially ideal. But he'd always assumed that Tilfords didn't get divorces. Those kinds of things happened in *other* families. Not to people like them.

Twenty-four hours later, Pres was still in a mild state of shock. If his parents did split up, there was no way he could stay in Tarenton with his father. Without his mother to referee their arguments, he and his father would drive each other nuts in two weeks. On the other hand, he couldn't exactly imagine where he'd fit in Aunt Hildy's city apartment in St. Paul. And for that matter, his mom hadn't sounded as if she had any intention of inviting him along.

Pres enjoyed being the one in the family who kept things stirred up. But he didn't much care for being a passive pawn in his parents' quarrels.

His name hadn't even been mentioned in the conversation he'd overheard.

Pres drummed his fingers uneasily on the armrest of his seat and stared out at the snowflakes whipping past the bus window. He wondered when the other members of the squad would stop rehashing tonight's game long enough to notice that the weather had suddenly turned very nasty.

CHAPTER

2

"Hold on!" Ardith's warning rang out just in time. The bus, which had been in the middle of a winding downhill curve, suddenly slipped sideways into a skid. While the driver fought to regain control, the passengers stared ahead of them in open-mouthed helplessness. A car, that minutes earlier had been approaching them in the oncoming lane, hit another patch of ice and lurched directly into their path. By a combination of skill and sheer luck, their driver managed to guide the bus over toward the shoulder, missing the car's rear fender with only inches to spare.

"That was close," Pres said, whistling softly in relief. From his seat in the back row he'd had a good view of the face of the driver in the other car. He'd heard of people's eyes popping out in fear, but until now he'd always thought it was just a figure of speech.

15

"I thought I was going to lose that hot dog that I stuffed myself with at halftime," Angie said with a laugh.

"Don't be so gross," Nancy gasped. "And don't mention food. Not *now*. Please." The blood had drained from her face, leaving her normally tawny complexion a sickly shade of yellow.

"Please God, just let us get home safely," Mary Ellen prayed, addressing the general direction of the bus ceiling. "We'll be good from now on."

"Some of us have been good all along," Pres shot back, regaining his cool. "We don't have to bargain now."

"That's true," Olivia piped up. "But I don't see how you get the nerve to include yourself in that group, Preston Tilford the Third."

Mary Ellen heard a voice giggling loudly. It was her own. She had to give Olivia credit for her coolness. For someone who seemed like such a baby at times, Olivia always had nerves of steel when everyone else panicked.

"Cool it, everyone," Walt said. "We ought to be thanking the driver for saving our necks."

The bus driver, who so far hadn't said a word, acknowledged the round of applause led by Walt with a barely perceptible shrug. "We were lucky that time," he said. "I'm getting off at the next exit to wait for the salt spreaders. The road's a sheet of ice and I can't see a damn thing, what with the sleet coming straight at me."

"Well, that certainly instills confidence," Nancy

16

whispered in a voice that came out louder than she'd meant it to.

"Nonsense, Nancy," said Coach Engborg, reaching back to give Nancy a comforting pat on the shoulder. "You just haven't lived in the north country long enough. Winter storms are a way of life."

"That's why Ardith has the garage order a spare set of fenders for her car every October," Walt added. "Just to be prepared." Walt knew that the coach didn't always appreciate teasing, but he couldn't resist. Ardith Engborg was not really a bad driver, but her house had the steepest driveway in Tarenton and her fender-benders were legendary.

"What would you know about the problems of winter drivers?" Mrs. Engborg shot back, only half jokingly. "*You* have four-wheel drive, I notice."

Walt grinned in mock apology and headed for the front of the bus, to act as lookout for the driver. The others stared out the windows in silence. They reached the next highway exit and the bus picked its way around the cars stalled on the upgrade around the exit ramp, and began to proceed slowly but steadily toward a neon sign that blinked fitfully in the distance.

"Whadya know!" Walt crowed from his spot up front. "Great minds think alike."

Peering up ahead, the others saw that the Tarenton team bus had obviously just arrived in the same diner parking lot.

The manager had to unlock the door of the diner to admit the passengers from both buses. "You're welcome to wait out the storm here," he said, "but I can't serve you anything except sodas and coffee. I sent my help home early to avoid the bad roads."

"That will be just fine," Ardith agreed quickly. "We don't want to put you to any trouble."

The answering groan of disappointment from the players suggested that the sentiment wasn't unanimous.

"Personally, I could eat a horse," one of the guys said. "I always get this starved feeling after we win. But never mind. I'll starve quietly."

The diner's manager studied the size of the boy who had made this speech, and began to reconsider his terms. No doubt he was thinking of the check a six-foot-four teenager could run up in the course of satisfying a major hunger. "Okay," he relented, "I'll open the grill. But I could use an extra pair of hands helping me. There'll be all you can eat free for the first volunteer."

"I'm your man!" Jimmy Hilbert bounded over the counter before anyone else could answer.

As the others distributed themselves around the various booths and tables, Walt and one of the team managers began to organize the orders. Within minutes they had served cold drinks, hot chocolate, and coffee all around, and the first hamburgers were beginning to emerge from the kitchen.

For forty minutes or so, an impromptu party spirit reigned. Then the food was finished, and

18

everyone began to look restless. Finally, the driver of the team bus got up from his corner table and paid his check. "Looks like the visibility has improved," he said. "I think we can make it now with no problems."

"I'm staying put," the cheerleaders' driver announced. "One near miss a night is enough. We wait here until the road crews come through."

As the players prepared to reboard their bus, Nancy Goldstein looked at Ardith pleadingly. "Why can't we go with the team?" she suggested. "There would be plenty of room if we moved some of their equipment into our bus. Then our driver could bring the gear home whenever he's ready to start."

Ardith shook her head. "I don't think so. Our driver has gotten us here safely so far. I trust his judgment. We'll wait it out."

Half an hour later, the highway was still unplowed and even Walt Manners was beginning to show signs of impatience to get home. Angie, finishing off her third cup of hot chocolate, surveyed her companions and wondered if now would be a good time to break the news she'd been saving for tomorrow's practice. At this rate, the practice would be canceled anyway.

Angie tapped her spoon against the side of her empty cup. "You're probably all wondering why I brought you here," she joked. "But I've got some great news. Did any of you notice that cute guy who was sitting in the reserved seat visitors' section?"

"I saw him wave at you," Mary Ellen said.

"Wellll . . ." Angie announced, "he's my cousin. Thomas Gaetano!"

Mary Ellen looked disappointed, the others merely confused.

"Another deep, dark secret from Angie Poletti's sinful past," Walt said sarcastically. "You've got a million of them, Ange. But so what?"

Angie was undeterred. She never had been good at wording things, and had long ago learned to accept her role as the target of self-appointed wits like Walt.

"That part wasn't the news," she said, ignoring Walt's comment. "The news is, Tom's a great guy. And starting Monday he'll be teaching at Tarenton High! He's taking over Mrs. LeMoyne's English classes!"

"This *is* news, even to me," Ardith said. "What's happened to Gloria LeMoyne?"

"Oh, her husband's company decided to transfer him to the Philippines," Angie explained. "She knew for months that it might be coming, but couldn't say anything until the official decision came through."

"No wonder she always seemed distracted," Nancy said. "She never gave homework assignments."

"That," added Walt, "is why I'm not exactly ecstatic about Angie's secret. LeMoyne also gave me an A last semester. Finally, Tarenton gets a teacher who recognizes my natural flair and brilliance, and they have to ship her out of the country."

"An A!" Nancy howled in outrage. "But you never do any work. Mrs. LeMoyne just favors guys, I guess. Especially ones whose parents have a daily TV show."

Mary Ellen was feeling vaguely guilty that she'd been so quick to think that Angie was dating a man in his thirties on the sly, and she wanted to make amends. "Angie's cousin is a real dreamboat," she assured the rest of the group. "He looks nice, too. I wouldn't mind being in his class."

"Don't let that statement get back to Patrick's ears," Walt teased.

"Patrick!" Mary Ellen looked cross. "What does he have to do with it?"

"Everyone knows you and Pat are always lusting after each other," Walt said innocently.

"Patrick is a jerk!" Mary Ellen snapped. "And you can all tell him I said so for all I care."

If she hadn't felt so tired, Mary Ellen might have reacted less strongly. It annoyed her, though, that her real feelings for Patrick were common knowledge around school. She certainly hadn't mentioned them to anyone, so it had to be Patrick who'd been discussing her. That was part of the problem with him. Every time she let him kiss her, which she wanted to do constantly, he acted as if she was practically ready to get engaged.

Mary Ellen wasn't ready for a serious involvement with Patrick Henley. For one thing, he wasn't in the league she wanted to play in. For another, she found him all too attractive in spite of his deficiencies. She could well imagine that if she ever did give in and decide to become Patrick's girl, she'd be hooked for life. Then what would become of her dream of going off to New York in search of fame and fortune?

"Pres here is more my style," Mary Ellen added flirtatiously. "Tall, blond, and rich. He just hasn't figured out yet that we're right for each other."

Nancy Goldstein couldn't help smiling in admiration of Mary Ellen's nerve. Mary Ellen was so beautiful that she was confident that she could get away with saying just about anything. If there were any objections, she'd easily managed to pass off her remarks as so much kidding around.

A combination of tiredness and the exhilaration of tonight's events was beginning to wear away Nancy's own natural reserve. She'd been impressed by Ardith's speech on the bus, and the squad's being all together like this. Sharing a minor emergency only increased her feeling that Ardith had been right — a real team spirit was growing. These kids weren't just fellow cheerleaders, they were her friends.

"I have a confession to make, too," Nancy heard herself blurt out. "I'm in love."

The others looked at her in astonishment. Obviously, she'd sounded more serious than she'd intended.

"I didn't really mean *in love*," Nancy corrected herself grinning. "Just carrying a heavy yen."

"You're worse at giving news than I am," Angie said. "You can't stop there. Tell us who."

"Never mind," Nancy said, retreating. She was sure now that she'd made a mistake to speak up.

It wasn't even true. She wasn't in love. Her boyfriend Alex had gone home to England just weeks ago. She'd only said what she did because she'd been feeling flattered and happy that another guy had asked her out so soon, and because she'd wanted to feel more a part of the group.

"Come on, Nance. You can't cop out that easily. Now that you've gone this far, you've got to tell us the guy's name," Walt demanded.

Nancy felt trapped. "Okay. Okay. Who was the surprise savior of tonight's game?"

"Jimmy Hilbert?" Angie, Walt, and Mary Ellen asked in chorus.

"Does he know?" Olivia asked in astonishment. "I mean, have you gone out with him?"

"Of course," Nancy said. "I went out with him just two days ago."

Two days ago! Olivia couldn't believe it. That was the same day Jimmy had called to invite her to the dance! She'd known Jimmy had a reputation for playing the field, but until now she'd managed to convince herself that his interest in her was different. Irrationally, she focused her jealous anger on Nancy. "One date is *certainly* undying love," she snapped. "Just remember to invite me to your wedding."

"What about you, Olivia?" Walt challenged. "As long as we're playing true confessions, what about you and Michael?"

Alone in the group, Walt Manners seemed oblivious to the fact that not everyone was enjoying the rap session as much as he was. Walt wasn't cruel, but he loved gossip and loved keeping

23

things stirred up. To him, it was a game.

Olivia had no desire to talk about Michael, though. Thinking fast, she decided to say something that would deflect the question. "Forget me, guys," she lied. "My only secret is that my love life is nonexistent. A big zero."

"That's funny," Walt said, not unkindly. "I was sure that you and Michael were a case of true love." Then he gave an exaggerated shrug. "What's wrong with the youth of today, anyway?" he asked in mock agony. "What happened to the good old days when true love lasted forever?"

Pres's hand slammed down onto the formica table top so hard that the sugar server flew up into the air and went flying off into Angie's lap. "I've had just about enough of you!" he yelled at Walt.

Walt looked bewildered. "What did I do?" he asked the group in general.

"For starters," Pres answered, "I notice that for a guy who's eager to hear everybody else's personal business, you never tell us anything about your private affairs."

"Honestly," Walt protested with a grin, "I haven't had any private affairs in *weeks*. If I do, you'll be the first to know."

But Pres was in no mood for humor. "In that case, you've got no right to stick your nose into other people's business. So put a lid on it."

Pres pushed his chair away from the table and stood up. His face was flushed with anger.

Angie had gone to school with Pres since the elementary grades and couldn't remember ever seeing him lose his cool this way. "Are you all right, Pres?" she asked.

"Do I look all right?" Pres groused. "It's just that I've had it with this dumb talk about romance. True love is a farce. The whole world is filled with people busy looking out for number one. The sooner you all wake up and realize that, the better off you'll be."

Having said his piece, Pres turned his back on the group and stormed out of the diner to wait in the unheated mini-bus.

Ardith, who had been on the far side of the room chatting with the bus driver, saw Pres's dramatic departure and approached the table. "What's going on here?"

"Who knows?" Mary Ellen answered on behalf of everyone. "We're just as confused as you are."

Ardith sighed. That's what she got for opening her big mouth to make a speech on friendship and togetherness. When would she ever learn?

CHAPTER

"Did you notice those cute little dimples that pop out every time he smiles?" one of the freshman girls asked.

"Did I ever!" her friend exclaimed. "And what about his teeth? They're gorgeous. He's definitely the handsomest teacher Tarenton High ever had. Maybe the handsomest guy in the world, period."

The two freshmen went giggling out of the girls' bathroom, leaving Vanessa Barlow to stew in her own curiosity. "I can't imagine who they're talking about," she said slowly. "Certainly not Mr. McGoughey. Not unless standards have changed since I was a freshman."

Cindy Hartman interrupted her application of mascara to give Vanessa a sideways glance. Was it possible that she knew something about school business that Vanessa didn't? "They're probably talking about the new English teacher, the one who replaced Mrs. LeMoyne."

"Oh. Him." Vanessa recovered in time to pretend to know what Cindy was talking about. Silently, she berated her father for not bothering to keep her informed of goings-on at school. What was the point of being the daughter of Tarenton's superintendent of schools if you were the last to know about important developments, like the arrival of a new teacher in midyear?

Cindy put away her mascara wand and studied her face critically in the mirror. She couldn't decide whether Vanessa was putting her on or not. "Then you know about Gaetano?" she pressed.

"Sure. I just forgot." Vanessa threw back her head and started brushing her hair vigorously.

"Then you know who's cousin he is?" Cindy went on.

Vanessa stared at Cindy.

To describe Cindy as Vanessa's friend would be too strong a word. Vanessa Barlow didn't have friends. She had sidekicks. It was understood, by Vanessa at least, that anyone who associated with her had to be ready and willing to play a supporting role in the enthralling drama of Vanessa Barlow's life and times — enthralling to Vanessa, at least. Cindy had been her number one sidekick for several weeks now, ever since she whipped up some great food for Vanessa's last party and let Vanessa take most of the credit. But Cindy's term appeared to be quickly running out. So far she'd been abjectly loyal in public, but in private she'd begun to challenge Vanessa's bossy ways.

This time around, Vanessa decided to give Cindy a second chance. "Of course I know who's cousin he is," she huffed. "But I bet you don't. So prove it . . . you tell *me*."

Cindy smirked, Vanessa's trick being so obvious. "Angie Poletti's. Can you imagine plain, potato-faced Angie having a cousin who looks like that?" Cindy knew she wasn't being fair. Angie, though no great beauty, was hardly a potato face. In fact, she had so much vitality, so much healthy exuberance, that she was almost beautiful. She was a cheerleader who loved every minute of every routine. Cindy couldn't resist the opportunity to swing back into Vanessa's favor, though.

"So what else have you heard?" Vanessa had now dropped all pretense and was eagerly pumping Cindy for information.

"Angie thinks her cousin is the greatest thing since the invention of sliced bread, naturally. But I hear he's very strict. He gave his first period class *days* of homework to do, and this is just his first day. I bet he'll be a tough grader, too. I heard that the other English teachers were upset because Mrs. LeMoyne gave so many A's last semester. She was a real softy, you know. She just couldn't stand to give a low grade to any kid she liked."

This was news to Vanessa, who'd received a B-minus. It also infuriated her that Cindy knew so much more faculty gossip than she did. Silently, Vanessa promised to take the matter up with her father that very day.

"I suppose we'll find out for ourselves, when fifth period rolls around." Cindy suppressed a giggle. "It will be interesting to see whether Walt Manners can wrap this new guy around his little finger the way he did LeMoyne. The only work he did all first semester was when he arranged for the class to visit his house while his folks were doing their TV show.

"It certainly will be interesting." Vanessa gave her hair ten more hard strokes with the brush. Then she studied the results in the mirror. She couldn't decide whether the effect was worth it or not, since her scalp tingled harshly.

By the time lunch period arrived, Vanessa had formulated her plan. Dragging the none too eager Cindy with her, she made sure that they left the cafeteria a few minutes early and arrived in Thomas Gaetano's classroom well ahead of the rest of the class.

"How do you do, Mr. Gaetano?" Vanessa proclaimed as she swooped down on the desk where the new teacher was reviewing his lesson plan one last time. "I want to be one of the first to welcome you to Tarenton High. I'm Vanessa Barlow and my father is Dr. Frederick Barlow, the superintendent of schools here in Tarenton."

Mr. Gaetano appeared to take the momentous news in stride. Turning toward Cindy, he managed to extract her name from her, and then politely note that he was looking forward to having both girls in his class.

29

"We certainly hope that you'll be giving us more work in writing," Vanessa said. "Of course, there are always a few students in any class who are lazy. But most of us feel that writing practice is very important. In preparation for college, I mean."

"That's good to hear," Tom Gaetano said, hiding a smile. "In fact, I intend to do just that. I feel that no matter how much reading you do, knowledge is wasted if you can't communicate your ideas in clear English prose."

"I couldn't agree more," Vanessa said. Tossing her long hair over her shoulder in a gesture that Vanessa hoped reeked of mature glamor and self-assurance, she headed back to her usual seat in the rear of the classroom.

As Cindy settled in across the aisle, Vanessa looked her way and confided in a stage whisper loud enough for Mr. Gaetano to hear, "What did I tell you? He's *very* nice, no matter what Walt Manners says."

Cindy thought at first that Vanessa had gone too far, but a glance at Mr. Gaetano's face made her wonder. It wasn't easy being a new teacher, especially when you had to come in during the middle of the year, replacing someone who had made life all too pleasant for her students. Cindy felt sure that no matter how hard Gaetano tried to forget Vanessa's remark, he'd be driving himself crazy wondering just what Walt had been saying about him.

By the time Walt Manners arrived in class, he

already had one strike against him. Only he didn't know it.

Walt took his seat near the door, wearing his usual all-purpose cocky grin and listened as Mr. Gaetano announced his plans for the class.

"One new project I want to introduce starting right now," Tom Gaetano explained, "is a daily journal. *What* you write is not important, as long as you fill at least one notebook page a day. You will be graded on clarity of expression. And, naturally, on grammar and spelling. That goes without saying."

Walt felt his stomach do an automatic flip-flop. Just what he didn't need! So far, he'd managed to get through Tarenton High without revealing to anyone the extent of his problems with spelling and grammar. Most teachers gave multiple choice tests and his mom made a habit of practically rewriting his typed papers. Since Gaetano wanted on-the-spot writing, Walt wasn't sure how he could get around this particular assignment. He frowned.

"Is something wrong, Mr. Manners?"

Walt swallowed hard. "Yes. I mean, no. I was just wondering if it would be all right to type our journals instead of writing them by hand."

"No go. I realize that handwriting is becoming a lost art," Mr. Gaetano said, "but you'll be doing this journal in the classroom. I'm setting aside the first fifteen minutes of every class. The reason for that is that I want you all to develop fluency. I want to see your first attempts."

What Walt saw was disaster staring him right in the face. He'd never manage to pass English with this guy, much less get the mark he needed to stay on the cheerleading squad.

Unfortunately, the worst was yet to come. The journal writing period was starting that very day. "Remember, you don't have to write your deepest personal feelings, although that would be fine. Any topic is acceptable," Mr. Gaetano explained, as he announced the start of the session.

All around Walt, students bent over their fresh, unmarked notebooks. Some started almost immediately and wrote at a furious pace. Others stared at the blank page and then began making a few tentative scrawls with their ball-points.

Walt watched the activity around him intently, dreading the moment when he would be the only one in class who had yet to put a word down on paper. He felt frozen with fear and, as often happened when he got nervous, his grin kept getting broader and broader.

"I'm glad you're finding this so amusing, Mr. Manners."

Walt looked up and saw Tom Gaetano standing beside his desk. He didn't know what to say. Maybe he could save himself with humor. "Yeah. Ha-ha. It's the funniest thing, but my mind just went totally blank."

"Oh, come on, Mr. Manners. I'm sure you must have some opinions — about teachers, for example. Just put them down."

What's happening? Walt wondered numbly. First Pres blows his stack for no reason, and now this new teacher seems determined to ruin his life. What had he done to deserve all this trouble?

While Walt continued to study the ceiling helplessly, in the back of the classroom Vanessa Barlow was polishing off her third paragraph on the importance of communication. She felt very satisfied with what she had accomplished so far.

Vanessa wouldn't have been quite so pleased with her day's work if she could have seen what took place in the Tilford home late that afternoon. Pres and Kerry Elliot were seated in the Tilford library, snuggling on the oversized leather couch in front of a roaring fire.

"I think fireplaces are just dreamy," Kerry said happily, as she rested her head on Pres's shoulder. "Imagine having this to come home to."

"I never enjoyed it much until now," Pres said.

And it was true, too, even though Pres couldn't quite believe that he was feeling this way about little Kerry Elliot.

During the last two years, Pres had dated scores of girls, mostly the more glamorous types Tarenton had to offer. It hadn't bothered him very much that none of his romances had ever seemed to last very long. Life was easier that way, especially considering the girls he always seemed to fall for.

Pres still often found himself fantasizing about Vanessa Barlow's lush mane of dark hair and curvaceous figure. Admittedly, however, the nonphysical side of their dating hadn't been too satisfactory. How could it be, when any man, even

33

one who wanted her, would have had to admit that Vanessa had the morals of a rattlesnake. Although she'd never used her venom on him, it was no fun watching her scheme.

Mary Ellen had been another mistake. Her blonde good looks were so much his own type that they seemed made for each other. But Mary Ellen never had figured out what kind of person he was inside, and she really wasn't interested. Pres was fairly sure that if she ever did psyche him out, she would be very disappointed. She wanted someone who would fulfill her fantasy of a man for her.

Neither of these lost chances had bothered him too much. There were plenty of other good looking girls in the world. Even in Tarenton. But the last girl he ever figured he'd find himself interested in was Kerry. Kerry Elliot, with her plump figure and flyaway, curly brown hair and way of wearing clothes that showed just how little she cared about style. What Kerry had was a sweetness, a vulnerability that touched Pres.

When he first realized he'd fallen for Kerry, he was sure he'd never get anywhere with her. She was dating Andrew Poletti at the time and only saw Pres as a distant, inaccessible, though desirable, upperclassman. Then Kerry had discovered the extent of her attraction to Pres. He could still remember the first time they kissed, how excited and nervous he'd felt all at one time. How soft and yielding she had been. After that, Kerry had decided to break up with Andrew.

But though Kerry was bewitched by Pres, she also was worried.

"If I could stop caring about Andrew so fast, and fall in love with you," Kerry explained, "then I probably wasn't ready to be dating just one person in the first place. I think I need time before I let myself get serious about anyone else."

That sounded logical, except that from Pres's point of view the decision to get serious was history. It had been made before he'd had time to even think about what it meant.

Pres kissed Kerry, gently, sweetly. He wanted her, but he also wanted to protect her from his strong attraction toward her. She was so young, so inexperienced that he kept his own feelings under control. He was not aware of the fact that Kerry, for all her outward softness, knew exactly how far she was willing to go with Pres.

Pres leaned down and kissed the top of Kerry's curly head. Tarenton's number one ladies' man was turning into a real softy. And at times like these, he didn't even mind.

"Why, look who's here!"

Pres felt the tension shoot up his spine. From the tone of his mother's voice he could tell that she'd been indulging in afternoon cocktails and was at least halfway to being drunk.

Until a few months ago, he'd never known his mother to drink during the day. But lately she had been doing it more often, and with every time her behavior became more strange. First she'd acted just depressed. The last few times, she'd been hostile.

35

"Hi, Mom." Pres disengaged himself from Kerry and stood up. His mother entered the room wearing a floor-length hostess gown of purple velvet. It was obvious she hadn't gotten dressed yet that day.

"Sit down, I don't want to disturb you," his mother said, plopping herself into one of the leather armchairs that faced the couch.

"You're not disturbing us," Pres insisted.

Mrs. Tilford waved her long magenta fingernails in a 'never you mind' gesture. "That's a lie. But I don't care. All Tilford men are liars." She fixed her gaze on Kerry as if noticing her for the first time. "You'll learn that soon enough, young lady."

"Uh, Mom, this is Kerry Elliot. I don't think you've met her before," Pres said, doing his best to change the direction of the conversation.

"Hello, my dear. A pleasure." Mrs. Tilford's gracious tone evaporated quickly as she turned back to Pres. "I don't suppose you know where your father is."

"No, I don't."

"I'm sure he's working late again," Mrs. Tilford said to no one in particular. "Busy, busy, busy, you know."

There was a pause while everyone tried to think of what to say next.

"You have a lovely home, Mrs. Tilford," Kerry said in a timid voice. "I love this room."

"It is lovely, isn't it?" Mrs. Tilford looked around vaguely, as if noticing the room for the first time. Then she giggled maliciously. "All of my son's little floozies just love it."

"*Mother!*" Pres begged.

He would like to have said a lot more, but he knew getting into an argument would just do more damage. The look of pain on Kerry's face made him want to protect her at all costs. And the best way to do that would be to get her away from his mother as soon as possible.

Fortunately, Mrs. Tilford made that easy. As if realizing that her barb had hit the wrong target, she got up and swept out of the room, leaving Pres to undo the damage.

"My mother's been upset lately," Pres explained hurriedly. "Don't take anything she says seriously. She just isn't herself."

"It's okay," Kerry said, not very convincingly, in a quivering voice. "I just want to go home now. Get me out of here, Pres."

"I will, Kerry. Just don't be upset."

On the drive home they were both silent.

Pres wished there were some way he could erase his mother's words from Kerry's memory, but he couldn't think of a way. Why, of all the girls who might have witnessed that particular scene, did Kerry have to be the one? Pres knew that Kerry already had trouble believing that his interest in her was sincere. She couldn't shake the suspicion that he was just looking for an easy conquest. He'd worked hard to get Kerry to trust him, and now his mother had undone his efforts in one minute.

"Please don't be upset, Kerry," he said again, as he dropped her off in her own driveway. "Promise me you won't."

Kerry smiled back, but she looked anything but calm. "I'd better go inside," she said. "I can't talk now, Pres. I'll speak to you later. Just let me be alone for a while."

When Pres got back home, his mother had retreated into her bedroom. A "Do Not Disturb" sign, taken from one of the hotels where she and his father had stayed on one of their trips to Chicago, hung on the doorknob. That evening, Pres and his father ate dinner alone, served by the cook. His mother never appeared downstairs.

CHAPTER

Mary Ellen leaped out of the passenger seat of Patrick Henley's truck and led the way into Burger Benny's, hoping that no one had noticed her and Patrick driving up.

Now that there was snow and ice on the ground, Mary Ellen's plan of bicycling home from practice had gone from impractical to physically impossible. Most nights, she took the public bus from school after practice ended, and met her mother in the downtown office where she worked as a clerk. Then they both caught a ride home with the co-worker who usually drove Mom. This system took an extra forty minutes or so, but Mary Ellen found it too humiliating and embarrassing to ask for a ride, when so many of the other kids in school had cars of their own. This afternoon, when Patrick Henley offered her a lift home in his garbage collection truck, she had felt almost grateful. That just showed how desperate she was.

Inside Benny's, Patrick ordered diet sodas for both of them and got around to saying what was on his mind.

"So what's this about me being a jerk?" he asked.

Mary Ellen stared at him, feeling her face redden. There was no point in denying she had said it. Patrick was no fool, and people who lied only made him more determined to get at the truth. "Who told you that?" she asked.

"I have my sources," he said coolly.

For some reason, Mary Ellen immediately thought of Olivia. She'd seemed in a strange mood the other night at the diner. But why would she go out of her way to tell Patrick about Mary Ellen's comment? Maybe she's jealous of anyone who has a boyfriend who doesn't fade away, Mary Ellen speculated. Now that Michael is so involved with running, maybe she wants to see the rest of us suffer, too.

Of course, it didn't have to be Olivia. It could have been Nancy, or Walt, or even Angie, who made no secret of her disapproval of Mary Ellen's opinion that a boy with a part-time job slinging garbage was not good enough for her.

Patrick watched Mary Ellen's confusion with amusement. In fact, his source had been the bus driver, who also happened to work part-time for Henley Trash. It never occurred to most people that bus drivers had ears. But this one did, and he'd wasted no time in informing Patrick what

Mary Ellen had said about him. Actually, he'd called her the stuck-up blonde, but Patrick had no doubt who he'd meant.

Unable to avoid the issue, Mary Ellen decided to try logic. "I didn't mean that you were a jerk," she began. "It's just that you get me all confused by coming on so strong. I'm not sure I want to be anyone's special girl right now, and you're always in such a rush to get serious."

Patrick thought this over. He'd always taken it for granted that Mary Ellen was the kind of girl who expected to be swept off her feet. Maybe he'd been wrong. "Okay," he said agreeably, "what do you want?"

Mary Ellen hadn't expected cooperation, and she hadn't bothered to think ahead that far. "I've told you before. We could see each other once in a while. On a friendly basis. But sort of low profile, you know."

Patrick lifted his palms upward in a gesture that said, "anything you want."

"Great!" Mary Ellen said, but secretly she was disappointed that Patrick hadn't pushed for something more serious. And exactly what did seeing each other "on a friendly basis" mean? The feelings she had for Patrick were not just friendly. They came from need and physical yearning.

Before she got out of his truck when he brought her home, Patrick took Mary Ellen in his arms and kissed her, lingeringly, slowly. When he pulled back, he grinned and said, "Just a friendly kiss."

Mary Ellen leaned toward him and he kissed her again, making her wish she had never said anything discouraging to him.

When she went into her house, her younger sister Gemma was seated in front of the TV. "Mary Ellen! Did you get a ride home?" she asked excitedly. "Who with? Was it Patrick?"

Mary Ellen dumped her coat and books in the nearest chair and made a face. "I'm afraid so. Patrick again."

"So why aren't you happy?" Gemma asked. "I think Patrick is awfully cute. And he's crazy about you. He even worries about you. I saw him on Saturday and he wanted to know if you got home safely from the game."

When Mary Ellen didn't answer immediately, Gemma assumed a knowing expression. "I get it," she said. "Patrick likes you. But you like Pres . . . and his Porsche."

"Gemma!" Mary Ellen couldn't believe that her own loyal sister would say such a thing.

"Oh, I don't blame you," Gemma said, turning her attention back to the old *Barnaby Jones* re-run. "What's wrong with preferring a Porsche to a smelly old truck?"

Mary Ellen strode into the kitchen and started throwing together the preparations for the family dinner. Sometimes she wished Gemma wasn't quite so smart. What was wrong with wanting to improve yourself, and thinking seriously about the future? When she put it that way, Mary Ellen was convinced her ambition was justifiable. But

Gemma's offhanded comments reduced everything to the crassest level possible.

Mary Ellen surveyed the ingredients for the night's meal: a head of iceberg lettuce, leftovers from last night's meatloaf, a can of generic peaches with a black and white label. Was there something wrong with her, because she didn't want to settle for a lifetime of coming home after work to meals like this one?

Vigorously tearing into the lettuce, Mary Ellen started to feel a bit better about herself. It wasn't that she didn't truly like Pres. She did. So from now on, she wasn't going to let herself feel the slightest bit guilty about keeping Patrick Henley at arm's length.

On the other side of town, Olivia was sitting in the front seat of a very different vehicle from Patrick Henley's garbage truck — Jimmy Hilbert's spanking new, white Mustang. Instead of the parking lot of Benny's, the two were parked on a lovely scenic overlook above Narrow Brook Lake, with a view of a group of ice fisherman's huts below them and a ruddy winter sunset taking shape on the far horizon. But while the setting may have been a lot more glamorous, Olivia Evans was feeling even more confused than Mary Ellen had been.

All weekend long, Olivia had scarcely been able to think about Jimmy Hilbert without feeling angry and hurt. Had he invited her to the dance because Nancy had turned him down?

Olivia knew that Jimmy had a reputation as a happy-go-lucky type. But her pride rebelled at being anyone's second choice.

It had taken all Sunday afternoon for her to get up her nerve to call Jimmy and ask that they get together Monday after practice to talk. But when Jimmy heard her voice over the phone, he'd seemed completely oblivious to the possibility that she wasn't happy.

"Terrific!" he'd said right away, when she suggested a meeting. "You haven't had a chance to ride in my new car yet, have you? I'll pick you up at the gym, and we'll go for a little spin before I take you home."

Jimmy's confidence that Olivia only wanted to congratulate him for Friday night's game began to melt her resolution. So what if Jimmy dates other girls? she asked herself. You wanted a guy who'd be a lot of fun. Now, before you've even had an official date with him, you're acting possessive. Like a real wet blanket. You have no right to expect anything from him yet.

So Olivia didn't say anything about what she had been feeling on the drive out to the lake. When the car pulled onto the overlook, she decided that she'd better speak now or the chance would be gone forever. Timidly, she asked Jimmy whether it was true that he'd been out with Nancy Goldstein last Wednesday.

"Sure," Jimmy admitted.

He turned and stared into Olivia's eyes with practiced sincerity. "You aren't letting that worry you, are you? Nance and I are just good pals. Nothing serious. Now, my feelings about you are a different thing altogether."

As if to prove the truth of his words, Jimmy reached over and caught Olivia in his arms.

Olivia gasped with surprise, then responded mechanically to Jimmy's kiss. A small voice in the back of her head told her that she ought to be skeptical about Jimmy's explanation. It had been just a little bit too pat, as if he'd used that line before on a number of occasions.

For the time being, however, Olivia had a different problem. She wanted to enjoy making out with Jimmy. She'd been telling herself for days that when the moment came, she would. Now, however, she felt nothing. Nothing at all.

Olivia caught hold of Jimmy's left hand, which had been slowly but steadily moving from the back of her sweater.

"Come on. Don't be a spoilsport, Livvy," Jimmy pleaded.

Olivia pushed him away and sat as upright as possible in her seat. The word *spoilsport* ruined any chance she might have had of getting interested. It made her suspect, uncomfortably, that Jimmy regarded what they were doing as just another game, like basketball — a chance for him to score.

"I just don't think we know each other well enough, Jimmy." Olivia said.

"So? I was trying to get to know you better."

Olivia stared out her window. "You know what I mean."

"Yeah, I know." Jimmy reached for the ignition key and started the motor. "I just can't figure you out," he said. "First you're jealous because you think I might have a thing going with Nancy. Then, when I show that I'm really interested in you, you turn into an instant icicle. How can a guy win?"

Olivia couldn't think of an answer to that one, so she rode in silence the rest of the way around the lake. At least part of what Jimmy said couldn't be argued with. She didn't know *what* she wanted.

By the time they reached Olivia's street, Jimmy's good spirits seemed to have recovered. "Tell you what," he said, "why don't we go to a movie tomorrow night?"

"On a Tuesday?" Olivia usually spent Tuesdays studying for her Wednesday biology quiz.

"Sure. Live dangerously for once," Jimmy laughed. "There's a movie at Cinema Mile that I've been wanting to see and tomorrow's the last night it's playing. *Vartan the Viking.*"

Sword and sorcery epics weren't normally Olivia's favorites, to say the least. But there was no way she could say so, and have any hope left of shedding her ice princess image. Thinking fast, Olivia remembered that her mother would be out tomorrow night, attending a fundraising meeting for the Heart Fund drive.

"Why not?" she told Jimmy. "As long as I get home at a reasonable time, there's no problem."

During the next twenty-four hours, Olivia changed her mind a hundred times. Not about

46

the movie. She was sure about that. But what would she do when Jimmy, inevitably, suggested going home by way of the scenic lake drive? If he stopped at the overlook again, would she be more encouraging than she'd been on Monday night? Or would she play icicle for a second time?

Olivia knew that other girls went through the same mental debates. But she was convinced that her case was unique. Others might have doubts about specific guys. Or about the wisdom of getting physically involved too soon. Or about going too far. Olivia knew, though, that other girls *enjoyed* kissing. She'd heard Angie talk about her dates with Marc, and about how tough it was sometimes for her to say no. And the other girls in the group had all seemed to know what Angie was talking about.

Olivia had never felt that way. Well, maybe just a little bit with Michael. But he was so elusive that she hadn't had much of an opportunity to sort out her emotions on that score.

With Jimmy, she'd been sure it would be different. He was handsome, suave, and confident. But at close range he left her cold. She was sure it must be her own fault. Nancy certainly wouldn't feel that way.

After school on Tuesday, Olivia dressed with special care. She wore corduroy slacks, a cotton shirt, and a blazer — nothing too dressy. But she had carefully put on eyeliner to accentuate her wide-set brown eyes, and she wore her best pair of earrings: tiny garnet posts that had been a birthday gift from her favorite aunt. Fortunately, her mother wasn't around to insist that she bundle up in three layers of sweaters under her winter coat. Olivia had told her mother that she was going to the movies, and received her grudging permission. But if Mrs. Evans had been home to supervise her preparations, Olivia was sure she'd have ended up looking as if she were headed for an assault on the South Pole instead of a simple trip to the movies.

Jimmy seemed to appreciate the results of her efforts. "You look great," he said as they headed for the line that had formed inside the theater lobby.

"Thanks," Olivia said apologetically. "It's nothing special. I'm too short to wear sophisticated clothes, unlike some of the girls on the squad."

Olivia wished she could bite off her tongue. Why had she said that? Actually, she loved chic clothes. She just didn't have any. And everyone knew that the only sophisticated dresser on the squad was Nancy Goldstein.

Jimmy hadn't missed the reference. "Yeah," he agreed, "Nancy's a very sexy girl. Uninhibited, if you know what I mean."

Olivia felt herself tighten. She clamped her jaw firmly shut. Did that mean what she thought it did? Was it true? She'd certainly never thought of Nancy in that way. But then, what did she know about that whole side of life? For all she knew, every single one of her acquaintances at Tarenton was miles ahead of her when it came to sex. She was the freak.

48

"Speaking of sophisticated dressers," Jimmy commented as they edged their way toward the waiting ticket taker.

Vanessa Barlow, with her friend Cindy in tow, had just entered the theater. She was wearing a short, fun-fur jacket, with a high neck and a fringe of tan, black, and white fur tassels along the bottom edge. Underneath, her legs were encased in skintight black pants of a shiny, satin-like fabric. High heels — which must have been tricky to walk in across the snow-encrusted parking lot — finished off the outfit.

"I think calling that sophisticated is an understatement," Olivia said mildly.

"What I can't figure out," Jimmy said, "is why a girl gets herself up like that and then never appears in public without at least one tag-along chaperone."

Olivia was about to answer, when they reached the head of the line and entered the dimly lit theater. Jimmy firmly steered her toward the tiny balcony set above the entrance door. "We'll be cozy back here," he grinned, draping his arm heavily around her shoulders.

Olivia squirmed. Naively, she hadn't thought about the possibility that Jimmy intended to concentrate on something other than watching the exploits of *Vartan the Viking*. She wasn't ready for this. Not yet. Not *here*.

"Well, hey there!" Vanessa's greeting rose above the hushed conversation of the other moviegoers.

Without asking whether she was welcome, Vanessa staked out the other two seats in the row and motioned for Cindy to join her. "Imagine running into you guys here," Vanessa said all too cheerfully. "I never suspected that you were a beefcake fan, Olivia."

Olivia mumbled something inarticulate.

"I think I must be Harvey Schlembarger's biggest fan in the whole world," Vanessa gushed on. "He was Mr. Universe, you know."

"In about 1956," Cindy grumbled disloyally.

Vanessa ignored this. "And I hear he's dated just about every starlet in Hollywood. I can see why, too. He can have my number any time."

With that, the theater went black and the movie began. Olivia tried to watch the picture, but within minutes she was hopelessly confused. For one thing she couldn't figure out just who was the enemy that Vartan had set out to conquer. At first, she'd thought the setting was England. But the enemy queen wore a semitransparent gown of green sequined material that looked as if it came straight out of a *Star Trek* rerun. And the queen's army was composed of strange dwarflike creatures with pointy ears. Worse still, Vartan's loyal lieutenant and the actor who played the queen's chief henchman looked a lot alike, which made the fight scenes very confusing.

The action back in their row of seats was almost as complex. Not long after the movie started, Jimmy had all too casually rested his hand on top of Olivia's own. Then as the first fight scene reached its peak, the hand moved to Olivia's knee.

Olivia had stared at it as if it was some sort of exotic insect. Jimmy pretended not to notice, and began planning his next move.

The hand had just begun to squeeze Olivia's knee a bit more familiarly when Vanessa turned toward both of them to comment on the action. "Isn't this juicy," she said. "Don't you just find these battle scenes *riveting*."

Distracted and embarrassed, Jimmy returned to square one.

The same routine was repeated at least three times before he gave up in total defeat.

Vartan had better success. By the time the film ended, he had vanquished the empress's army and rescued a blonde Viking princess who had been held captive by a large mechanical bird in a cave.

As Vartan and his bride sailed off into the sunset in their Viking ship, Vanessa applauded enthusiastically. "Jimmy, I really hate to ask," she said, ignoring Olivia's presence entirely, "but do you suppose you could give Cindy and me a lift home? We both live just off Connell Drive. It isn't very far past Olivia's. Cindy's dad dropped us off here, and I was supposed to call my folks for the ride home. But I don't dare since it's so late."

"Uh, sure. Why not," Jimmy agreed.

At first, Olivia felt indignant. How had Vanessa and Cindy planned to get home if they hadn't run into her and Jimmy? Besides, it wasn't late at all. Just the normal time that the movie had been scheduled to end: shortly before ten. At

51

least Vanessa could bother to think of a more logical excuse, Olivia thought.

As they piled into the Mustang, Olivia calmed down enough to savor the amusing side to the situation. No doubt it had never occurred to Vanessa that she was rescuing Olivia from an uncomfortable situation. It was probably the first good deed Vanessa had ever done in her life — consciously or not.

Not only had Vanessa's presence kept Jimmy at bay during the movie, but Olivia decided that it gave her the perfect excuse to end the date early. She'd already warned Jimmy that she wanted to be home before her mother returned that evening. And Vanessa and Cindy both lived a good bit farther from the mall than she did.

Olivia waited until they were about to turn into the entrance to Connell Drive before announcing her decision. "I guess you'd better let me off first," she said sweetly. "My mother doesn't like me to be late, any more than Vanessa's father does."

Jimmy, looking perplexed and totally defeated, let her off in her driveway and Olivia ran inside without a backward glance.

Inside the house, Mrs. Evans was waiting, home early from her meeting on purpose to monitor the time of her daughter's return. "You didn't mention that one of your friends was a boy," she said accusingly.

"I thought I did."

"Well, maybe you did say something," Mrs. Evans corrected herself, reluctant to let go of her suspicions. "But you shouldn't have gone out without a warm hat. You've got to watch your health."

"Mom! We were in the car or the theater the whole evening. I don't need a hat just to walk across a parking lot!"

"That's what *you* say, young lady. Suppose the car broke down on the road. Suppose you had an accident. What then?"

Olivia gave up. If she were in an accident, the last of her worries would be needing a hat. The first would be figuring out how to break the news to her mom without bringing on an hysterical scene.

Up in her room that night, Olivia tossed and turned, unable to sleep. Everyone said that high school was supposed to be the best time of your whole life — nothing but parties and laughs and good times. She wanted those good times. So why couldn't she just relax and enjoy herself? She was sure the problem must be unique.

CHAPTER

5

Vanessa wasted no time in informing the world of Olivia's date with Jimmy Hilbert.

The next day at lunch, she made a point of joining one of the crowded tables at the front of the cafeteria, setting her tray down immediately across from Olivia's old boyfriend, Michael.

"You'll never guess who I saw at the movies last night, taking in the last showing of *Vartan the Viking*," she announced to no one in particular.

"King Kong," someone suggested.

"Mrs. Oetjen," said someone else, naming Tarenton's principal. "She wants to revise the dress code and was taking notes."

Vanessa milked the suspense as long as possible, then dropped her bombshell. "Jimmy Hilbert and Olivia Evans! Can you believe it! Jimmy's so cool, and Olivia's such a little mouse! I wonder how she manages to keep Jimmy interested in her." Vanessa rolled her eyes wickedly, in case anyone present should miss the implications of her remarks.

But Michael, however he felt about the news, was not about to fall into Vanessa's trap. He peered across the table, studying Vanessa as if she were speaking a foreign language he'd only just begun to pick up. "Would you like my dessert?" he said after a long pause. "It's stewed prunes."

The boy seated beside Michael let out a loud guffaw, which was echoed the length of the table, as Michael's put-down began to sink in. Vanessa, slinging her hair over her shoulder in a demonstration of wounded dignity, picked up her tray and left in search of more appreciative company.

Only one person in the group had failed to see the humor in the incident. Nancy Goldstein, seated quietly at the far end of the table, was mulling over the meaning of Vanessa's revelation. Just last Friday she had confessed her interest in Jimmy. And on Tuesday Olivia Evans had gone out on a date with him. *Olivia*, of all people — Olivia, who rarely dated at all!

As far as Nancy was concerned, Olivia was a traitor. Why else would she pick out the one guy that Nancy had just developed an interest in, out of the hundreds at Tarenton High?

Choking with hurt and anger, Nancy grabbed her own tray and dumped the remains of her un-eaten lunch into the nearest garbage bin. She had no idea where she was headed, but her homing instinct took her straight to her locker where she could at least recover her composure and undo the damage done to her makeup by the tears of rage that had welled up in her eyes. She combed her thick, dark hair and outlined her dark eyes. Feeling more composed, she decided to restrain her impulse to find Olivia and strangle her on the spot. Instead, she went back to the lunchroom and located Angie Poletti.

"Ange, can I talk to you?" she hissed.

"Sure thing."

Angie followed Nancy out into the hall. "What's wrong? You look just awful, Nancy," she said.

"Thanks." Nancy smiled wanly and repeated the story she'd just heard from Vanessa.

"I'm sure there's some explanation," Angie said after hearing the tale. "Let's not jump to conclusions."

"Like what?" Nancy demanded.

Angie searched her mind for possibilities. "Well, maybe she had already agreed to go out with Jimmy *before* Friday night," Angie suggested. "That would be different, wouldn't it? You couldn't expect her to break a date just because you mentioned liking him."

Even in her present mood, Nancy could see the logic of that. "But that wasn't the way it was," she insisted. "I remember Olivia saying right then that her social life was zero. She had nothing going for her at all. Why would she say that so definitely if she already had a date with Jimmy? Besides, for once Vanessa spoke the truth. Jimmy isn't Olivia's type at all. If anything, she's attracted to quiet, serious types like Michael. And Jimmy Hilbert is definitely *not* that kind."

Angie pondered the situation a little more, reluctant to see evil in anyone's motives. Except Vanessa's. . . .

"Vanessa!" Angie said aloud. "Has it occurred to you that Vanessa might have made the whole thing up? You know what a schemer she is!"

Nancy considered this. "I don't think so. I'm sure Vanessa was trying to stir up trouble by telling Michael what she saw, but I don't think it was a lie. For one thing, Jimmy would be furious with her if she made the whole story up. And Vanessa wouldn't want to have that happen. She'd never let herself get on the wrong side of a guy who drives a new Mustang."

Angie giggled. "I suppose you're right. That means there's only one explanation left — Olivia Evans is a creep."

Nancy arrived at cheerleading practice that afternoon, still boiling with anger but hoping that she could manage to get through the practice and save her grievances for a private talk with Olivia later on.

Changing hurriedly into her practice clothes, she entered the gym and joined the others who were already seated in a circle listening to a pep talk from Coach Engborg.

"I don't have to remind you," Ardith began, "that we've got the Grove Lake game coming up in a little less than two weeks. Now this is an important basketball game, not just for you students but for alumni as well, so we really want to be on our toes. Some of your parents and older brothers and sisters may recall, even if you don't, that Grove Lake used to be Tarenton's traditional grudge rival."

Ardith smiled at the looks of noncomprehension that went around the group. "That was back in the old days," she explained, "before 1963, when the conferences were reorganized. But a lot of us old folks still remember it. And you can bet that Grove Lake remembers — and the local newspapers and media, too. We might even get coverage of the game on TV news, so I want to make sure that our cheerleading squad is in top form."

Everyone looked suitably impressed, except possibly Walt, who had made bit appearances on his parents' TV show since he was three and was completely relaxed about appearing on camera.

At the other extreme, Mary Ellen was excited over the possibility of TV coverage. Even if the squad only appeared for a minute or so, she was determined to make the time count. "We'll need a new attack cheer," she pointed out to the others, "since we don't normally play Grove Lake during the regular season."

"Grove Lake's mascot is the grizzly bear," Walt mused. "So we will have to refer to that."

"How about 'Grind the Grizzlies'?" Mary Ellen suggested.

"Okay," Walt said encouragingly. "Go on. How will the rest of it go?"

Mary Ellen thought for a few seconds. "I don't know. Maybe 'Grind the Grizzlies. Mash 'em to a pulp. . . .' "

Olivia made a face. "Do we always have to have so much violence in our cheers?" she asked. "I mean, that's awfully *graphic*."

"It's an attack cheer," Mary Ellen said, exasperated. "What should we say: 'Hug the Grizzlies! Aren't they cute?' "

"No, of course not." Olivia looked ready to give up. "I just thought it might be nice to have some cheers that emphasize positive values."

"You mean like loyalty?" Nancy said sarcastically.

Everyone stared in her direction. No one knew what Nancy was talking about, but the challenge and hostility in her voice were unmistakable.

"Sure," Olivia said weakly. "Why not?"

"Because I don't think you know anything about the meaning of the word, that's why," Nancy retorted.

Ardith Engborg looked stern. "If this has to do with the squad, we'll hash out the problem right now," she announced. "If it's personal, I trust you two will be mature enough to settle the dispute between you. I won't have personal feuds getting in the way of our work."

Ardith left no doubt that she meant business. Nancy wilted a bit under her glare. "That's okay with me," she said, trying hard to keep her voice even. "I can wait till later."

"And you?" Ardith looked in Olivia's direction.

"Sure," she said in a tiny voice. "I don't even know what this is about."

With peace restored for the time being, at least, Ardith suggested that the squad work on a trick they had discussed in the past but never got around to trying. It involved the girls doing tumbling runs through a large hoop, held by Walt and Pres.

"When we actually do the trick," Ardith explained, "we'll have tissue paper stretched over the opening of the hoop. The first girl to do a forward roll through the hoop breaks the paper."

"Sounds great," Mary Ellen said. "It certainly will be a dramatic entrance onto the gym floor. But isn't it difficult to get through the hoop?"

Ardith shook her head. "It's much easier than it looks. And the two fellows holding the hoop make it easier still. They can adjust the position of the hoop a bit if it looks as if the tumbler is going to hit wrong. All it takes is a little cooperation on their part."

Cooperation, unfortunately, was not in the works between Walt and Pres that afternoon.

For three days in a row now Walt had sat in silent protest, never so much as picking up his pen during the journal-writing segment of Mr. Gaetano's class. If he had been anyone else, his passive resistance might not have attracted much attention. But Walt was accepted as a class leader, the catalyst of every prank and every new trend. His behavior was not only noticed, but it had distracted the rest of the class so much that very little journal writing was getting done by anyone. Most of the students scribbled something in their books just to get by, all the while devoting most of their attention to the silent battle of wills going on between Walt and Mr. Gaetano.

In the beginning, most of the class had been on Walt's side. He was well liked, and there was always a tendency — cruel perhaps, but all too human — to challenge a new teacher and enjoy studying him or her for signs of cracking under pressure. Every day, however, the mood of the class seemed to be moving slowly but perceptibly in the other direction. Mr. Gaetano was clearly a decent guy, and the better students were becoming annoyed with Walt for disrupting what could have been an interesting project.

Today, as the class period ended, Andrea Markley, one of the honor students, had gone up to Walt in the classroom and confronted him openly. "So, what's the point of all this?" she had asked. "If you want to flunk, go ahead and do it. We don't care. But at least put your name in the silly notebook. Or don't come to class at all."

For a second, Walt had been speechless. The fact was, his original reason for not writing in the journal had already begun to seem pointless. No matter how badly he wrote, he had nothing to lose. Total noncooperation was the way to a sure F. Somewhere along the line, however, his refusal to write had turned into a gesture. With a capital G.

Feeling too silly to tell the truth, Walt had searched around for some explanation for his behavior that Andrea might buy.

"I just don't think creative people can be forced to perform on cue," Walt had told her. "How can I be inspired to write sitting here in this dingy classroom? And if I did have a good idea, I wouldn't want to be interrupted by Gaetano's stopwatch, would I? It's stupid. The man just doesn't understand how creative minds work."

Andrea hadn't looked as if she thought much of his excuse. "Thinking that one up was your most creative act in months," she said, turning her back on Walt. But a few bystanders had seemed mildly impressed, and Walt had calculated that he had picked up at least a couple of new sympathizers.

In his own mind, though, he was in silent agreement with Andrea. His own parents were in television, and he knew very well that they got up every morning and did their show on time no matter what. Waiting for inspiration had nothing to do with it.

The fact was, Walt felt trapped. If he kept on his present course, he was sure to fail English. If he gave in, he'd look as if he were backing down. And Mr. Gaetano would have no reason whatsoever to give him a break in grading his lousy grammar. He was headed for disaster either way.

None of this made it any easier for him to concentrate during practice. The first time Angie came in too low for her forward roll through the hoop, Walt failed to respond to Pres's tug adjusting the hoop downward, and Angie's toe caught the lower edge of the hoop as she went through, pulling the hoop out of the boys' hands and sending it flying.

"Are you all right?" Walt asked Angie absentmindedly as she lay in a heap on the mat, the hoop tangled between her legs.

"I guess so," she laughed. "Just surprised, that's all."

"If you were paying attention, dummy, it would never have happened," Pres told Walt.

Pres's rebuke reminded Walt of their run-in the previous Friday, an incident he had almost forgotten in the wake of this classroom troubles. "Why don't you stop needling me," he shot back.

"All I want is for you to pay attention to what you're doing for a change," Pres groused.

"Look, I've had problems lately," Walt explained in a halfway sort of apology. "I can't help it."

Pres was unmollified. "Has it ever occurred to you that you aren't the only one with problems? Just because some of us don't put on a big act, doesn't mean we don't have difficulties, too."

"Come on, you guys," Angie said, jumping to her feet and moving between them. "It's no big deal. We can't do every trick right every time. I'm sure everyone's personal problems will get straightened out, too."

"That shows how much you know," Walt retorted. "It's your stupid cousin who's making my life miserable. And you think he's *so* wonderful! Maybe you'll change your mind when I get kicked off the squad on account of my grades, and you have to find a new guy to take my place."

Angie blinked in surprise. She was used to playing peacemaker in other people's quarrels, not to being a partisan herself. And being in a different English class from Walt, she had somehow managed to remain oblivious to the great journal-writing war between him and Gaetano.

"Walt's just sore because we finally got a teacher who won't give him A's for charm alone," Nancy put in, not helping things any.

"That doesn't even deserve a reply," Walt retorted. Then he added, on second thought, "Of course, if you had to get by on charm, Nancy Goldstein, you wouldn't get far."

Olivia, who had been strangely silent since her own run-in with Nancy, let out a burst of laughter.

"Come on, gang, let's bury the hatchet and get back to work," Angie pleaded. "We need every practice session we've got between now and the Grove Lake game."

For once, however, Angie's mediation attempt had no effect. Walt announced that he didn't feel like doing any more practice routines that day, and Nancy and Olivia all too readily agreed. Finally, giving in to the inevitable, Ardith Engborg suggested that they break up early for once. "Let's just write this practice off as a lost cause," she said wearily. "Perhaps by tomorrow we'll all be in a better mood."

* * *

"Poor Ardith," Pres said later, as he helped Mary Ellen into the passenger seat of his Porsche.

Mary Ellen was doubly surprised — first, that Pres had thawed in his recent coolness toward her enough to offer her a ride; second, that his sympathies seemed to be focused more on their long-suffering coach than on the imminent disaster facing the squad.

"I feel bad for Ardith, too," she agreed. "But what about us? Here we are facing the biggest game of the season, not to mention a chance to appear on TV, and it's all going to be ruined because we're bogged down in a lot of petty quarrels and personal problems."

"Maybe they're not so petty," Pres mused. "That's just *your* point of view."

That was easy for Pres to say, Mary Ellen thought. He left practice, jumped straight into this wonderful sports car, and headed for a mansion by the lake. Cheerleading was just a game for him, a way to pass his spare time and simultaneously infuriate his father, who hated the very idea of a Tilford heir making a spectacle of himself leading cheers.

"I don't see how you can say that," she finally protested aloud. "This is our big chance! Ardith said there will even be TV cameras at the game!"

"Big deal!" said Pres, unimpressed.

"Maybe that's how *you* feel about it," Mary Ellen retorted, "but it certainly matters to me."

She was glad that she'd asked Pres to let her

65

off on Spring Street, near her mother's office, instead of at her house. A lot of times she thought she was silly to be sensitive about living in a tacky, turquoise-painted, frame house in one of Tarenton's poorer neighborhoods. But a few minutes with Pres when he was in one of his haughty lord-of-the-manor moods always reminded her that she had good reason to be sensitive. If Pres thought appearing on TV, on a game that would be telecast all over the state, was unbearably small-time, she could imagine what he'd be thinking about her house and family!

"You wouldn't understand how I feel," Mary Ellen announced defensively, "but cheerleading is the most important thing in my life. It's important to all of us. Except, apparently, to you."

Pres wished he'd never brought the subject up. Mary Ellen only talked that way because she had nothing really important to worry about, he told himself. Only a week ago, he might have told anyone who asked that the most important thing in life was his car, or learning a new gymnastic trick, or even having a date with a sexy girl. When you were facing the break-up of your home, though, things like that no longer seemed to matter much on a scale of one to ten.

Unable to put his thoughts into words without sounding corny or mysterious, Pres decided to change the subject. "How's Patrick?" he asked innocently.

Mary Ellen was guarded. "Why do you want to know?"

"Good grief!" Pres sighed. "No reason. I was just making conversation."

"He's okay. We're still talking. No thanks to whoever went out of his way to tell Pat what I said on Friday night."

"Don't pin that on *me*," Pres said defensively.

But that was exactly what Mary Ellen was doing. Up until now, she'd felt that it must have been Olivia, or possibly one of the other girls. On second thought, however, she felt sure that Pres must be the creep. She wasn't sure why he would do something like that. Except that Pres's ego was so large, he probably wouldn't want Patrick to be dating her . . . even though he really didn't want her for himself.

"I'm not making any accusations," Mary Ellen lied, "but in the future, don't think you have to be my messenger. I can start enough arguments with Patrick without help from you."

The Porsche had just come down the hill onto Spring Street, three blocks of old-fashioned brick and stucco commercial buildings quite different from the rest of Tarenton, which was a picture-book pretty resort town. To Mary Ellen, Spring Street would always epitomize the small-town dullness of Tarenton. A store like Millie's Fashions managed to survive year after year, featuring a window display of mannequins draped in "house dresses" that Mary Ellen felt sure would have looked dumpy and old-fashioned forty years ago. Who wore such things? Someone must, since Millie's stayed in business. The brightest spots on the three-block long street were the two hardware stores — Olaffson's and Murtries, avid competitors who had stuffed their respective front windows with brightly colored displays of power tools, lawn mowers, and tractor accessories.

Pres is just a tourist in this world, Mary Ellen told herself. He drops by from his house on the peninsula when he feels like it. But his family doesn't know this street exists, you can be sure of that.

Pres's bland smile and his show-off moves as he steered the Porche one-handedly into a parking space between two old pickup trucks tried Mary Ellen's determination to say no more. "You think all of life is a joke," she blurted out accusingly, "but to some of us, it isn't!"

That did it! "Just because I don't go around whining all the time," Pres snorted, "everyone seems to think I have no feelings. And don't blame me for your problems with Patrick, Mary Ellen Kirkwood," he added. "You treat that guy like a yo-yo, reeling him in whenever it suits your purposes. I won't take the blame for your guilty conscience."

Mary Ellen was too furious to even think of a reply. Jumping out of the passenger seat, she slammed the door behind her hard — a move she knew was guaranteed to set Pres's teeth on edge. She headed off toward her mother's office without a backward glance. She didn't have to look back actually. She could tell from the sound of the Porsche, as Pres all but burned rubber making the turn back toward Route 21, that he was just as furious as she was.

As she entered the office of the Great North Insurance Company where her mother worked, Mary Ellen made sure that her face gave no hint that she was anything but totally carefree. Smiling broadly, she greeted Miss Petrasson, her mother's friend.

"You look beautiful as usual, Mary Ellen," Miss Petrasson said as she buzzed Mrs. Kirkwood in the back room to signal that it was time to leave for the day. "You make me wish I was back in high school, without a care in the world."

If she only knew! Mary Ellen thought. Why do all adults remember high school as four years of smooth sailing?

As she waited for her mother to gather up her things, Mary Ellen found herself counting off the problems that were dividing the squad:

Olivia and Nancy were feuding over Jimmy Hilbert.

Walt was angry with Angie because of his problems with Mr. Gaetano, her cousin.

Nancy was peeved with Walt because she felt the classroom stand-off was all his fault.

Pres was upset with Walt, and now with her, Mary Ellen. *Why* was a mystery, but then most things that went on in Pres's mind were a mystery to the rest of the world.

And now she was furious with Pres, since he must be the one who had gone out of his way to start a quarrel between her and Patrick.

Coach Engborg might kid herself that everyone's differences would get worked out in time for the play-off game, but Mary Ellen couldn't see any prospect of that. The feuding spirit seemed to be contagious, like an epidemic of chicken pox or flu. The squad was tearing itself apart.

CHAPTER

Nancy Goldstein had already considered her priorities. Which came first, squad loyalty or Jimmy Hilbert? The answer did not take long for her to figure out. "Loyalty is worthless unless it's a two-way street," she told Angie Poletti. "The squad can fall apart for all I care. I won't take Olivia's betrayal lying down."

In fact, Nancy was physically lying down as she spoke, stretched out on her bed simultaneously watching a rock video on MTV, blow drying her hair, and talking on the telephone to Angie. After years of being dimly aware of rock music at best, she had become an avid fan during her romance with Alex, the British exchange student who had played with a local new wave band. The drawn out routine of washing, conditioning, and styling her hair was a bad sign, though. Nancy was one of those girls who got compulsive about her hair when she was depressed.

"Don't you think you're jumping to conclusions?" Angie was arguing, raising her voice to compete with the whine of Nancy's blow dryer. "You should at least try to talk this out with Olivia before you condemn her. There's probably a good explanation."

Angie had a steady boyfriend and could afford to be philosophical on the subject of jealousy.

Nancy didn't see matters so coolly. "What explanation could there be?" she wondered aloud. "I've even been inviting Olivia to my parties, and seeing that others invite her, too. All for the sake of the squad. How can you make excuses for her? She's trying to steal my new boyfriend right out from under my nose!"

"I'm not making excuses," Angie explained patiently. "I'm just suggesting that a six-foot-three, 190-pound male isn't that easy to steal . . . unless he *wants* to be stolen."

Nancy didn't want to hear what Angie was trying to tell her. "It's just *got* to work out with Jimmy," she wailed. "He's the first guy my folks have approved of right from the start, since I came to Tarenton."

"I don't get it," Angie objected. "Since when has parent-appeal been a must quality in guys?"

"Since lately. For me, at least. I'm tired of battling with my mom and dad all the time."

Angie giggled. "It's funny to think of Jimmy Hilbert being any parent's dream. The word is, he has fast hands, and I don't mean just on the basketball court."

"It's true, too," Nancy laughed. "But I can handle that."

There was a long silence on the other end of the line. "So how come your folks like him? He isn't Jewish. Or is he?"

It tickled Nancy that the issue of being Jewish, so crucial to her parents, was a total mystery to Angie. For months her new friend had gone on the assumption that Nancy Goldstein was Catholic.

"No, Angie, he isn't," Nancy explained. "But that's the only strike against him. Otherwise, he's my parents' dream: a preppy dresser, a smooth talker, and his father happens to be a prominent lawyer who's active in politics and writes articles for national environmental publications. If that isn't enough, Mrs. Hilbert graduated from the University of Michigan, just as my mom did, and they're both active in alumni affairs."

"It's hard to imagine Jimmy Hilbert being the son of two real go-getters," Angie mused. "He isn't the studious type, that's for sure."

"So?" Nancy objected. "I'm studious enough for both of us."

After she had hung up the phone, Nancy switched off the blow dryer and lay back on her peach-colored bedspread, staring at the ceiling. It was probably true that her parents liked Jimmy even better than she did. From that point of view, it wasn't such an ideal romance. But she *was* tired of fighting every battle with her parents. Mom and Dad weren't ogres. They usually gave in when she truly wanted something, and they liked her friends well enough when they got to know them. But being an only child wasn't easy. Her folks had such high expectations. Nancy couldn't help envying Mary Ellen and Angie, who had younger siblings to distract their folks' attention once in a while.

Of course, that's the way life worked, Nancy reflected. If you wanted anything, you had to be a fighter. So why was she holed up in her room moping about Jimmy? Why not take the initiative?

On impulse, Nancy reached for the phone again and dialed Jimmy Hilbert's number.

She hadn't figured out what she was going to say. If she'd bothered to think out her strategy ahead of time, she'd have lost her nerve. So when Jimmy's voice answered, she just blurted out the first suggestion that came to mind.

"I called because we have this history quiz tomorrow," she explained into the mouthpiece.

"We do? Oh, yeah."

Nancy found Jimmy's total indifference to schoolwork exciting but a bit scary.

"It's on the Civil War, remember?" Nancy reminded him.

"Well, who won?"

"The north, silly," Nancy giggled.

"Great," Jimmy said. "Now that we have that out of the way, how would you like to go skiing tonight? They have night skiing up at Brinley Mountain."

"Sure. Let's live dangerously."

Nancy was sure her mother would say no. But she was wrong. Telling her that the invitation came from Jimmy Hilbert worked wonders. Permission was granted.

Nancy didn't go skiing often, but before her last outing she'd bought a new ski suit that she was eager to show off. The pink stretch pants and pink and gray jacket were topped off with a matching striped cap that showed off her thick, dark hair to advantage. Jimmy's reaction, when he picked her up on her doorstep a little later, told her that she looked as good as she felt.

It took less than an hour to get to Brinley Mountain. Only one intermediate slope was floodlighted for night skiing, but it was a good run, just tough enough for Nancy to demonstrate her skills. The crowd was mostly made up of college kids from the state university nearby, and there weren't too many of them. By nine-thirty, Nancy and Jimmy were completing their second good run of the night.

"Whew! That was terrific!" Nancy exclaimed, as she caught up with Jimmy at the bottom of the hill after a brisk second run. "Didn't I do great? Did you see my form on the big turn up at the top?"

"Your form is great all the time, if you ask me," Jimmy said, looking at the way her figure filled the skintight ski pants.

Nancy made a face. She was beginning to find Jimmy's need to make comments like that a real turn-off. Not that she was a prude, but there was something insincere about the way Jimmy kept pushing the subject of sex constantly. Like he was trying to prove something.

"What you need is to cool off," she joked out loud. Scooping up a handful of snow, she fashioned a crude snowball.

Jimmy pretended to run away, but soon let himself be caught.

Nancy playfully lobbed the snowball at his chest, and giggling, let herself be tackled into the bank of soft snow that lay piled against the side of the ski lodge.

After a few seconds of mock tussling she was ready to get up. But not Jimmy. He seemed determined to turn the game into an impromptu grope session.

Out of the corner of her eye, Nancy noticed that two college guys passing by on their way to the refreshment stand were staring at them with funny smirks on their faces. "Youth," one of the guys said in a loud voice. "I sure do miss it!"

His friend laughed and stared harder.

"Jimmy!" Nancy hissed. "Good grief, let me go. Not here. It's gross."

Jimmy ignored her protests and kissed her hard. Nancy was aware that her heart didn't beat faster, and all she could think of was that he was being a jerk.

Then he let her go and stood up, laughing, not

caring that Nancy had not been responsive to him. "Well, how about a hamburger, then, before we head home."

Inside the high-ceilinged lodge, Nancy and Jimmy found a table and ordered burgers and fries. Ravenous from the exercise, Nancy polished off the food with no trouble at all, while Jimmy conducted a monologue on his other favorite topic — himself.

To hear Jimmy tell it, he was about to write a new chapter in the history of Tarenton basketball. Hank had never been as good a center as everyone thought. In a way, his injury was a stroke of luck for everyone. Come the Grove Lake game, Jimmy would show everyone that he had deserved to be in the starting lineup all along.

Nancy pushed the remnants of her French fries around her plate and yawned.

Jimmy was the perfect guy for her in so many ways, she scolded herself. The two of them made a great-looking couple. Her parents were putty in his hands. She usually found him very sexy . . . at least she would if he'd only stop pushing so hard and let her feel that it was partly her own idea.

So how could she spoil it all by admitting to herself that there were times when she found him to be a big bore?

Annoyed with herself, Nancy pushed the thought to the back of her mind. She decided that she wasn't going to bring up the subject of

Jimmy's movie date with Olivia either. They weren't going steady or anything like that, so why make a fuss? Maybe when they got to know each other better, her doubts would evaporate. For now, she'd just keep quiet and hope for the best.

When he stopped his car in front of her house, Nancy put her arms around his neck when he kissed her, letting herself enjoy the feelings he could arouse in her when they had some privacy.

CHAPTER

The squad's Friday afternoon practice was turning out to be even more of a disaster than Wednesday's had been.

At first, Mary Ellen had thought that everyone was settling down to work. But the trouble started when Olivia made a sarcastic remark about Nancy's awkward attempt at a split at the end of the "We're number one!" cheer.

"It's supposed to look easy," Olivia said, as Nancy hauled herself up off the floor, grimacing with the effort.

Mary Ellen couldn't decide who to sympathize with. She herself didn't find splits that easy and felt a good deal of envy over Olivia's ability to turn herself into a pretzel at will. On the other hand, Nancy did seem out of shape today.

The explanation wasn't long in coming. "Sorry, everyone," Nancy groaned. "I went skiing the other night and now my muscles are getting their revenge."

This was no news to Olivia. Although Jimmy hadn't mentioned the ski trip to her, Vanessa had been quick to notice the lift tag on his jacket the next day and point it out just when she knew Olivia would overhear.

Olivia had promised herself that she wouldn't say a thing to Nancy. She didn't want to get in a jealous snit. But Nancy's bringing the subject up right to her face was the final straw.

"Maybe your social life is starting to interfere with the squad," Olivia huffed.

Nancy felt defensive. She hadn't meant the excuse as a dig at Olivia, but Olivia's criticism went too far.

"My social life is my own business," she snapped.

"Does anyone mind if we get back to work?" Ardith intervened. "There's going to be an important game next weekend, whether you all have your personal lives in order or not."

"How can we go through our drill without Walt?" Angie wondered aloud. "He's twenty minutes late."

"He should be here soon," Ardith said.

It seemed that earlier that day in Mr. Gaetano's class, Walt had complained out loud that he couldn't possibly write in his journal with so many people around. He needed privacy. So Mr. Gaetano had offered to solve that problem by making Walt stay after school every day for twenty minutes of detention. The sentence was to last until he wrote at least one paragraph in his journal for every day he'd missed so far.

No sooner had Ardith finished explaining this than there was a commotion outside in the hall. The double doors of the gym swung open and Walt backed through them, waving good-bye to a group of cheering freshmen out in the hall.

Then he turned around and proudly displayed to the squad the reason for the laughs he'd been getting. His bright orange T-shirt bore the custom-lettered motto: FREE WALT MANNERS.

Pres, Mary Ellen, and Olivia couldn't help laughing.

Angie felt her heart sink to her feet. She could just imagine what her cousin Tom had thought of this gesture. Walt had always liked to play the role of the rebel and class jester. But up to now, he'd never let his little jokes go too far. If he had to get involved in something like this, why had he decided to pick on a nice guy like Tom?

It was Nancy who put into words some of what Angie was feeling. Relieved to be distracted from the awkward situation with Olivia, which she didn't really know how to handle, she turned her annoyance on Walt.

"I, for one, don't see the joke," she said. "If you want to express yourself, all you have to do is write something in your journal. *Anything.* What's the big deal?"

It was easy for Nancy to talk, Walt thought. She got A's without even trying.

"Thanks for the support, Nancy," Walt drawled. "I knew I could count on you."

"Enough!" Ardith's one word comment left no doubt that she meant business. "Back to work, and I don't want a single other interruption this afternoon."

The squad did manage to get in a straight half hour of practice after that. They went through some of their old cheers and then Walt started to teach a new halftime routine he'd worked out that involved a series of break dancing moves. He and Pres loved the routine because for once, they got to do flashy, acrobatic moves instead of just lifting and supporting the girls.

Mary Ellen was a bit less enthusiastic. Walt had long ago perfected his Michael Jackson imitation and was constantly looking for ways to work it into their routines. By now, the others had pretty much caught up with him. When they moved their feet, it looked as if they were gliding on roller skates. Mary Ellen was the only one on the squad who couldn't seem to get the hang of the moves. She knew she looked ridiculous.

Fortunately for Mary Ellen's ego, Nancy was having problems today, too. Every time the steps called for a sideways kick she grunted in agony. Her muscles were so stiff from skiing that she could barely move.

If I look like someone trying to swim out of the water, Mary Ellen thought, Nancy looks like a windup toy soldier.

"What a pair you two make! I love it!" The derisive comment echoed Mary Ellen's thoughts exactly. Startled, she looked toward the door of the gym just in time to see Donny Henderson taking her and Nancy's picture with a telephoto lens.

"Perfect!" Donny crowed again. "Mary Ellen's expression couldn't have been better. The agony and embarrassment of being caught in the act!"

"Would you care to explain what you're doing?" Ardith snapped. "No one said anything about taking yearbook pictures today. We're trying to work."

Donny, who was in charge of yearbook photography, was not used to being challenged. "We just need a few candid shots," he explained unabashedly.

Coach Engborg looked none too pleased. "Does it have to be now?" she asked, giving in. "We've got work to do."

"Oh, don't mind us," Donny said. "Just go right ahead. That's the whole point. We don't want poses. We want to show a glimpse of the hard work that goes into putting your great routines together."

Angie and Pres, standing safely out of Ardith's view, rolled their eyes in appreciation of Donny's line. He could really sling it.

"Well, I suppose it's all right," Ardith agreed. "Just don't get in our way."

Mary Ellen, meanwhile, was slowly taking in just what Donny had meant by the use of the word *we*. Behind him, with another camera slung around his neck, was Patrick. Bad enough that she had just been captured in the most embarrassing photo of all time, but Patrick seemed to be finding the whole situation wildly amusing. She felt the blood flow to her cheeks.

For the rest of the practice, Mary Ellen did her best to ignore Patrick's presence. It wasn't easy, though, with him darting in and out of the line to snap pictures every few minutes. More than once, he pointed his camera right in Mary Ellen's face and snapped away. The more flustered she got, the more he seemed to be enjoying himself.

When Ardith finally called a merciful end to the session, Mary Ellen made straight for the locker room and changed into her street clothes as fast as she could manage it. She was planning to escape through the other door that led from the girls' locker room directly into the downstairs hall. But Patrick had anticipated that and was waiting for her when she emerged, leaning against the lockers that lined the opposite wall.

"Gotcha!" he laughed. He caught her in his arms and just held her, close to him. She felt the warmth of his body and the nice smell of his aftershave lotion. He didn't try to kiss her, just enclose her in his arms.

When he released her and saw her surprise at being caught, he said, "You can't escape me, you know."

"Apparently not," Mary Ellen said coolly.

"So why keep trying?" Patrick asked. He was smiling, but he was serious.

"I thought we agreed to just be friends," Mary Ellen replied. "If this is your idea of how to go about it, it's not a very good one."

"Okay, I admit that," Patrick said. "But we never agreed to stop talking. You've hardly said a word to me since we made that agreement."

"It's only been a couple of days," Mary Ellen pointed out.

"But it seems like centuries to me," Patrick countered. "It feels like the next ice age has started."

She gave him a look that said, "you're crazy." But Patrick was not about to let her off that easy. As she started past him, he reached out and held her by the arm.

"I wouldn't bother you, you know, if I didn't know that you really like me, in spite of how hard you try to pretend otherwise."

"What makes you think I like you?" Mary Ellen said, but the words were not very convincing. The pressure of Patrick's hand on her arm made her forget the meaning of "friends." His touch always did that. And she knew he felt it, too.

Patrick moved even closer and Mary Ellen felt what resistance she had left begin to melt away. He kissed her sweetly, tenderly, and she let him. But when she pulled away, her glance fell on Patrick's T-shirt. Back in the gym it had been partially hidden by the camera gear he wore around his neck. Now she could see the words printed across his chest: HENLEY TRASH.

Involuntarily, she made a face of disapproval.

"What's wrong with my shirt?" Patrick said. "If Walt can advertise his silly games, I can wear this."

"I didn't say anything," Mary Ellen protested.

"You don't have to." For once, Patrick decided, he was going to speak his mind. "You know damn well that if my dad's business was Tarenton Fabricators, you wouldn't mind me wearing a shirt that said so."

"I don't know what you're talking about."

"Yes you do, Mary Ellen. Be honest."

Mary Ellen felt miserable. Why did Patrick insist on forcing the issue?

"I just want you to know that I'm not ashamed of my dad, or our business. Why should I be? He and Mom got married when they were just seventeen years old. They couldn't even afford to have an apartment of their own. And now my dad has his own business. What's wrong with that?"

"Nothing," Mary Ellen said honestly, "for *them*."

"For anyone," Patrick countered.

"Even the part about getting married at seventeen?" Mary Ellen wanted to know.

"Why not? If you're in love."

"That's fine if you want to spend the rest of your life right here in Tarenton. Raising babies and paying bills."

Mary Ellen pulled her arm from Patrick's grasp and strode down the hall, leaving him standing there looking after her. From his point of view, paying bills and raising babies was just part of life. Ordinary, everyday life. It didn't mean not being happy. Mary Ellen had a way of making the prospect sound like some sort of prison sentence.

And to Mary Ellen, that's just what it was.

Grabbing her coat from her locker, Mary Ellen ran out of the school building and headed toward the public bus stop. As always, she did her best to put the confrontation with Patrick out of her mind. She knew exactly what she wanted out of life, and for the most part her plans were right on course. She planned to go straight from high school to New York. She would break into high fashion modeling there. Maybe she'd even try working in Europe for a while, if she could manage it. And in the meantime, she'd take acting lessons.

None of this agenda seemed the least bit doubtful to her, until she let herself get distracted by Patrick. Being with him always made her feel confused and flustered. Not only were his plans completely incompatible with hers, but he was the one guy she knew who was every bit as determined to have his way as she was.

Mary Ellen was grateful when the bus pulled up ahead of schedule and she could get on board, leaving school behind for one more day.

The bus, just like the one her own father drove for a living, was always a reminder of the part of her life she wanted to leave behind. Settling into one of the rear seats, Mary Ellen reached into her bag and pulled out a copy of *Pizzazz*, her favorite fashion magazine, and began to study the full-color layouts. One featured a spread of slinky, hand-beaded evening dresses. Another showed five models with short, upswept hairdos demonstrating all-white play clothes by one of the avant-garde Japanese designers. There was no reason in the world why Mary Ellen couldn't be modeling clothes like these some day. And living the life that went with it. She was *not* going to let Patrick ruin that dream for her, no matter how attractive he was.

Patrick, meanwhile, was dropping off his camera equipment at the yearbook office when he ran into Vanessa Barlow.

"Hi there," Vanessa said, eyeing his camera. "Are you going to take my picture for the yearbook?"

Dressed in simple white shorts and a tennis team jersey, Vanessa was headed for her after-school lesson on the indoor court.

"Sure, why not?" Patrick agreed.

"How's this?" Standing sideways to Patrick, Vanessa cradled her racquet in one arm and looked over her shoulder at the camera lens.

It was hardly a candid shot, Patrick thought, but why argue. He focused the camera and snapped the shutter.

"Thanks," Vanessa said as she prepared to go on her way. "Oh, by the way, that's a cute T-shirt."

"Glad someone likes it," Patrick growled.

If he hadn't been feeling so low about Mary Ellen, maybe he would have been more cautious. Mary Ellen was just afraid of being trapped in Tarenton, but Vanessa was a grade-A snob.

Normally, her reactions to guys were in direct proportion to their importance or their family's bank balance. For the moment, however, Patrick let himself forget this.

"I don't suppose you happen to be free for next week's dance?" he said, turning up his Patrick Henley charm to full volume.

"Is that an invitation?" Vanessa asked casually. Needless to say from her reaction, she didn't have a date yet.

"You bet it is."

"It's a deal," Vanessa said in a low, husky voice.

"Great. We'll go to the game together and then hit the dance from there," Patrick said.

Whistling happily, Patrick locked up the photography storage room and left the school, headed for his late afternoon stint of work on his trash collection route. He felt triumphant. He had figured out a way to make Mary Ellen suffer for her attitude. Imagine how jealous she'd be when she saw him out with another girl — and Vanessa Barlow of all people! The girl she really hated.

Not that he was dumb enough to think that Vanessa was honestly interested in his company. No doubt she had some reason of her own for wanting to go to the dance with him. But that had nothing to do with him.

CHAPTER 8

"Angie, hurry up and don't forget to bring that salad that's in the refrigerator. And Papa's present, too."

Angie, who was already carrying three dozen homemade cookies, her snow boots, and her brother's eyeglasses, which had been left behind on the coffee table, stuffed the salad bowl into a shopping bag, grabbed her grandfather's birthday present, and staggered downstairs to the garage where her mother and brothers were waiting for her.

She didn't really mind spending her Friday evening with the family, celebrating her grandfather's seventy-fifth birthday. Her only regret was that Marc was not going to be home this weekend to attend the family party with her.

She'd been counting on seeing Marc, only to face disappointment when he had called earlier this afternoon to cancel the trip.

"Sorry, Ange," he had explained, "you know I'm dying to get home. But my electrical engineering prof gave us a whole batch of problems to work out by Monday."

"Can't you do them here?" Angie had asked.

"Not really. I need to use the computer lab. Sorry, but school's got to come first. Otherwise, there's no point in my being here."

Angie knew that it was useless to argue. Marc had been lucky to be able to go away to college at all. It was his big chance to escape a life of dead-end jobs, like the one servicing vending machines that he'd had when he and Angie first met. Besides, she'd broken dates with Marc for reasons a lot less important than studying. Her commitment to the cheerleading squad, for example. So she was just getting a dose of her own medicine.

"I'll miss you, Marc," she said, accepting the inevitable.

"Same here, baby. You know I miss you."

"Well, there's always next weekend," Angie said consolingly. "You'll be here for the Grove Lake game and the dance, won't you?"

There was a pause on the other end of the line. "I can't make any promises right now," Marc said finally. "I'm sorry, Ange. But these courses I'm taking are tough. It's hard to predict how much work I'll have, even a week in advance."

"Sure. I understand," Angie agreed.

She did understand, too. But understanding didn't stop her from being worried. Marc had a whole other life at college. She knew he loved her.

Right now. But could any romance last when the two people involved were so far apart, with different schedules and different responsibilities? She wasn't sure.

At least, Angie told herself, her grandfather's party would give her something to do tonight. Anything was better than sitting home and moping about Marc. By the time the Polettis' car pulled up in her grandparents' driveway, she was actually starting to look forward to her evening.

Grandfather and Grandmother DeAngelo — their family called them Papa and Mama — lived in a frame house surrounded by two acres of land, just beyond the city limits. Though not exactly a farm, Papa and Mama's place had always seemed like one to Angie when she visited there as a child. In those days, Mama had kept laying chickens and sold eggs at a nearby farm stand. Papa had raised rabbits.

The story of Papa's rabbits was one he never got tired of retelling every time the family got together, and tonight would be no exception.

"You look beautiful, Angie," Papa said, greeting her from his favorite reclining chair in the living room.

Angie put down her armloads of stuff and gave Papa a hello kiss.

An assortment of a dozen or so aunts, uncles, and cousins was already gathered in the room around Papa's chair, and sure enough he wasted no time regaling them with his favorite story about Angie. "When this one was small," he chuckled, "she loved to feed my rabbits. She was crazy about them. Then one day she found out that my customers didn't buy them for pets; rabbit stew was more what they had in mind. Little Angie didn't say anything at the time. But the next morning when I came out to feed the rabbits, they were all gone. Angie had gotten up before dawn and opened the doors of the cages."

Papa laughed at the memory. Though he'd been angry at the time, he'd later decided to give up selling rabbits altogether. "To me, there was nothing wrong with it," he explained, laughing at the memory, "but I couldn't have my own little granddaughter thinking I was a bunny killer." He looked at Angie with affection. "She's tenderhearted, this one."

Angie grinned in embarrassment and moved into the kitchen where her mother and her brother Andrew were already helping Mama set the table.

"At least we won't go hungry," her mother said in understatement, surveying the covered dishes that were arrayed on every counter and tabletop. Mama DeAngelo had been cooking all week, and the relatives hadn't arrived empty-handed either. There were baking dishes filled with lasagna and manicotti, loaves of garlic bread ready for the oven, a cold seafood salad, a veal roast, and assorted other goodies too tempting for diet-conscious Angie even to allow herself to think about.

If it weren't for the menu, Angie thought, you'd never guess that this family was Italian. Mama and Papa's offspring ranged in looks from honey-blonde, green-eyed Angie to the black hair and olive complexion of the Gaetano branch of the family. But there was something else the family had in common, too, even if it wasn't visible to the eye. They were very close-knit. No one in the family had been particularly surprised, years ago, when Papa gave up his rabbit business to keep from hurting the feelings of a little granddaughter who loved animals. It was taken for granted that every member of the family looked out for the happiness of all the others.

That was the reason that Angie didn't hesitate to take aside her cousin Tom for a talk. She felt sure that if only they could talk the situation over, the two of them could work out some solution to the Walt Manners problem.

Fifteen years older than Angie, Tom Gaetano had always been her favorite cousin. Though barely five-foot-ten, he'd been a basketball star in high school and college, known for his gung-ho attitude and his jumping ability, which made up for his height. He and his wife Sandy were high school sweethearts who'd managed to keep their romance going, even though they waited to marry until Tom had completed his master's degree and a hitch in the Army. Just looking at them now, happily married with two cute daughters, Angie felt reassured that there was some hope for her and Marc.

Confidently, she sought out Tom before dinner and found him in the basement playroom, keeping an eye on his little girls while discussing basketball with Uncle Ernie and Aunt Alice.

"What do you think of Tarenton's chances against Grove Lake?" Ernie was asking Tom.

Tom shook his head. "Not so hot. It looks as if Hank Vreewright is out for the rest of the year."

Angie joined her aunt on the couch. "But aren't you forgetting Jimmy Hilbert?" she asked. "He looked great in last week's game."

Uncle Ernie shook his head. "A hot dog if I ever saw one."

"He's right," Tom agreed. "Jimmy's one-man show worked for a few minutes, but it won't be enough to stop Grove Lake. They're a well-coached team, and it won't take them long to figure out that Jimmy hates to give up the ball. They'll make sure he's so fenced in that he never gets within shooting distance."

Angie was surprised. The kids she knew at school were so euphoric about last week's victory that they hadn't stopped to think that Jimmy's magic might not work a second time. When you thought about it though, you could see that Tom and Ernie's logic made sense.

In the meantime, though, there was something else she needed to discuss with Tom. "Can I talk to you alone for a minute?" she asked her cousin. "It's about school."

"Sure." Tom retreated with Angie to a pair of chairs in the far corner of the room.

"It's about Walt Manners," Angie began.

"Speaking of showboats, he's another," Tom said, making a face. "Don't worry, Angie, he's not going to ruin my enjoyment of teaching. If it comes down to a contest of wills, you can be sure of who'll win. I'm the one who gives out the grades in the end."

"Does that mean Walt will flunk English?" Angie asked, aghast. If he did, that would be disaster for the squad, not to mention Walt personally.

"He sure will if he keeps on the way he's been going," Tom said.

"But that's awful!" Angie exclaimed. "Can't you give him another chance? Walt's my friend. I'm sure there's just some misunderstanding between the two of you."

"You're damn right there's a misunderstanding! Walt thinks he can get away with murder. And if I let him, my chances for getting any respect as a teacher are nil."

The look in Tom's eyes reminded Angie of the temper she knew he had.

"I really don't believe that Walt meant to get into a battle with you," Angie said more calmly. "I know he must have had a reason for not wanting to keep a journal, even though I don't know what it was. And I'm sure that from there things just got out of hand. I bet he'd give anything right now to end this whole argument, if he could just do it without backing down in front of the whole class."

Tom considered this possibility. "You're probably right," he agreed, "but I'm not responsible for Walt's problem. I'm ready and willing to let him make up the assignments he's missed so far. But I can hardly let the rest of the class think that Walt is going to get away with writing nothing and still pass English. That wouldn't be fair to them. And it would make it completely impossible for me to demand any work from my classes in the future. There's no way I can save Walt from having to admit that he's in the wrong."

"Tom! Angie! Everyone! Dinner is ready!" Sandy's call from upstairs brought the conversation to an abrupt halt.

The only good thing that could be said for the rest of the evening was that Angie, for once, had no appetite for all the fattening food that was on the table. The knotted up feeling in her stomach came from the fact that she knew Tom was basically right. She'd been counting on him to come up with some magical solution that would end Walt's problems and save the squad. But this time there was no magical solution. When the grading period ended two weeks from now, Walt would have an F on his record, and his cheerleading days would be over.

On Saturday morning, Angie woke up at six A.M. and took a long, luxurious shower. She still hadn't thought of a solution to Walt's troubles, but she felt more optimistic than she had the night before, if only because things always looked brighter in the early morning hours.

Her father had been killed in an accident when Angie was a baby, and she had always taken over a heavy share of the responsibilities for running the house and looking out for her younger brothers. Her mother, busy running the beauty salon that she operated out of the small shop on the lower level of the Polettis' split-level house, relied on Angie to keep the household going.

Angie had never minded the responsibility, but she had soon gotten into the habit of getting up earlier than the rest of her family, just to give herself a few hours of privacy. In fact, the only good part about Marc's not being home for the weekends was that she wasn't staying out late with him and missing out on her only chance to spend time on herself, free from the demands of her family. She had a full schedule of errands planned for later that day, so this morning she intended to make the most of her private time.

Quickly drying herself after the shower, Angie pulled on her running pants, sweatshirt, and down vest. In the kitchen she gulped down a glass of orange juice while tying up her running shoes. As she headed down the outside steps and up the road, she couldn't help thinking how shocked Mary Ellen and some of the other girls at school would be if they knew that she, Angie Poletti, was a secret jogger.

In spite of her being a cheerleader, which belonged in a different category, Angie had always been the first to joke about how she was too lazy to enjoy any kind of physical exercise. Most of her friends took it for granted that Angie's athletic ability just came naturally, without any effort on her part.

In fact, Angie had started jogging reluctantly, knowing that it was either exercise or give up the chocolate and rich food she loved. She was still less than fanatical about the sport. But after a while, she'd come to look forward to her solitary morning runs.

On this particular morning, the air was clear and cold. Twenty minutes after leaving home, Angie had reached her goal — a small town park that sat on the hill overlooking the old downtown section of Tarenton. As usual the park was empty in the early morning hours, and Angie circled the paved pathway that ran along the promenade, enjoying the view of the village below. After her second time around the path, she felt she deserved a rest and plopped down on a bench, her eyes closed in a moment of solitary meditation.

The moment ended all too abruptly with the feeling of a wet, slobbery tongue licking at Angie's face. Blinking in shock, Angie opened her eyes in time to see a very large and very friendly labrador retriever in the process of settling himself right in her lap.

"*Freddie!* Mind your manners!" shouted the dog's owner, Kerry Elliot.

Freddie grudgingly moved off Angie's lap and settled between the two girls on the bench, blissfully unaware that in the opinion of some, dogs belonged on the ground.

Kerry gave the dog a fond look. "He's so spoiled. I know I should lay down the law sometimes, but I just can't stand to say no."

"That's okay." Angie was glad to see Kerry. Although she'd been disappointed when Kerry decided to stop going with her brother Andrew, she liked the way Kerry had managed things so that she and Andrew were still friends.

"How's everything with you?" Angie asked.

"Oh, fine," Kerry said, unconvincingly.

Angie had figured as much. She knew very well that Pres Tilford was the real reason Kerry had stopped going with Andrew. Pres had come on really strong about Kerry. It had even seemed that, for once in his life, he had lost his head over a girl. But lately, he'd been acting awfully strange.

Based on Pres's past history, Angie felt she knew the story. Pres had changed his mind yet again, and now Kerry was feeling betrayed and depressed. It was so typical of Pres.

"Oh, that's not it at all," Kerry insisted after Angie had gently questioned her about Pres.

"It isn't?" Angie was more confused than ever. "So what's gone wrong?"

Kerry sighed and began filling Angie in on the scene that had taken place in the Tilford library.

"I was so upset at being called a floozy," Kerry admitted. "I guess it bothered me because I know Pres's reputation. I don't want to end up as just another girl that Pres Tilford loved and left.

"Now that I've thought things over, though, I realize it wasn't Pres's fault," Kerry went on. "He can't help what his mother says, and she *had* been drinking. But I'm not sure I'm going to get a chance to talk it over with him. I told him to take me home and wouldn't talk about it. Ever since then, he's been avoiding me."

"You have to talk to him, Kerry," Angie said. "But at least now I know why Pres has been strange recently. Family problems can make people weird."

After Kerry and Freddie left, Angie sat for a while on the park bench, thinking over what she'd just learned. In theory, there was no reason why she should be interested in helping Pres and Kerry get back together.

Still, Pres was her friend. It bothered her to think that, like everyone else, she'd accepted his golden boy image as the whole truth. How could anyone as handsome and rich and *lucky* as Pres have problems?

Now, as it turned out, Pres seemed to have problems that made the rest of their troubles seem petty. Walt's feud with her cousin Tom, the cheerleading squad's difficulties, even her own tendency to feel sorry for herself at having to get through the weekend without Marc, didn't amount to much after all. Pres was the one with *real* troubles.

CHAPTER

 9

If Pres Tilford lived in the biggest house in town, Walt Manners inhabited the most unusual one.

Located deep in the woods outside town, the Manners' house was an architect-designed contemporary fantasy, complete with an entire glass wall with a view of the woods and distant Narrow Brook Lake; a kitchen illuminated by a huge skylight; and a big, airy room, over the studio his parents used for broadcasting, which Walt had turned into a cozy hideaway for himself.

Modern as it was, however, the Manners' house came equipped with old-fashioned, wood burning stoves. And stoves needed fuel to burn. So that's how it happened that Walt had become quite an expert at chopping wood, a chore his parents had turned over to him as soon as he was old enough to manage an ax safely.

One thing about cutting wood was it gave Walt a chance to think out his problems. On this particular Saturday, as he attacked the problem of reducing a large pile of logs to firewood, he was also mentally dissecting his own situation.

Even though he was only wearing a thin flannel shirt, Walt had managed to work up a good sweat, partly because of the heat generated by his hard work. But at the moment, Walt would have been plenty hot even if he had been standing still. The dull thwacking sound of the ax as it bit into the logs usually had a calming effect. Today, Walt felt himself getting more agitated the longer he worked.

Walt had started out feeling sore that he should be in all this trouble over his little problems with spelling and grammar. No one outside of school considered these things important. Walt knew that his own father was a less than perfect speller, and this failing hadn't kept him from working all his life in television. When he needed help with his writing, the station sent out a secretary to clean up what Dad wrote. So what was the big deal?

As hard as he tried, though, Walt couldn't seem to build up a good head of resentment over the demand that he improve his English. Even *he* knew, when he thought about it, that his weakness in this area wasn't the real reason he refused to keep a journal. The real reason was that the very idea of a journal threatened his sense of privacy.

Mr. Gaetano had said that no one had to write

103

down his deepest secrets. But it was hard to write in a journal without revealing something about yourself. And Walt was of no mind to reveal his personal thoughts to anyone.

As far as Walt was concerned, he had good reason to be touchy. All his life, he'd been in the spotlight. Practically his first memories were of running across the living room in front of the TV lights and sitting on his mother's lap, while she introduced him to the audience of the Manners' breakfast talk show.

All the time he was growing up, his parents had used his most personal problems as material for the discussion segment of their show. If Walt wet the bed, his Mom and Dad would be sure to do a segment on bed-wetting and discuss his habit in detail with some psychologist they'd invited to join them on the air as an expert guest. Later, when Walt had problems adjusting to school, these too had been hashed over at length for the local TV audience. And the same for his first crush on a girl, which became the basis for a cute, nostalgic segment that drew scores of letters of praise from adult viewers — but made the object of Walt's crush so embarrassed at having her name mentioned on the air that she didn't speak to him for months.

After that episode, Walt had finally learned his lesson. Practically growing up on TV had made him a confident performer, who knew how to make himself the center of attention and enjoy every minute of it. But he kept his deeper feelings to himself. Walt Manners had plenty of good pals, but not a single deep friendship. The girls he'd dated all agreed that Walt was a cute guy and lots of fun to be with, but looking back on their dates with Walt, not a one could honestly say that she knew Walt any better when the relationship ended than she had when it began.

Walt's strategy for surviving at Tarenton High had been so successful that he was reluctant to do anything that might change his luck. "Try writing about your own life, a kind of autobiography," Mr. Gaetano had suggested the first day he handed out the journals. But the very idea of writing about Walt Manners made Walt break out in a cold sweat. On paper, the happy-go-lucky person he pretended to be would surely be exposed as a fake.

It only made matters worse that the people he wanted most to like him had taken sides against him from the beginning. Nancy Goldstein, for one, was the kind of girl that Walt secretly admired, even though he probably would never ask her out. Nancy worked hard for what she got, not just in school but at making friends, too. Although the parties she gave always seemed relaxed and spontaneous, Walt knew that it took initiative to bring people together and hard work to make any party a success.

Nevertheless, Walt knew that very few of the kids at school saw this side of Nancy's personality. To most of them, she was a cute kid to whom everything came easy. Just because she was good looking and always wore the best clothes money could buy, it seldom occurred to anyone that Nancy had to try as hard as anyone else to get what she wanted.

Then there was Angie Poletti. If there was one person in the world that Walt had felt he could count on to be more than just a pal, it was Angie. Not that he'd ever tested their friendship, but he'd always felt that in a tight spot Angie would be the one to stick by him.

As Walt worked away at turning his pile of logs into fodder for the wood stove, he'd managed to work up a first-class case of resentment against Angie. By the time he'd finished stacking the wood in the shed at the rear of the house, however, he'd begun to have second thoughts. Angie could hardly help the fact that Tom Gaetano was her cousin, could she? Maybe he'd been too quick to assume that she was unsympathetic.

After finishing his chore, Walt poured himself a Coke and went to his room over the studio. The more he thought about it, the more he liked the idea of giving Angie a call. With any luck, he'd catch her in a mood to listen to his side of the story.

Angie Poletti really was happy when she picked up the telephone and heard Walt's voice on the other end of the line.

"I've been worrying about you all weekend," she told Walt honestly.

"Gee, that's nice to hear," Walt said, flattered.

Now that Walt had reached Angie and found her still willing to talk to him, he wasn't sure where to go with the conversation. For a few minutes, they chatted on about the routines they were preparing for the play-off game.

It was Angie who finally worked the discussion back around to the subject that was on both of their minds. "We really need you on the squad, Walt," she said. "Male cheerleading at Tarenton is your project. I can't imagine what the squad would be like without you."

Walt would rather Angie had worried about him as a person. What if he weren't a cheerleader? Would anyone in the whole world care if he flunked English?

"Why don't you just write something in that stupid journal?" Angie suggested, unaware of Walt's train of thought. "Write anything. Whatever your reasons are for going on strike, they can't be more important than passing English."

Walt was beginning to feel very defensive. What did Angie know about how important his reasons were? She'd never even asked him what they were.

"It's no big deal," he said, resorting to one of his favorite all-purpose expressions. "I do all my other classwork, don't I? I can't believe Gaetano would flunk me over just this one assignment."

"Believe it," Angie warned. "I talked to Tom just last night and he explained his side of the story to me. He didn't want to start a war over this, but if he doesn't keep his word and make the journal a requirement for passing English, he's afraid he'll never be able to make an assignment stick again."

"You talked to Gaetano about me? Good old cousin Tom! I can just see you hashing over my situation behind my back."

For Walt, who was feeling friendless to begin with, Angie's casual admission was the last straw. He'd been betrayed!

Angie, on her part, couldn't quite see why Walt was reacting this way. She'd only been trying to help. Why should she be made to feel guilty?

Like most people secretly afraid to admit any weakness in themselves, Walt vaguely understood that Angie's sympathy was there waiting for him. But to get it, he'd have to ask for it. Or at least show that he was ready to meet her halfway in the discussion. And asking for help of any kind was not something Walt knew how to do.

Instead, he retreated into his shell. "Anyway, I'm glad I called," he groused. "At least now I know for sure whose side you're on."

"Oh, Walt!" Angie groaned. "It's got nothing to do with sides."

"It sure does!" Walt countered.

Angie was losing patience. "Okay, you win," she agreed. "If you want to think that the whole world's against you, then go right ahead. There's no way I can change your mind."

Angie couldn't recall a single time in her whole life that she had ever slammed the phone down in the middle of a conversation. But this time she did.

Walt could hardly believe Angie's reaction. Suddenly the security of his own bedroom, with its carefully framed collection of theater posters, his professional quality stereo system — bought at a discount from one of his parents' DJ friends — began to feel like a prison. He couldn't wait to get back outside.

Grabbing his down jacket and the keys to his jeep, Walt headed out to the garage. When moods like this one hit him, the only cure he knew was to go for a long hike in the woods, and then maybe an even longer drive through country roads that snaked through the hills outside Tarenton. Eventually, he'd calm down enough to think straight. Maybe he'd even figure a way out of his dilemma.

While Walt had been out chopping wood, Olivia Evans had spent her Saturday morning at the Pineland Mall, looking for a new winter coat. Since her mother had insisted on coming with her, the chances of the expedition ending successfully didn't seem promising.

At the moment, Mrs. Evans was standing in front of a store mannequin that happened to be showing a coat Olivia would have given her eye teeth for. It was a trim, two-thirds length coat with padded shoulders that created a silhouette like an inverted triangle. The material was a nubby wool in starkly contrasting colors — black and a vivid purple.

"Looks like something an invader from outer space would wear," Mrs. Evans sniffed.

"I think it's great!" Olivia disagreed.

Olivia knew that she had no hope of ever

looking as sophisticated as tall, slender, Mary Ellen Kirkwood. But her short, wiry figure was suited to the new wave-influenced styles that were in fashion. In fact, Olivia's pale skin, dark eyes, and thick eyebrows, which gave her face a dramatic look even without makeup, were right in vogue. If only she could win a little cooperation from her mother, she would have been able to make the most of her natural assets.

"I know it might seem a little extreme to you," Olivia agreed, trying to be tactful, "but I'm the one that has to wear it."

"And *I'm* the one who has to look out for your interests," Mrs. Evans shot back. "For one thing, that coat is much too short for a cold winter's day. You'd catch the flu the first time you wore it."

"I would not. I'm as healthy as a horse and you know it," Olivia argued back.

Of course, it was useless to try to convince Mrs. Evans of that. Olivia's childhood operations had been a scare that she might be able to put behind her, but her mother would never get over the trauma. In her mind, her little girl would always be a delicate, semi-invalid. And protecting Olivia's health had become an excuse for protecting her daughter from just about every aspect of growing up.

Knowing that she and her mother would never agree on a coat that day, Olivia left Mrs. Evans to select a coat for herself, and drifted across the floor to check out a display of leather handbags in bright hues of red, plum, and sea blue. Although there was no way that a blue handbag could possibly be bad for her health, Olivia felt sure that her mom would think of some reason why it might be. Any style that was not one hundred per cent conservative rated as dangerous in Mrs. Evans' book.

"I hope you're not planning to buy *that* one," a voice behind Olivia said. "Because I just did. We don't want to look like twins."

Olivia turned around and saw that Vanessa Barlow was carrying a bag identical to the one she'd been looking at.

"Don't worry," she said. "I was just window shopping."

"I figured as much. Vanessa studied Olivia's appearance critically. "I mean, that handbag wouldn't exactly go with the rest of your wardrobe. It isn't brown or gray."

Count on Vanessa to turn every conversation into a dig, Olivia thought.

"That's right," Olivia agreed, with mock modesty. "That bag is a little too tacky for me. It is more your speed, Vanessa."

Vanessa tossed her long hair to one side, managing to attract attention from all over the handbags deparment. "Really!" Vanessa said, her voice dripping with condescension. "Why take your disappointment out on me? Just because things haven't worked out between you and Jimmy."

"I don't know what you're talking about," Olivia replied. She wanted to walk away, but her legs felt as if they had turned to jelly. Whatever

111

bad news Vanessa had to deliver, she couldn't resist staying around to hear it.

"Oops! I guess I spoke too soon." Vanessa's attempt to pretend to be sorry didn't have a hint of sincerity. "I just couldn't help thinking that you must be out of the picture. Now that Nancy Goldstein is in it, that is."

"Well, you're wrong." Olivia hoped she sounded more confident about that than she felt.

"Do you mean to tell me that you and Jimmy are *still* going to the dance together?"

"Of course we are."

"Amazing!" Vanessa tossed her head again, a gesture that never failed to show off her cascade of dark hair. "It must be really tough trying to compete with Nancy," she added in feigned sympathy. "After all, she's so much more sophisticated. Especially when it comes to sex."

With that parting shot, Vanessa walked away. Olivia watched her go, feeling that Vanessa had at least cured her of the unrealistic desire to spend forty dollars on a bag she didn't really need. And a handbag wouldn't make her sexy, anyway.

But Vanessa's comparison of her and Nancy had hit home. No doubt about it, Vanessa had meant that Jimmy's interest in Nancy was based on Nancy's willingness to go a lot farther sexually than she was. How could Vanessa know a thing like that? Olivia thought suspiciously. Obviously, she couldn't. But that didn't mean that Vanessa hadn't guessed correctly.

For the rest of the shopping trip, Olivia felt

even more impatient than usual with her mother's attempts to steer her in the direction of the kind of clothes she associated with Girl Scouts and sensible, middle-aged ladies.

Maybe Vanessa was right, she told herself. She, Olivia Evans, was a case of retarded development in every department. Especially sex. Her only chance of proving otherwise was to make sure that Nancy didn't get away with stealing Jimmy right out from under her nose.

CHAPTER

10

"It's a beautiful clear Saturday here in the vicinity of Narrow Brook Lake. But tonight the temperature should plunge down into the teens. So all you music lovers take my advice: Make sure you have your honey by your side to keep you warm."

Pres flicked off his car radio in disgust. Not only was he not going to have his honey by his side tonight, he wasn't sure if he ever would again. Ever since Kerry Elliot's run-in with his mother, he hadn't so much as talked to her. The reason was simple, too. Fear. Until Kerry came along, it had never occurred to Pres that one reason for his great confidence with women was that he had never cared too deeply what a particular girl thought of him. Now, for the first time in his life, he knew what it was like to be tied up in knots, wondering if a girl still cared for him. He was so

114

afraid of finding out bad news, that it was almost easier to go on avoiding Kerry forever.

In the meantime, Pres had to do something to fill up his spare time, so he was concentrating on his second love — the red Porsche that had been his sixteenth birthday present from his folks. Pulling to a stop in the Keen-way parking lot, Pres left his car and made his way through the acres of groceries to the auto parts center at the rear of the market.

He had completed his errand and was returning by way of the delicious-smelling bakery department when he ran into Angie.

"Pres! Don't tell me you're shopping for groceries!" Angie exclaimed. "I can't believe it!"

"No way." Pres held up his only purchase, a can of winter-weight motor oil. "The only work I do is on my car. Otherwise, I'm totally useless to society."

Angie laughed. There were times when she was tempted to let herself be jealous of Pres for having such an easy life. But how could you resent anyone who was so totally honest about his own laziness? Would you ever know, either, just by looking at Pres, that he was the only son of the richest family in town? As usual, he was wearing jeans and a flannel shirt that had probably cost a bundle when it was originally ordered from some fancy sporting goods store in New York or Chicago. But that had been at least twenty years ago — not in Pres's lifetime. No one else that Angie knew would have worn their parents' hand-me-down clothes by choice.

"Guess who I saw today?" Angie said, as if she were bringing up the subject by the merest chance. "Kerry Elliot. She was walking her dog in the park."

"Kerry! How is she? Did she say anything about me?" His eagerness was so obvious.

Pres's response made Angie realize that he must be in a bad way. The old, casual Pres she had known most of her life would never have let it show that he cared about a girl.

"She's okay," Angie said. "But I think she's wondering why you haven't called or spoken to her for days."

Pres looked abashed. "Too embarrassed, I guess. Did she mention what happened up at my house the other day?"

"Just that your mom hadn't made her feel too welcome." Angie didn't want Pres to think that she had been gossiping with Kerry about his family, so she pretended ignorance of the details.

Pres wasn't fooled. "That's all right. I don't mind Kerry's telling you. But keep the story quiet, okay? My mother usually isn't like that. It's just that she's been unhappy lately. I think that she and my father might be having some problems."

"That's too bad," Angie commiserated.

"I don't know exactly what's wrong," Pres said. "I wish Mom had someone she could talk things over with."

"What about you?" Angie asked.

Pres looked surprised. "What do you mean?"

"I mean," Angie said, "why don't *you* talk to her? Or won't she discuss it with you?"

"To tell you the truth, I haven't had a chance. Mom's been avoiding me lately, especially since her scene with Kerry. She spends a lot of time in her room with a 'Do Not Disturb' sign on the door. And when we are together, usually the maid is there, so we can't really talk."

Angie was beginning to get the picture that Pres's home life did not remotely resemble her own.

"Well, I think you should at least let her know that you're worried about her," she said lamely. "In the meantime, what about Kerry? Aren't you going to call her? She cares about you Pres . . . and she's so sweet and vulnerable."

"I guess I will," Pres said thoughtfully, "if you think she'll be willing to talk to me."

"I know she will," Angie said.

"It's weird," Pres thought out loud. "I would have guessed that you'd be the last person to want to smooth things over between me and Kerry. Considering that she used to be Andrew's girl."

"I know," Angie admitted. "But seeing how upset Kerry was made me realize that what happened was no one's fault. Even Andrew doesn't think so anymore, so why should I?"

Pres looked relieved. "It's good to hear that at least *one* member of the squad isn't angry with me. What with my little run-in with Walt and my own worries, I haven't been much use at practice lately."

117

"Walt's been acting really strange, too," Angie said. "I just had the weirdest conversation with him on the phone. I only wanted to help, and somehow I ended up being the villain in his eyes."

"Yeah," Pres agreed. "I don't try to figure Walt out. He's too deep for me."

"Walt? Deep?" Angie practically choked on the words. "Walt's the last person I would call deep."

Pres understood Angie's reaction. But he'd always felt that Walt had a hidden side to his personality. "It's just a thought," Pres said, feeling unwilling to dissect Walt. "Anyway, I'd be the last one to ever figure out exactly what Walt's problem is. I'd be happy if I could just manage to remember that routine he was trying to show us the other day. There's no reason why the whole squad should make fools of ourselves next Friday, just because we're having our differences."

"I agree with you there." Angie was struck by a sudden inspiration. "Are you doing anything special this afternoon?"

"Me?" Pres held up his can of oil again. "I was just planning to spend the afternoon tinkering with the car. Not that there's anything that really needs doing. It's just my way of wasting time."

"Why don't you come over to my house and we can go over some of our routines on our own. I'll call Mom and tell her she doesn't need to pick me up here. We can both use the extra practice, and at least it would be a way of showing Walt

118

that we *do* care about making his idea look good."

"What about Andrew?" Pres frowned. "I'm not sure I'm ready to run into him."

"That's okay," Angie assured him. "Andrew's spending the day at a friend's house and staying overnight. He won't be around."

"Then you're on."

They were out in the parking lot, trying to figure out a way to stuff Angie's three bags of groceries into the tiny luggage space of the Porsche when Nancy Goldstein came by with Sue Yardley and two other girl friends.

"I don't think that car is exactly made for practical errands," Nancy giggled.

"That's never been a problem up until now. There's never been even *one* bag of groceries in it," Pres said as he frantically repacked one of the bags so that it would fit into the narrow space behind the driver's seat.

"So what's up?" Nancy's first thought was that Pres and Angie were planning a party of some sort and hadn't invited her. A quick inspection of the contents of the grocery bags made that thought seem doubtful — unless cornflakes and detergent were the new "in" thing to serve at parties.

Angie quickly explained that she and Pres were headed to her place for an impromptu practice session. "Want to come along?" she added.

"Sounds like a great idea. I sure didn't get much accomplished yesterday," Nancy admitted. "My body felt like a disaster area after skiing. I

could use a good workout to get rid of the kinks."
She glanced questioningly at Sue and the other
two girls she'd come with, all of whom indicated
that they wouldn't feel deserted if Nancy took up
the invitation.

"I'd love to come along," she said finally. "But
is there room?"

"Sure," Angie said. "You can sit on my lap.
There's plenty of room."

Pres rolled his eyes in mock distress. "My poor
car. It's never had to work this hard."

"Don't be silly," Angie laughed. "What's a
car for if you can't use it for practical things?"

Nancy could hardly keep from grinning ear to
ear, as she carefully lowered herself into the tiny
space between Angie's lap and the dashboard.
It was just like Angie to be oblivious to the difference in glamor quotient between a Porsche and,
say, a Dodge sedan.

Once Nancy was settled in, Pres headed out
onto the road, driving with extra care to avoid
sudden stops.

"I think my foot is already developing a case
of pins and needles," Angie observed cheerfully
after a few blocks. "But I guess it's worth it. I
just hope Walt Manners will appreciate the sacri-
fices we're making here so that his new routine
looks good on Friday night."

But Walt was in no mood to be appreciative.
Finishing a brisk hike along one of the trails
that followed the undeveloped side of Narrow

Brook Lake, Walt had driven his jeep aimlessly for nearly an hour, trying to make up his mind how to spend the rest of his Saturday. He had just decided to stop by the Pinelands Mall in hopes of finding some kids from school to hang around with, when he spotted Pres's red car on the road with Angie and Nancy crammed like a pair of sardines into the passenger seat.

What's going on? Walt muttered to himself.

A look at the grocery bags stuffed behind the car's seats suggested one explanation, the same one that had occurred to Nancy minutes earlier: Some sort of party was in the works, and Walt hadn't been invited.

If the Porsche hadn't made a right turn onto Crossways Road, Walt would no doubt have pulled even with Pres's car at the stoplight and gotten an explanation. As it was, he couldn't resist following the Porsche to see where the group was headed. After several blocks on Crossways, when the Porsche turned off onto Elm Drive, Walt was pretty sure that Pres and company were going to Angie Poletti's place.

Suddenly, the resentment that he had spent most of the afternoon trying to reason himself out of was back in full force. He had just talked to Angie a few hours ago and she hadn't mentioned anything about a get together at her place. And why was the squad, or at least 50% of it, meeting without him? Angie had seemed awfully sure that his battle with Mr. Gaetano was going to end with him flunking English and getting

121

bounced from the squad. Maybe the squad had decided not to wait for the inevitable. Maybe they were already taking it for granted that Walt was on his way out.

The last thing he was in the mood for right now was to confront Angie, Pres, and Nancy all at once. Instinctively, he dropped back into the line of traffic hoping that Pres wouldn't notice his all too conspicuous black Cherokee jeep. At the next light, he turned off to the right and headed along a roundabout route of back streets that he judged would bring him around past the Poletti house just about the time the others arrived from the opposite direction.

As bothered as he was by the suspicion that Pres, Angie, and Nancy were meeting behind his back, Walt was not too depressed to enjoy the fantasy of himself as a private eye, tailing a car full of suspects. In his daydream, moon-faced, stocky Walt Manners — the eternal joker who was always in hot water over some prank or another — was instantly replaced by his alter ego: Walt Manners, secret agent. This imaginary Walt was an ace spy who combined the suave good looks of Remington Steele with the macho ruggedness of Lee Majors.

The transformation felt terrific! Walt hunched over the steering wheel of the jeep, picturing how surprised Pres and company would be when Walt just happened to drive by and give them all an unconcerned wave, just as they were heading into Angie's house for their secret meeting. He would pretend total indifference, of course. But it would be a way of serving notice that you couldn't pull a fast one on Walt Manners.

By now, Walt had swung onto Henley Street, which ran parallel to the road where Angie's house stood. At each corner he peered up the side street to the right, checking to make sure that the Porsche hadn't picked up speed. By his calculation there should be just enough time for him to circle around and pass Angie's place in the opposite direction as the Porsche pulled into her driveway. The timing was critical, but Walt felt sure that he had figured out the maneuver perfectly.

Bang! The sound of his front bumper slamming into the rear of another vehicle jarred Walt out of his fantasy world instantly. Lost in his daydream and with his eyes glued to the side street, he hadn't noticed that the car ahead of him had not yet pulled through the stop sign. Fortunately, the jeep had only been going between five and ten miles an hour, but the impact was enough to shatter the right taillight of the car and give its occupants a good jolt.

There goes my perfect driving record, Walt thought automatically. Television private eyes never seemed to have to worry about little details like insurance. Not to mention the problem of how to break the bad news to their parents.

This automatic reaction was soon replaced by another — fear. What if someone in the other car had been hurt?

Leaping out of the jeep, Walt ran to the driver's

side of the other car, his face a mask of worry. "Are you all right?" he gasped.

"No thanks to you."

The familiar voice registered on Walt's consciousness, before he'd had a chance to recognize the driver.

"Why don't you watch where you're going?" the voice went on. "A car isn't some kind of toy. I've got my two daughters in here. They could have been hurt."

Walt listened with his heart sagging to his shoes as Mr. Gaetano let off steam. This time, Walt had no clever comeback to make. Gaetano's anger was all too justified.

Walt had always been quite proud of his driving ability. Now, he felt shaken to realize the mess he'd made by taking his eye off the road for a few seconds. What if there had been a bicycle on the road instead of a good-sized sedan? Or even a pedestrian? He could have caused a really serious accident.

"Look, I'm sorry. I really am," he apologized, when Mr. Gaetano had come to the end of his lecture.

"Good," Gaetano said, calming down considerably. "I just hope you've learned a lesson from this." Walking around to the back of his car, he examined the shattered taillight critically. "It could be worse, I suppose."

After a few minutes of discussion, the two agreed that Harry's Garage in town could look over the Gaetano car. If nothing was broken except the taillight, which seemed to be the case, Walt would pay the damage out of his own pocket. Fortunately, he had some money in his savings account left over from his summer job. It would be a lot easier that way than getting the insurance company involved, which was sure to set his parents on the warpath.

Walt followed the Gaetano car to Harry's, where it took fifteen minutes or so for a mechanic to look over the car and decide that there was no serious damage. Luckily, too, the garage was able to lend the Gaetano family a car so that they could do the repair work over the weekend.

By the time Walt left the garage and headed for home, he had decided privately that Tom Gaetano might not be such a bad guy after all. A lot of people would have been a lot less reasonable than Gaetano had been, particularly when the other driver was a teenager. More amazing still, Gaetano hadn't even referred to their problems in class, even though he had every reason to be fed up with Walt. For the first time since the battle over the journal started, Walt felt a twinge of guilt. Maybe he should have given the new English teacher a break after all.

As for the gathering at Angie's house, Walt was already beginning to lose interest. Even though he was still none too happy at the thought of being excluded, he had decided that his plan to make Angie, Pres, and Nancy feel guilty had been pretty silly from the beginning. If they hadn't cared enough to invite him in the first place, why should they feel guilty if he happened to drive past and catch them in the act? They probably wouldn't have even cared if they realized that Walt knew all about their little Saturday afternoon meeting.

Deciding to chalk up the whole afternoon's mess to experience, Walt headed on home.

CHAPTER

Vanessa Barlow had enjoyed a very successful Saturday.

By four o'clock in the afternoon she was headed home from the shopping mall, the backseat of her mother's car piled high with purchases. The total bill for her day's amusement had come to just over two hundred dollars — a bit breathtaking even by Vanessa's standards — but she was quite pleased with the way she'd managed to spread the damage over five different credit cards belonging to her mother.

Experience had taught Vanessa that credit card debts never seemed to affect her mother the way the news of cash outlays did. The bills didn't arrive for over a month, and then they trickled in one by one. By that time Vanessa had usually managed to figure out ways to convince Mrs. Barlow that at least some of her purchases had been dire necessities. And a certain percentage of the bills were never connected to Vanessa at all. An impulse shopper herself, Mrs. Barlow could never be absolutely certain that the forty dollars spent in Marnie's sportswear department in a given month hadn't been for some forgotten purchase of her own. Vanessa, of course, usually did her best to convince her mother that this had indeed been the case.

On this particular day, Vanessa was just a little worried that she might attract attention while sneaking her shopping bags up to her room. Just to play it safe, she'd decided to put some gas in her mother's car before returning it. That way, her mom might not even notice that Vanessa had been out in the car all day. And if she did see Vanessa coming home, at least Vanessa could score a few brownie points by bragging that she had actually replaced the gas she'd used.

Pulling into the full-service lane at Harry's, Vanessa automatically checked herself out in the mirror before ordering five dollars worth of premium.

"Sure you don't want me to fill it up?" the gas jockey asked.

"Are you kidding?" Vanessa looked at him as if he'd taken leave of his senses. "It isn't *my* car."

"I get it. Wouldn't want to give your folks a heart attack." The attendant, whose name was Duane Richards, chuckled at his own joke.

Vanessa ignored him. Although she'd been coming to Harry's ever since she got her license and Duane had always been friendly, she considered him beneath her notice.

128

Normally, everything that happened at Harry's was beneath Vanessa's notice. But today, as she gazed around while waiting for the gas, she saw something rather interesting.

"Doesn't that sedan over there belong to Mr. Gaetano?" she asked idly. "You know, the man who teaches at Tarenton High."

"That's right," Duane agreed. "Had a little fender bender. Just happened about an hour ago."

"Really! I hope no one was hurt."

"No one hurt at all. They were all in here getting an estimate. You just missed them."

"All? Oh. You mean the other driver? And who was that?" Vanessa's curiosity was always insatiable.

Duane was quite pleased to be making small talk with the very attractive Vanessa. If he noticed that he was being pumped for information, he didn't seem to mind.

"You know Walt Manners," he said. "He must be in your class at school. Ran right into the back of Gaetano's car down on Henley Street."

The gears inside Vanessa's head were already spinning, putting the scene together. "I bet his goose is cooked for sure," she thought out loud.

"Oh no, I don't think so." Duane disagreed. "I've known Tom Gaetano since he was a kid. He has a temper, but he isn't one to hold a grudge in the long run."

This last bit of news didn't particularly please Vanessa. She had rather been looking forward to seeing Walt's problems with Gaetano escalate to the point where he'd have to give up cheerleading. She had even begun to think that there might be an opportunity shaping up for her to make the squad after all. Naturally, Ardith Engborg *would* want to replace Walt with another guy. But who?

Most of the guys in school who were athletic enough for cheerleading had already gone out for a sport. Of the rest, Vanessa couldn't think of a single guy who combined the outgoing personality of a cheerleader with enough interest in the squad to make all those practice sessions worthwhile. And knowing Ardith, she'd restructure the entire squad before she'd consider taking on a cheerleader who was second best, male or female.

So far, Walt had been doing a great job of making trouble for himself. From Vanessa's point of view, it seemed unfair that the situation might resolve itself without benefitting *her*.

Following that line of reasoning to its natural conclusion, Vanessa decided that she would be justified in helping things along. The plan was already formulating in her mind. It was going to be so easy that Vanessa couldn't help feeling rather pleased with herself.

Walt Manners was in the studio, where his parents stored the equipment used for their broadcasts from the house. The accident momentarily forgotten, he was hard at work putting together a tape of dance music that he had thought of using for a squad routine. Since the school band didn't play at basketball games, the squad used recorded music, at least before the game when the crowd was waiting for the action to get underway.

Walt knew he'd have his hands full selling the new routine to Ardith and the other members of the squad, but he was used to that. Compared to putting male cheerleaders on the squad in the first place, his routines would be a minor departure from tradition.

Walt's ideas for the squad were always more theatrical than anyone else's, and he had to admit to himself that for him cheerleading would always be a substitute for dancing and acting, two activities that there weren't a whole lot of chances to pursue in Tarenton. Most likely, he'd never get the chance to pursue them fulltime anywhere. His chunky body was not what most choreographers looked for in a dancer, and his round, cheerful face would never qualify him as a leading man. No doubt he'd end up like his father, who had given up a stalled career in acting to become a local TV emcee and "personality." Or else, he'd drift into some form of behind-the-scenes work in the theater or broadcasting. That wouldn't be so bad, really, but for the moment Walt was enjoying his chance to be on center stage as a varsity cheerleader.

He enjoyed it so much that he knew he'd eventually have to find a way to pass English — even if that meant giving in and writing in that journal. Although he hadn't thought it through, his decision was already half made. All he needed was a graceful way of giving in.

Walt had just finished splicing the last song onto his master tape when the ringing of the phone sent him sprinting into the kitchen. "Hi!"

said a honeyed voice on the other end of the line. "It's me. Vanessa."

Walt frowned. There was nothing routine about Vanessa calling him at home at six o'clock on a Saturday night. Something was definitely up. But what?

"I just heard about your accident," Vanessa purred, "and I want you to know that I, for one, intend to stand by you. No matter *what*."

Walt glared at the phone. "How could you know about that? It just happened."

Vanessa was glad he'd asked. So far, her script was unfolding according to plan. "Well, you know how it is," she said evasively. "When your father is the school superintendent, you hear things."

Just as Vanessa had hoped, Walt jumped to the obvious conclusion. "But how could your old man know? Did someone tell him?"

Of course, Vanessa had never quite said her father did know. Could she help it if Walt read too much into her words? "I don't want to say too much," she went on. "I could get in trouble." All of which was only too true.

Then she added her parting shot. "They say Mr. Gaetano has a reputation for having a short fuse."

"That snake! I can't believe it." Walt was totally indignant. "He promised he wouldn't make a big issue of the accident, and not two hours later he's already complained about me to the superintendent of schools. And why? Don't tell me he's trying to claim that what happened had something to do with our not getting along in class!"

Until that moment, it hadn't occurred to Walt that such a claim would be all too easy to make. After all, he'd run into the Gaetano car from behind, when it was stopped for a stop sign.

Vanessa was so pleased with her success that she had to bite her lower lip to keep from laughing out loud. "Well, *I* will never believe that it was anything but an accident," she said.

"But it *wasn't* anything but an accident," Walt protested.

"Uh oh. I gotta go now. My dad just came in," Vanessa replied. And she hung up, just in time to keep Walt from hearing the bursts of laughter she could no longer hold inside.

Walt, for his part, was in no mood for humor. He'd been more or less resigned to going to see Gaetano on Monday morning to find out how he could make up the days he'd missed doing his journal assignment. Now he just couldn't see doing any such thing.

As one who'd been a few steps ahead of disaster before in his school career, Walt knew that there was no point in apologizing before he knew exactly what the charges against him were going to be. Until he found out, he'd just keep on as before.

CHAPTER

12

Vanessa was not the only one in Tarenton who was busy on he phone that weekend.

Pres had finally gotten up the nerve to call Kerry.

"I had a long talk with my mom today," Pres was saying. "She's really sorry if she upset you."

"I couldn't stand what she said about me, Pres," Kerry said. "She made me feel as if I was just another girl in a long line of Pres Tilford conquests."

Pres gripped the phone tighter. "That's not true, Kerry. You're special to me. You have to believe that. I've had a lot of girls, I admit it. But I've never really cared about one of them. Not like you."

"I don't know, Pres. I feel out of your league. Maybe we should just —"

"Mom didn't have anything against you personally," Pres interrupted. "She said that sometimes she's actually jealous of all the girls I go out with, because they get more attention than she gets from Dad. Anyway, she and Dad are trying to work things out. Things will be better from now on."

"That's great." Kerry said wearily. "I'm happy that everything is better for you. Really."

"What about you and me?" Pres asked softly. "You aren't angry are you? Will you come to the dance with me after Friday's game?"

Kerry hesitated. "No to the first question. I'm not angry. I don't know about the second part. Maybe we shouldn't go out anymore."

Pres felt his heart drop. He needed Kerry. "But why?" he sputtered. "Unless you really are angry."

"It's hard to explain." Kerry said. "But I guess I know what your mom means about being jealous."

Women! Pres thought. "How can you be jealous when I can't get you out of my mind? You don't think I'm fooling around with anybody else, do you? I can tell you I'm not."

"Not now," Kerry admitted. "But in a couple of days, or a couple of weeks, maybe, you will be. I haven't been walking around Tarenton with blinders on all these years. Just about the time I'm really hooked, when I've let myself fall in love with you, you'll lose interest. And I'll be left to drive myself crazy wanting you."

Pres was dumbstruck. No girl he could remember had ever raised this objection before. And now, when for once he had found someone he wanted to love forever, his past was coming back to haunt him.

"Trust me, Kerry." As soon as the words were out of his mouth, Pres knew they wouldn't be enough. He'd said that to at least two dozen girls in the past year. Even to him, it was starting to sound like a line.

The best Pres could do was to get Kerry to promise not to make a decision right away. He'd wait until Friday if necessary. He certainly didn't want to go to the dance with any other girl.

At the other end of town, Mary Ellen had been daydreaming about Patrick.

On Sunday morning, she'd awakened early, clutching her pillow for dear life. The heat was already on in the house, and she'd been dreaming that it was summer and she was at the Narrow Brook Lake public beach. She'd been stretched out on the sand with the dreamiest guy in the world beside her. At first, she hadn't been able to see his face. She'd been gently rubbing suntan oil onto his chest and muscular back. Then she'd decided that what she really wanted to be doing was kissing him.

It was only after the endless dream kiss was finished that she'd suddenly been able to see the face of her companion.

Patrick!

As soon as she'd recognized him, Patrick had started to dissolve. Although she tried to grab him and hold on as tight as she could, the dream Patrick slowly but surely slipped away from her.

She was left wide awake, clinging to her pillow.

Mary Ellen didn't need a psychiatrist to tell her what the dream meant. She'd known all along that Patrick was the one guy who really turned her on. That was exactly the problem!

If she and Patrick ever became a couple, it would be only a matter of time until they were sleeping together. There would be no half-way relationship for them. Then, knowing Patrick, he would want to get engaged. To get married, even.

What scared Mary Ellen was that she might want that, too. If she couldn't forget Patrick now, how would she ever manage to break off with him once they were lovers? And if she couldn't, all her dreams of a modeling career and a life in New York would go right down the drain.

Mary Ellen had been through this a hundred times before. This time, however, she was coming to a different conclusion. Why should she turn her back on love just because of something that might happen months from now? Or years? She'd make those decisions about the future when the time came.

It took half a dozen tries before she got hold of Patrick, who had been out helping his father repair the Henley Trash truck. By then, Mary Ellen had rehearsed what she wanted to say so many times that she couldn't possibly back down.

"I was thinking about our conversation a few days ago," she began. "The one after cheerleading practice. And I've decided to declare an end to the ice age."

"Terrific!" Patrick yelled.

Mary Ellen waited for the expected followup. "So," she said at last, "how about celebrating by inviting me to be your date for the dance Friday night?"

Patrick was silent and then he said slowly, "I'd love to —"

"Good —"

"The thing is," Patrick interrupted her, "I can't. I've already got a date."

"You do! Who with?"

"Vanessa Barlow, actually." Patrick sounded sheepish, not a usual mood for him. "I guess I just sort of fell into it."

"I bet you did!" Mary Ellen was choking with anger and humiliation. "Well, when you manage to claw your way out of whatever you 'just fell into' don't call me." She slammed down the phone.

It took several hours before she was ready to admit that she was really angrier with herself than with Patrick. She'd played hard to get for too long. And now. . . .

No sooner was the thought formed, though, than she changed her mind. Her reasons for resisting Patrick had never been a game. They were very important to her. How could he have hung around for so long, pleading with her to change her mind about him, only to dump her for Vanessa?

That was the end. The ultimate betrayal.

Mary Ellen snatched the pillow from her bed and pounded it with her fists. If that pillow really had been Patrick in the flesh, he would have been black and blue for a week.

Of all the kids who were having problems with dates for Friday's dance, Jimmy Hilbert was unique. Nancy and Olivia were both under the impression that they were going to be his date that night.

Not that Jimmy had a guilty conscience. For one thing, Jimmy's conscience was the only muscle in his body that he never exercised. For another, he was too carried away with congratulating himself for having two girls fighting over him.

In Jimmy's mind, the solution to the problem was simple. Two girls were competing. All he had to do was make up his mind who the lucky winner was going to be. Fortunately, he didn't have to think too hard to come up with the perfect test. On Wednesday afternoon, Mr. and Mrs. Hilbert were leaving for a bar association convention in Chicago. They were planning to be gone overnight and were leaving Jimmy to take care of himself and the house. Jimmy was sure he *could*, too.

Thinking it over, Jimmy had decided that Nancy Goldstein was the girl who would be most likely to understand and appreciate the possibilities opened up by his parents' trip. On Sunday night, right after he got the news himself, he dialed Nancy's number.

He started by suggesting that Nancy come over Wednesday night for dinner. "My folks have an electric grill in the kitchen," he said. "I can cook us up some steaks. It'll be great. Just the two of us."

To Nancy, it sounded good. All except the timing. "I'd love to come over," she said, "but I've got cheerleading practice. It's the last one before the Grove Lake game, too. No way I can miss it."

"How about after practice?" Jimmy suggested.

"Okay, but we won't have much time," Nancy said. "My mother will want me home by ten-thirty at the latest."

"I think we can solve that problem." Boldly, Jimmy suggested that Nancy just might tell her mother that she was planning to stay overnight with a girl friend. "That way," he went on, "we could go out to some of the late-night clubs in Grove Lake. I'm sure we'd get in. I've even got some borrowed ID."

"And then what?" Nancy's voice was dripping with suspicion.

Jimmy decided not to push his luck. "That's strictly up to you. You know what *I'd* like," he said softly. "But it's a big house."

"It couldn't be big enough to suit me," Nancy snapped.

Jimmy couldn't believe it. The conversation had been going so well. "Does that mean you won't do it?" he asked.

"That's *exactly* what it means," Nancy shot back. "We've only gone out a few times. And meanwhile, you've been dating Olivia Evans, too.

140

Don't think I haven't heard about that."

The sound of Nancy slamming the phone down was so loud that Jimmy held the receiver at arm's length. So much for his hunch that Nancy would be a willing date, he told himself. Or maybe not. Maybe he just hadn't been subtle enough. What girl in her right mind would turn down Jimmy Hilbert, if the offer was made in the right way?

As he picked up the phone again to dial Olivia, Jimmy decided that this time he would play it cool. He wouldn't mention his idea about her spending the night. He'd just stick with the invitation to dinner for the time being.

Olivia turned out to be a different kind of surprise. Shy, unsophisticated Olivia — Olivia who had so far been totally untouchable — agreed without an argument to Jimmy's plan for dinner at his house on Wednesday.

Jimmy was so amazed that he was almost, but not quite, suspicious that Olivia had missed his broad hints about the advantages of their having the *whole* house to themselves.

Olivia was if anything even more surprised to hear herself say yes. In fact, if Jimmy hadn't automatically suggested making the date for *after* cheerleading practice, she probably would have agreed to skip practice — something she never did.

Olivia's problem was that she was desperate. Not for Jimmy personally. Not for dates. Or even for male interest in general. She was desperate for a chance to build up her sagging self-confidence.

She was tired of hearing Angie talk about how special Marc's kisses made her feel. She was tired of watching Patrick and Pres and half the guys in school chase after Mary Ellen. She was tired of wondering how she could possibly compete with a sophisticated, sexy-looking girl like Nancy.

Olivia had begun to feel that sexual experience was like a kind of secret club ritual that all her friends knew about except her. Of course, even Angie, who was practically engaged to Marc, said that she would never actually go to bed with him. But Olivia wasn't even sure that this was the truth. For all she knew, everyone did it except her. She and Michael had been so shy that they'd barely gotten to square one, and she was sure her total ignorance must be obvious to the whole world.

Olivia wasn't stupid. She knew that Jimmy's plans for the evening included going beyond the good-night kiss stage. Just how far beyond, she wasn't exactly sure. But at this point anything was better than being a total babe in the woods. She only wished that she could look forward to Wednesday night. She liked Jimmy. At least she'd been telling herself for weeks that this was the next thing to being in love with him. Still, she felt as if their upcoming date was not so much a chance to enjoy each other's company as a kind of club initiation that she would have to grit her teeth and get through, one way or another.

Olivia walked through the first three days of the school week in a numb daze. She barely heard what went on in classes. She jumped and yelled like a robot at cheerleading practice. Luckily, no one noticed. At practice, the whole squad had been on the stiff side. Everyone was still mad at everyone else, but the need to be prepared for Friday's game had triumphed. No one had any good humor left over for kidding around, so Olivia's moodiness didn't attract any attention.

After practice on Wednesday, Olivia spent longer than usual getting dressed. She didn't wear anything special, just slacks and a nice plum-colored sweater. But underneath her sweater she had on a shrimp-colored silk camisole that she'd bought for her cousin's wedding and never worn since. It was the closest thing she owned to sexy lingerie and, best of all, it hid the three vertical scars from her operations. No matter what happened, she was determined not to let Jimmy get a look at those scars.

By the time she was finished making up and went outside to meet Jimmy, she was really nervous. It was the kind of nervousness that always made Olivia talkative and giddy.

"You're in a good mood today," Jimmy said approvingly as he drove. "What happened to quiet, serious Olivia Evans?"

"Oh, I don't know." Olivia laughed. "I guess she isn't here tonight." If she were, Olivia thought silently, she'd be screaming at me to forget this nonsense and go home. The thought made her laugh even more.

At the Hilbert house, Jimmy immediately disappeared into the kitchen. "Wait till you try this," he shouted out to Olivia in the living room. "My folks have a great cellar."

"Cellar?"

"You know. For wine." Jimmy reappeared, carrying a bottle of red wine and two crystal glasses.

Olivia took a tentative sip of the wine Jimmy poured for her, and put the glass down. "I guess I'm not thirsty," she said.

Jimmy howled with laughter. "You don't have to be thirsty to drink wine." And to demonstrate, he finished off his glass in one gulp.

Then, all of a sudden, Jimmy pounced. His mouth clamped onto hers in a clumsy, unappealing kiss. Olivia felt herself pushed backward into the corner of the couch. It was all happening so fast! It didn't take her long to decide that she didn't care for Jimmy's style.

She liked it even less when she felt his hand begin to move under her sweater. She pushed his hand away, but Jimmy was not about to be discouraged.

The sensation of his cold hand on her warm skin jolted Olivia back to the unpleasant reality of the situation she was in. What am I doing here? she thought. I don't really *like* this boy, no less *love* him. I don't have to prove anything to myself *or* him. I am who I am, and it's okay.

Olivia squirmed free, nearly dumping Jimmy on the floor in the process.

Jimmy's face was a mask of surprise. "What's going on?" he gulped.

Olivia reached for the first excuse that came

to mind. "I think I don't feel so good," she said. "Maybe it was that sip of wine."

Just hearing herself say it, Olivia felt stupid. All her life she'd hated it when her mother used her little girl's health as an excuse for why Olivia shouldn't do things. Now she was doing the very same thing. Then and there, Olivia made a decision.

"No. That's not true!" she said. "I'm not sick at all. What I am is mad."

Jimmy, sinking into the depths of the sofa, looked almost funny to her. His sauve macho act interrupted, he had suddenly turned to Jell-O.

"You don't care about me at all," Olivia went on accusingly. "You just wanted to take advantage of your parents being away. Any girl at all would do. All you want is a *body*. You're really a creep."

Olivia didn't wait for an answer. Grabbing her coat and scarf, she stormed out the door of the Hilbert house. She was halfway down the driveway before it occurred to her that she was going to have a very long walk home. But she felt free, as if she had done something important.

CHAPTER

13

For someone who was in deep trouble, Walt was feeling awfully triumphant.

All week long he had been waiting for Mr. Gaetano to show his true colors. Today, when Walt reported for his after school detention it had finally happened.

"On Friday I've got to turn in my preliminary list of students in danger of failing English," Gaetano had explained. "It's up to you, Walt, to decide whether you want to be on it or not. If you want to pass, you'll have to give me your word that you'll make up the journal assignments you've missed so far."

Mr. Gaetano was trying to give Walt one last chance. What Walt heard was a threat. And the phrase "give me your word" struck an especially sour chord.

"*My* word!" Walt said. "What good is a promise to you? You said you wouldn't get me into

146

trouble about the accident. And not an hour later, you'd reported me to the superintendent of schools."

"I have no idea what you're talking about," Mr. Gaetano protested. "I haven't even talked to Dr. Barlow."

"Maybe not. Maybe you reported me to Mrs. Oetjen and she told Barlow. What's the difference? I still can't trust you."

Now that Walt thought he wasn't to blame, failing English no longer seemed so bad. It proved what he'd been feeling. The whole world was against him. His only real friend was himself.

Even though Walt was busy congratulating himself, he was still paying careful attention to the road. The bill for fixing the Gaetano car had been large enough to teach him one lesson at least. He noticed the small, fast-moving form of Olivia Evans as soon as he came over the crest of Robin's Hill. She was just starting up the hill coming toward him, her face already red from the effort.

Walt drove down the hill and came to a stop at Olivia's side. "What are you doing way out here?" he asked.

"What does it look like I'm doing?" Olivia puffed. "Walking."

"Want a ride?"

Olivia shook her head. "No thanks. I'm perfectly capable of taking care of myself."

Walt grinned. "I never said you weren't. That doesn't mean you can't accept a ride, does it?"

Olivia looked longingly at the passenger seat

of the jeep. It was more than three miles to the nearest bus stop. Most of them uphill. And it was already beginning to get dark. "Okay," she agreed. "But don't ask me what I'm doing out here on this road."

"I wouldn't think of it," Walt assured her. But that was one promise no mere human could keep. Less than a mile up the road, his curiosity was already getting the better of him. "I can't help it," he said. "What are you doing out here?"

"You'd never understand," Olivia said, "because you've always been part of the in-crowd. But when you go through life feeling that you have something to prove, you can end up getting into some dumb situations."

Walt winced. Somehow the problem Olivia was describing sounded all too familiar. "Maybe I would understand," he said. "Try me."

Half sputtering with embarrassment and half laughing, Olivia related the story of her wrestling match with Jimmy Hilbert. "At least it was an instant cure for my crush on him," she giggled ruefully. "Jimmy is a jerk. But I hate to think that he'll tell the story all over school and make me look ridiculous."

"I have the idea that he won't do that," Walt said. Only that day after English class, he explained, he'd heard Nancy Goldstein tell Susan that she'd been invited to Jimmy's house that evening and turned him down. "So far Jimmy has been playing the two of you against each other," Walt added, "and it worked like a charm. You were mad at Nancy. Nancy was mad at you. Neither of you was mad at Jimmy. Which you would have been, if you and Nancy had ever thought of talking the situation over with each other."

"I guess you're right," Olivia agreed. "This whole argument never would have gotten started if I'd just trusted my friends on the squad."

As Walt's jeep pulled up in front of the Evans house, Olivia reached over and gave him a big hug. "Thanks for the advice," she said. "I won't forget. Squad loyalty forever!"

Squad loyalty!

That was all very well for Olivia. But Walt still wasn't sure how that motto was supposed to apply to him. He was still wondering where, if anywhere, he fit in.

Walt was almost home when he remembered that his parents were going to be working late at the broadcasting studio that evening. There would be no dinner waiting for him. Turning his jeep around, he headed back toward the Burger King near Pineland Mall and went inside for a hamburger and shake.

The Burger King was almost empty except for one woman who was with her three children at a table in the far corner. Walt took a table at the opposite side of the room and sat down to eat. Although he loved being the center of attention in any group, for some reason he always felt awkward and conspicuous when he had to be in a public place alone. To pass the time, he started watching a blonde girl in a Burger King uniform and hat who was busy cleaning up the mess left by departed patrons.

His hamburger was almost gone before he finally realized who she was. Cindy Hartman from school! Although he'd been in classes with Cindy for years, he'd never really noticed her before — except lately, as Vanessa Barlow's newest shadow.

Cindy's looks made her perfect for that role. She was Vanessa's opposite in almost every way. In fact, if Vanessa were a photograph, Cindy might have been the negative. She had natural white-blonde hair and very pale skin, in contrast to the tawny, dark Vanessa. Her figure was lanky and angular, where Vanessa's was all curves. And she was as quiet as Vanessa was melodramatic.

Noticing her now, Walt couldn't help thinking that Cindy looked interesting. Not pretty maybe, but interesting. It was too bad that she was tied to Vanessa's apron strings.

It was almost as if Cindy was able to read his mind.

Looking up from her work, she smiled shyly in Walt's direction. "Hi," she ventured. "I'm in your class at Tarenton High."

"Of course," Walt grinned. "I know who you are. Cindy Hartman."

Cindy looked pleased. Walt, meanwhile, breathed an invisible sigh of relief that he remembered her name in time. All of his good friends, whatever problems they might have, were class stars. He could hardly imagine what it would be like to think that other kids in his own

150

class might not remember who he was.

"Can I sit down?" Cindy asked nervously. "I think I ought to talk to you."

"Sure." Walt had no idea what was coming.

"I guess I shouldn't tell you this . . . but I've been feeling guilty for days."

"Guilty?" Walt repeated dumbly.

"Yeah. See, I was in the room when Vanessa called you last Saturday. We planned it ahead of time."

"Planned it?"

Cindy laughed. "You're starting to sound like an echo."

Bit by bit, the story came out. Cindy told about how Vanessa had found out about the accident. Not from her father, who never heard about it, but from the garage man at Harry's. It was Vanessa, too, who'd planted the idea in Tom Gaetano's mind that Walt was insulting him behind his back.

"Why are you telling me this?" Walt asked, amazed.

Cindy shook her head in confusion. "I don't know for sure. I suppose I'm being disloyal to Vanessa. But I don't think she deserves my loyalty. And I guess I started to feel guilty. I always thought you were a nice guy. Now you're getting in trouble and it's all our fault."

"I don't think so," Walt said. "I made some of that trouble for myself. Vanessa just helped me out along the way. Come to think of it, if my head had been on straight I'd never have believed any rumor I heard from her."

"I hope you're not angry," Cindy said.

"Funny thing. This is just about the first time in weeks I *haven't* been angry," Walt answered. "But I do have some important questions to ask you."

"Me? Important?" Cindy looked confused.

"Sure. Number one: Do you like to dance? And number two: Are you busy Friday night?"

Cindy laughed. "I was expecting hard questions. Those are easy."

By the time Walt left the Burger King, he had his answers.

CHAPTER

14

"Here we go . . . ready or not!" Ardith Engborg announced, prepared to flip the switch connecting Walt's tape machine to the auditorium sound system.

The stands were nearly filled. A sell out crowd of home-team fans had turned out to see the Tarenton Wolves try to beat the Grove Lake Grizzlies. There was even a camera crew from the local independent TV station busily conferencing at the other end of the players' bench, waiting for the action to begin.

Out on the court, Walt and Pres had just finished arranging a long gym mat that the squad planned to use for its pre-game pep routine. After debating the matter for two days, Coach Engborg had decided to go with Walt's idea after all and do the break-dance style drill that he had worked out.

"Our practice sessions have not been exactly inspired," Ardith had announced at the pre-game meeting. "Maybe what we all need is a challenge to pull this squad together again."

Nancy Goldstein nervously fingered the red-and-white pleats of her cheerleading skirt as she waited for the music to begin. "I just hope I don't trip and fall while the camera's on me," she said.

"You'll do fine," Olivia Evans patted her on the back. "You've got the moves."

Which I don't, Mary Ellen thought nervously, as she took her place at the end of the line. Somehow, though, she felt more elated than nervous. The prospect of being on camera was enough to make her forget her reservations about this routine. It was even enough to make her forget, temporarily, that Patrick would be at the dance with Vanessa Barlow.

When Walt and Pres had returned to take their places at the head of the line, Ardith flipped the switch to start the music.

"Baby, do the Beat Street strut . . . it's so hot. . . ."

Its attention grabbed by the unusual music, the home crowd burst into applause. Then, as the squad took the floor, one by one, the crowd began clapping in unison.

As she waited, the last to join the line, Mary Ellen noted the others' movements admiringly. Walt, of course, was the best. His stocky body looked so unsuited to this kind of dancing that his high kicks and sinuous steps were all the more breathtaking. And when he sank to the floor for a dramatic break dance solo, the crowd burst into spontaneous applause. Even the TV crew, which had been standing around looking bored at being stuck for the evening at a mere high school game, came to life and started the cameras rolling.

Olivia, who joined Walt on the floor next, was a natural at this routine.

And Nancy, who came third, was almost as good.

Even Pres, and then Angie, did respectably. Obviously they had been getting in some extra practice.

Here goes! Mary Ellen told herself as her turn came to go out onto the floor. Giving herself up to the music, she imagined that she was the girl on the rock video, learning to dance this way for the first time. To her surprise, the make believe started to work. The pasted smile on her face started to feel real. She was enjoying herself! And for the first time, she felt natural doing the high sideways kicks and strutting steps.

The response of the crowd and the continuing interest of the TV crew, as it kept the cameras rolling, told the entire squad that the routine had caught on. About halfway through the record, a voice-over that Mary Ellen recognized as Walt's strong tenor broke into the song with a new lyric: "The *Wolves* are *so hot . . . do the Beat Street strut. . . . Beat the Grizzlies.*"

The crowd clapped wildly, then sang along.

As the tape came to an end, Mary Ellen ran to the sidelines and grabbed the megaphone, determined to keep up the pitch of excitement.

> "Hear ye . . . hear ye
> Read all about it. . . .
> We got a team.
> No doubt about it. . . .
> Clap your hands! Stamp your feet!
> The WOLVES are the team
> That can't be beat!!!"

The spirit was there. The squad was its old self again.

The action on the court, meanwhile, was not going quite so smoothly. Mary Ellen had been wondering before the game just what would happen when it came time to give individual cheers for Jimmy Hilbert's baskets. She had envisioned Olivia and Nancy practically at each other's throats vying for the honor. As it turned out, there was no opportunity for competition on that score.

After allowing a few baskets to Jimmy in the first quarter, the Grizzly defense simply double-teamed Jimmy, rendering him helpless.

"That's just what my cousin predicted," Angie muttered during an early time-out. "It's going to take more than one hot shot to beat this opponent."

"Gaetano was right about that," Walt agreed.

"Glad to hear you say so, old buddy," Pres

added. Now that his own problems were beginning to straighten out, he was finding it hard to recall exactly why he'd been so down on Walt lately. As usual, it didn't occur to him to put his change of heart into words. Pres wasn't the type to talk about his feelings more than he had to. But Walt had been around Pres long enough to recognize a peace feeler when he heard it. "See," he announced to the others, "even the great Preston Tilford III agrees with us. We must be right."

Instead of bristling at this, Pres grinned serenely. Walt was definitely back to his old self again, making wisecracks and dishing out backhanded insults.

Even Ardith Engborg couldn't help smiling with satisfaction at Walt's recovery — but only for a second or two. "We're not here to be basketball critics," she reminded everyone. "We're cheerleaders, in case you've all forgotten."

"We've got the T-E-A-M that's on the B-E-A-M. . . ." Angie shouted, leading the others into the cheer.

When the time-out ended, however, Angie really had something to shout about. Her own brother, Andrew, was being sent in to replace Jimmy Hilbert. "Andrew, Andrew, he's our man! If he can't do it, no one can!" she yelled.

Andrew's entry into the game did change the Wolves' luck. From lagging ten points behind, the team caught up to within a basket of the Grizzlies. Unfortunately, for the next three quarters it was a question of playing catch-up. Every time the Wolves narrowed the score, the Grizzlies would get a spurt of energy and pull ahead again.

Mary Ellen had never cheered so hard in her life. She cheered for Andrew. And she cheered even louder, if possible, when Hank Vreewright came into the game with his bandaged knee to make one last try for the team. The final results of the contest were in doubt right up to the last play. With just seconds to go, the Wolves had pulled to within two points of the Grizzlies once again, and Hank was loping down the floor with time for one more shot. The entire Tarenton section rose to its feet as Hank let the ball fly. Then they watched in agony as the ball lazily rolled around the hoop and dropped to one side. A moan of dismay arose spontaneously from fans and cheerleaders alike.

Oddly enough, the loss didn't seem to dim the fans' spirits. After the final buzzer sounded, the entire Tarenton section stayed on its feet while Mary Ellen and Pres led them all in the "Growl, Wolves, Growl!" cheer. Next came the Tarenton High fight song, and still no one left. Finally, after a good five or ten minutes of cheering, the fans slowly began to disperse.

"You can all be proud of yourselves tonight," Ardith told the squad as they huddled for a brief post-game meeting before going to the locker rooms. "It's easy to keep a crowd cheering for a winning team. But not every squad can keep up the energy when their team is lagging behind."

Ardith's judgment turned out to be shared by the TV news crew. That evening, on the local ten o'clock news, the clips of the game featured more than a few shots of the Tarenton cheerleading squad in action. "Tarenton basketball fans showed up in force tonight for a game that marked a new stage in the town's old rivalry with Grove Lake," was the way the sportscaster framed the story. The fact that the Grizzlies had actually won the game was mentioned only as an afterthought.

Mary Ellen, watching on a portable TV in Ardith Engborg's office, was the only member of the squad to see the news report. The rest had all gone downstairs to the cafeteria where the after-game dance was already underway.

Even Ardith was surprised that Mary Ellen was willing to miss the dance just to see the report on TV. "I'm saving this all on videotape so we can watch it tomorrow," she reminded Mary Ellen for what seemed like the hundredth time. "There's no need for you to miss the dance."

"I haven't missed anything," Mary Ellen finally said as she got up to leave after the report ended.

Before Ardith could ask for an explanation, Mary Ellen fled to the showers. She did not plan to go to the dance at all. At least that's what she'd been telling herself all day. Plenty of girls went to Friday night school dances without dates. There was no couples-only rule. But going solo to a dance was not an experience that Mary Ellen

Kirkwood ever had to face before. Nor was it one that she had any desire to go through for the first time.

Knowing that Patrick would be at the dance with Vanessa, after she'd actually broken down and suggested he take her, only made the prospect less appealing.

If she hurried, there would still be time to ask Ardith for a ride home. Mary Ellen showered and changed quickly and went over to the mirrors by the sinks to fix her hair. "Coward!" she said accusingly as she faced her own image in the mirror. "You know very well that if you don't show up at the dance, Patrick will think you stayed away because of him and Vanessa."

Of course it wasn't true.

Then, too, there was the prospect of having to explain to Ardith why she was going straight home and skipping the dance. Ardith's speech after the game had reminded everyone that the coach had no respect for quitters.

Mary Ellen studied her appearance in the mirror critically. Since the dance was being held right after the game, there was no dress code at all. Some girls would be dressed up, but others would no doubt show up in casual clothes. Still, the outfit that she had on was not what Mary Ellen Kirkwood would normally be expected to wear to a dance: tan slacks and a long-sleeved blouse that she had often worn to school, and a hand-knit vest of gold-toned wool that her sister Gemma had made and given to her for Christmas.

"Not great. Not great at all," she told herself. But it would have to do. Even if she just stayed at the dance for five minutes, it would be better than not showing up at all and letting Patrick Henley think he'd kept her away.

CHAPTER

15

For the after-game dance, the high school cafeteria had been transformed into an ice-castle fantasy. The formica tables and ugly tan chairs were gone, banished to the storerooms. The dull green walls were hidden under yards of gauzy white material. Even the old tile floor was unrecognizable, covered with silver spangles that glittered like snowflakes under the bluish spotlights.

Angie Poletti had more to be happy about than just the decorations. At the last minute, Marc had decided that he could make the time to come home for the weekend after all. As she stood near the main entrance, watching the other couples arrive, Angie felt Marc's strong hands resting lightly on her shoulders. She had all but resigned herself to attending the dance alone. Now, having Marc here with her was almost better than if it had been planned that way all along.

Angie knew why *she* was happy.

She knew why Pres was happy, too. A few minutes ago, he had come through the door with Kerry Elliott at his side, beaming proudly. No one could say Pres and Kerry were a natural couple: Pres, the golden boy, and shy Kerry, who hated the limelight. But for tonight at least, Kerry had overcome her doubts. She leaned her head against his shoulder as they danced, determined not to let all the still unanswered questions in her head drive her crazy.

It was a lot harder to figure out just what Nancy and Olivia had to be so thrilled about. By Friday afternoon, Nancy had managed to spread the news all over school that she and Jimmy Hilbert had a date for the dance that night. Angie had expected Olivia to be throwing tantrums of jealousy. Instead, the two girls had seemed to get along awfully well during tonight's game.

And in the locker room afterward, they had gone into one of the changing rooms together and come out, giggling, wearing identical dresses. Chic-looking shifts of jersey wool with raglan sleeves and wide, hip-hugging sashes. Only the colors were different. Nancy's dress was a soft shade of rose that made her dark complexion look all the more radiant; Olivia's, a vibrant purple, the kind of bright, dramatic color she seldom wore, but which made her youthful looks seem suddenly very sophisticated.

163

"You both look great," Angie had said admiringly.

She had not wanted to ask why both girls were wearing the same dress. Maybe it had been a coincidence, in which case the less said, the better.

But the impish looks on both their faces told her otherwise. Something was up. "So what's going on?" Angie had teased. "Are you doing an Eismar twins imitation?"

Angie hadn't gotten an answer then. Just a pair of knowing grins that said, "wait and see." But when Nancy and Olivia showed up at the door to the cafeteria still arm in arm, Angie caught on right away. She knew what was going to happen even before Jimmy Hilbert, who had been lounging by the ticket desk, happily waiting for the arrival of his date for the evening.

"Hi, Jimmy," Nancy said, ignoring the confused looks he was shooting her way. "I knew you wouldn't mind if I brought Olivia along for the evening. Since you're such good friends and all."

Without further explanation, each of the girls took one of Jimmy's arms and ushered him up to the ticket desk.

"Jimmy loves the idea of having two girls chasing him," Angie said, explaining the situation to Marc. "But I guess he didn't count on having both of them catch him at exactly the same time."

His face a picture of total resignation, Jimmy danced first with Nancy, then with Olivia, then with Nancy again.

By the end of the set, though, he was alone. While he was taking his turn with Olivia, Michael calmly strode onto the floor and cut in. Nancy, meanwhile, had begun dancing with Andrew Poletti.

Jimmy stood in the middle of the floor for a minute or two, looking bewildered. Then he slunk off in the direction of the refreshments.

Angie and Marc, who were taking a break themselves, noticed Jimmy's fate. "I almost feel sorry for him." Angie said. "Or I would if the whole thing weren't so funny."

"Vanessa won't like this," a voice from behind them predicted. "She was counting on Nancy and Olivia to cancel each other out by making a scene. Then she would swoop down and steal him from both of them. Somehow, though, I don't think this was the kind of scene she had in mind."

Angie turned around. The voice belonged to Cindy Hartman, who was looking unusually pretty in a pale blue blouse and black, ankle-length slacks. And with her was Walt.

"You'll be happy to know I'm not flunking English after all," Walt announced. "Thanks to Cindy here."

Walt explained that he had turned in the first installment of his journal, and would be catching up by doing extra writing after school for the next two weeks. "Your cousin is actually a pretty nice guy after all," Walt conceded to Angie. "I'm sorry I ever doubted it. It was my fault, but my feud with Mr. Gaetano did get a little boost from

Vanessa. It took Cindy here to remind me of who my friends were."

Angie looked at Cindy questioningly. "But aren't you —"

"Vanessa's shadow?" Cindy suggested, finishing Angie's thought for her. "I was, but no more. I've resigned."

"Speak of the devil. . . ." Marc's deep baritone voice boomed out louder than he had intended. All eyes turned toward the door.

Vanessa had arrived. She was wearing a full-skirted red dress with a plunging neckline and ankle strap shoes. At her side was Patrick Henley. Judging from the way Vanessa posed in the doorway, Patrick was no more than just another part of her get-up for the evening. And not the most important part, at that.

When Vanessa accepted Patrick's invitation to the dance, she had never intended to stick with him all evening. And certainly she didn't plan to be taken home in the Henley Trash pickup truck. Her original plans had called for her to dance with Patrick the first hour or so. Just long enough to set up her move on Jimmy Hilbert.

Vanessa hadn't known earlier in the week who would end up being Jimmy's date for the dance — Nancy or Olivia. But she had bet that either girl would be driving Jimmy crazy with jealous questions about the other. Maybe they'd even end up quarreling. And that would be her golden opportunity.

Scanning the room from the doorway, Vanessa

realized that part of her plan hadn't worked out. Mary Ellen was nowhere in sight. So her entrance on Patrick's arm had been at least partly wasted.

On the other hand, Jimmy was standing all alone over by the punch bowl.

Vanessa saw no reason to hang around with Patrick a minute longer. "See you later," she said, dismissing Patrick without regret. And she made a beeline across the floor in Jimmy's direction.

Marc, Angie, Walt, and Cindy all watched with interest the look of rising panic on Jimmy's face. When Vanessa was five feet away, he suddenly turned around and bolted out the door.

"Gee," Angie said, "what got into him? I thought he and Vanessa would make the perfect couple."

"Some other time, maybe," Marc mused. "If you ask me, Jimmy has had too much girl trouble for one day. He just wasn't ready to take on Vanessa, too."

Marc put his arm around Angie's shoulder and steered her back out onto the dance floor. "Let's forget about Vanessa for now. We're together. That's what counts."

"Right you are," Angie agreed. And she closed her eyes and rested her head on Marc's shoulder. For the rest of the evening, being with Marc was enough to put her on top of the world.

At the moment, togetherness was the last thing on Mary Ellen's mind.

She had purposely waited out in the hall until

a slow dance started, hoping to time her solo entrance so that it attracted the minimum attention. At the moment when the lights were at their dimmest, she judged that her chance had come. Straightening her spine and squaring her shoulders, she stepped through the door.

"Melon!"

The sound of the nickname she hated, booming out in Patrick's idea of a normal conversational voice, made her want to cringe. But it was too late. Patrick had spotted her entrance immediately and was already at her side.

"Where's Vanessa?" Mary Ellen asked coldly, forgetting for a second that she was not supposed to care.

"I got dumped," Patrick said cheerfully. "I should have known that Vanessa had an ulterior motive for coming with me. I guess I just got carried away, thinking she was mesmerized by my great body. Anyway, forget Vanessa. Let's dance."

Mary Ellen yearned to be in his arms. But her feelings were in a turmoil. I'm the one who's mesmerized, she thought. "Why should I dance with you," she said aloud, "after you turned me down for another girl?"

Patrick shrugged. "No reason. Unless it's because you want to. You know I only came with her to make you jealous."

Mary Ellen watched in confusion as Patrick began to walk away from her. The fact was, she did want to. There was no use pretending otherwise.

"Hey, wait a minute!" she said, calling him back. "Don't tell me you're going to give up so easily."

"What do you think?" Patrick asked. And without another word, he swept her into his arms and out onto the dance floor. Neither of them spoke again for as long as the song lasted. For two people who could barely have a conversation without getting into an argument, they danced smoothly together, as if they belonged in each other's arms. Mary Ellen's blonde head next to Patrick's dark one made a handsome contrast.

As the last strains of the music died away, Patrick cupped Mary Ellen's face in his big, work-hardened hands. "You really are an impossible girl to figure out," he said. "Does this mean you're going to stop fighting your feelings for me? Is tonight a beginning for us? Or is this only a temporary truce?"

For one heart-twisting moment, Mary Ellen felt tempted to give Patrick the answer he wanted to hear. She opened her mouth to speak, only to see him shake his head in warning. "Forget it," he said. "I guess I'm not ready for an honest answer to that one. I'd rather just enjoy being with you right now."

The music started up again, another slow song. Mary Ellen rested her head dreamily against Patrick's muscular shoulder. For the moment, being close to Patrick felt completely right. She tried her best to pretend that the feeling would last forever. But she knew herself too well. Tomorrow all her old yearnings for a different kind of life would start again. But just for tonight, Patrick's arms around her and his lips against her cheek were all she wanted.

Caroline B. Cooney

CHEERLEADERS

5

All the Way

CHAPTER

1

Mary Ellen Kirkwood stepped out in front of the other five cheerleaders; placed her long, slim legs in a V; tossed her head; and cupped her hands around her mouth.

The eyes of five hundred basketball fans were fixed on her, waiting for the cheer. The crowd was screaming already. They were full of energy and excitement, and the cheer would channel their screams into a pounding rhythm.

She knew how beautiful she was with her golden hair gleaming under the hot lights of the Tarenton High gymnasium. No colors could be better for her fair complexion than the white and scarlet of her uniform.

How I love being a cheerleader! Mary Ellen

thought. "All the way!" she yelled at the crowd.

The din in the gymnasium was deafening. Nobody could possibly have heard those three words, not even the other five Varsity cheerleaders facing Mary Ellen. But they could read her lips, and Tarenton fans knew all the cheers and loved them. They would join in.

She did not glance behind her. She knew the coaches were arguing fiercely with the referee, the boys tensely poised to continue the game or come to blows. Whichever side lost this decision was going to fly into a rage.

But Mary Ellen herself was winning.

This hour, this moment, she was Number One. She had it all.

Looks, figure, brains — those she had worked on all her life. But this year she was captain of Varsity. She was the girl with the scarlet carnation pinned to her white wool sweater. Four hundred thirty-seven girls in Tarenton High and she — only she — had such a badge of success.

But there was more.

Behind her, pacing, was Donny Parrish, captain of the basketball team that would take Tarenton to the regional and state championships. Donny Parrish, with more points this season than any single boy in the region — except the co-captain of the opposite team, Ben Adamson.

Donny: tall, muscular, handsome, and — maybe — hers.

Donny had not dated in the six months since

his beloved girl friend moved away. Last week he had invited a girl on his first date after all that time.

And the girl was Mary Ellen Kirkwood.

She smiled with delight just thinking about it.

Beaming at the crowd, thrilled with herself, Mary Ellen started the cheer rhythm with two sharp, geometric gestures. At either end of the squad lineup, the two boys who made Varsity so spectacular stepped farther out, motioned high and wide, and then each girl did a quick sidestep. Mary Ellen stepped into the opening this created. On her third gesture, they swiveled as sharply as a color guard turning a corner, raised their fists in a victory salute, and began the cheer that Tarenton fans wanted to scream:

> Roadway, runway, *rail*way!
> Make this game our vict'ry day.
> *Alllllll* the way!   *Alllllll* the way!
> *Not* just halfway — *cut out* the horseplay!
> Make this game our vict'ry day.
> *Alllllll* the way!   *Alllllll* the way!
> *Yeaaaaah, Tarenton!*

But the finest cheering in America wasn't going to sway this referee. The decision went against Tarenton. Garrison, the enemy, would get two free throws.

A massive scream of protest rose from the throats of five hundred Tarenton fans on the west side of the gym, matched by shouts of triumph from the Garrison crowd.

They had a particularly stupid pair of referees this game. Of all games to draw dunces! Garrison had bitterly fought Tarenton for the regional championships for years now — high school basketball was very important in their part of the country. So you would think that the league organizers would have been sure to send their best to this game. But no. They had sent two men who couldn't distinguish between a basketball and a bowling ball.

Tarenton was on its collective feet, yelling unprintable names and waving fists. The three policemen assigned to the game were shifting from the gymnasium doors to the edge of the bleachers. Everyone knew that the worst thing would be for the cops actually to get involved. That would be the spark that would set the actual fire. So far it was only words and gestures. One more problem and there would be fists.

Now the score was close. There were dangerously few moments left in the game. This decision might well end in an enemy victory.

Enemy.

A word for war.

But this year, it was true.

The animosity between Tarenton and Garrison had reached an appalling level. Although there were decades of traditional rivalry between the two schools, there had never been a time when there was so much open anger at games.

It began during football and soccer. Fistfights, bloody noses, a dislocated jaw, and a lot of anonymous obscenities screamed from the sidelines.

The local paper ran editorials: "What is happening in our schools? Are we teaching our children violence?" The principal, the vice-principal, coaches, teachers — they all lectured the kids. Nobody knew what to do about the situation. With each game the hostility relentlessly accelerated.

Right now you could feel violence in the air, ready to explode into an attack.

Mary Ellen had devised a particular signal for her squad. As the Tarenton fans stood up in their seats, and several older boys gave every sign of being about to stomp down the bleachers and beat the referee to a pulp, she got her squad started in a very complex, wide-ranging cheer. It involved twists and spins, side slides and pikes.

What it was was a moving fence. A human barricade of waving arms, scarlet-wrapped legs, and rustling pompons — six Varsity cheerleaders effectively blockading the court and distracting the eye.

Actually, this wasn't an appropriate time for the cheer. In fact the words to this particular cheer were rather stupid and had nothing to do with anything. But then, Mary Ellen reflected, a lot of cheers were like that. What did roadways, railways, and runways have to do with basketball games? But they kept the fans happy.

Hopefully this cheer would keep the fans off the gym floor as well, and help prevent the spill of blood.

Especially, Mary Ellen thought adoringly, Donny's blood.

Donny was in a peculiar position. Having brought Tarenton to victory in every single game so far this season, he was expected to do so again tonight, against Garrison. If they lost, even by a single point (especially by a single point) Tarenton would be furious with Donny. No matter that he'd racked up nineteen points in this game; no matter that he so carefully helped the others set up their own plays.

What counted was winning.

Winning against Garrison.

Mary Ellen shivered inside her thick, white wool sweater. The pressure was almost unbearable. She felt responsible for the game, as if her throat, her cries, her flashing colors could clinch the score. How must Donny be feeling? *He* had to beat Ben Adamson of Garrison.

The two captains were somewhat alike. Both towered over the rest of the players. Ben was probably a few inches taller and quite a few pounds heavier than Donny. But Ben was beaky like a hawk, with oddly stooped shoulders near the top of his six-and-a-half-feet height. Ben looked like a burned-out criminal. The cheer-leaders had once joked about Ben.

"Not a future athlete of America," Olivia said. "A future *felon* of America."

Donny was rather wholesome looking. Rather. Not completely. Both boys had developed a need to win that surpassed their other characteristics. It came through in everything they did. There was nothing sweet or friendly in their dispositions.

Mary Ellen loved that antagonism, that determination. She had much the same spirit herself, although it didn't show so clearly. All her life she had wanted to be Number One. Mary Ellen — the poor kid in the lousy neighborhood, whose mother was a clerk and whose father drove a bus. Mary Ellen — who did laundry for the neighbors to earn spending money.

Well, tonight, Mary Ellen truly was Number One. There could not be a single girl in the huge audience who was not eaten up with envy over Mary Ellen Kirkwood.

She had known she would love such a position, but she had not known how *much* she would love it. It permeated her every thought, spreading through her life like a gas. Invisible, but everywhere. She breathed it in like oxygen. It was her own private victory over the world.

The game continued.

The fans relaxed slightly, their wrath slowed by the outlet of cheering.

Mary Ellen signaled the squad to take a much-deserved rest. All six sank to the bench in utter exhaustion. Anybody who thought cheerleading was a wimpy sport should have watched Tarenton's Varsity Squad tonight.

No sooner had they hit the wooden seats than Garrison's cheerleading squad leaped to their feet, taking instant advantage of a time-out.

Mary Ellen kicked herself. She should have seen this coming and been ready for it. Now Garrison's cheerleading squad could run out on the floor and do a display, not just a sideline cheer.

Sure enough, the twelve girls from Garrison ran out on the gymnasium center, spread themselves across it, and proceeded to steal the show.

Tarenton had a most unusual squad. First of all, it was coed. There were only a handful of squads in the entire state with boys. Boys added tremendous strength to the squad and allowed for all sorts of lifts and tosses that girls alone could not do. But Tarenton had only six on Varsity, with the rest of the would-be cheerleaders on Pompon Squad.

Garrison had twelve girls. Clad in bright green and vivid yellow, the girls were garish and gaudy. But extremely effective. Unlike Tarenton, which went in for gymnastic-type moves, Garrison was more of a dancing unit. Their moves were intricate but delicate. They were extremely feminine in a totally traditional way. The contrast between the two squads could not have been greater.

Six Garrison girls faced the Garrison side of the gym, and six faced Tarenton. They linked arms, alternating directions, and began one of the most impressive high-kick routines Mary Ellen had ever seen. There was not a single person in the gym ignoring them. Let the basketball players have their huddle! Everybody was taking a break from basketball to appreciate the sight of brilliant symmetry among twelve lovely dancing girls.

Two rows behind her, Mary Ellen heard a Tarenton fan exclaim, "That squad is better than ours!"

If they had accused Mary Ellen of war crimes, she could not have been more upset. *She was Number One!* And therefore, so was the squad she captained.

To her utter horror, several voices agreed. "They're wonderful," came the admiring remarks.

At a time when Garrison was the enemy, people were saying that Garrison's cheerleaders were better. It was all Mary Ellen could do not to turn around and smack their faces. Stinkers, she thought, tears of rage and hurt pricking the back of her eyes. Rotten, no-good judges of cheerleading! What do you know about anything? You traitors. How dare you say Garrison's good at anything at a time like this?

Her eyes fixed on Garrison's performance.

They were a very fluid group with sinuous, sensuous motions. Like sirens on the rock, luring sailors to their deaths.

Her squad could never do that. Their two boys were not dancers and — naturally enough — lacked the feminine grace of those girls. Pres Tilford was handsome, dark-blond, muscle-bound male energy. Walt Manners was clown, technique, personality, and height. As for the girls, she, Angie, and Nancy were all dancers, but Olivia was a dazzling gymnast. Lightweight and wiry, Olivia had spectacular tumbling and flipping abilities.

Garrison positively slithered through a routine that seemed to Mary Ellen like pure sex.

"Hey, Kirkwood!" came a shout from way up in the bleachers. "How come *we* can't show off like that?"

Mary Ellen's cheeks burned with humiliation and anger. I don't *want* to show off like that, she thought. And if you were any judge of real ability, you'd put us so far ahead of Garrison it would be laughable.

With a flourish, Garrison wrapped up its display. When Tarenton clapped for them almost as hard as Garrison itself, Mary Ellen's chest tightened with pain. *We're* the best, not Garrison! she thought, agonized.

Vanessa Barlow, who had not made the squad and who was dedicated to getting even, smiled broadly. She threw back her dark, shining hair in a typical Vanessa gesture and called out, "*I* could have added something *you* just don't have — *sex.*"

Mary Ellen was not the only cheerleader to feel disgraced. All six moved closer together, deeply upset.

Olivia said, "We're going to learn new routines. I don't care how many hours we have to practice. *Nobody* is ever again going to say we're second best."

One of the very few people in the overheated, smelly gymnasium who was not watching the Garrison cheerleading squad was Nancy Goldstein. A cheerleader for Tarenton, she normally found cheerleading the most absorbing activity, no matter who was cheering. But tonight her dark eyes and her heart were elsewhere. She was gripped by the shoulders and head of Ben Adamson, who towered over everybody but Mary Ellen's Donny.

Nancy thought Ben was the most sexual person she had ever looked at. He claimed more space than other boys out there. Just the way he stood proclaimed ownership. He was like an astronaut putting a flag on the moon. Ben owned the floor, owned that ball, owned the entire game.

Nancy certainly did not want her team to lose. She loved victory and hated defeat; her entire purpose as a cheerleader was to assist in victory. But she found herself captivated by Ben. Stop this daydreaming that *he*'ll win, she ordered herself. You want him beaten. Creamed. Whipped. Stomped on. He's the captain of the opposite team, not your boyfriend!

But daydreams are not easily tossed aside. Nancy's dreams of Ben grew stronger. They were not wispy, vague dreams, either, but strong, thick, detailed ones of herself and Ben.

Like Nancy, Ben paid no attention to the cheerleaders' performance. Nor did he bother with the arguing referees and coaches. He never glanced at the hundreds of fans screaming his name.

His eyes were fixed on the scoreboard and the clock, as if he were measuring his future. His face was lean and angular. His chin was held high, so that his throat seemed exposed. His shoulders were very broad, and his Garrison T-shirt clung wetly to his chest.

Nancy shivered slightly.

Beside him all boys paled. There was no comparison. Even Donny did not compare. Donny was too ordinary-looking. Too milk-and-Oreo-cookies-looking.

Ben was unreadable. Tough.

Perhaps if I knew him well, he wouldn't be so attractive to me, she thought. But he's so aloof. So mysterious.

She yearned to know him well enough to find

out what was behind that mysterious toughness.

Around her the rest of Tarenton's Varsity Squad murmured tensely about the need to win, to cream Garrison and Ben. Nancy forced herself to think poorly of Ben. Be still my heart, she ordered herself.

But her heart was not still. It pounded for Ben.

Olivia Evans' family history was not a joyful one. The only child of worrying parents, she had had a heart defect at birth and undergone considerable surgery to correct it. Since first grade Olivia had been fine, but her mother could not yet believe it. Mrs. Evans had wrapped herself around Olivia, protecting, coddling, and smothering.

Olivia was on speaking terms with her mother, but just barely. No sooner would she fling her mother off her back than some upsetting situation would arise and Mrs. Evans would return, clinging and clasping.

For Olivia, cheerleading was the ticket to freedom.

Cheerleading was her first experience in a tight-knit group and Angie Poletti, Mary Ellen, and Nancy were her first close girl friends. She learned to unwind and let herself go. For the first time, Olivia had fun. It was like having childhood at the wrong end of the age spectrum — as a high school sophomore instead of a second grader.

But Mrs. Evans was sure that cheerleading was a corrupting influence.

Olivia protested constantly. "We're not wicked, Mother. We're a nice bunch of kids. Truly. Nobody drinks. Nobody does drugs. Nobody steals." Her mother would mention that terrible episode with Mary Ellen. "Mother," Olivia would repeat, "Mary Ellen was set up. She did *not* shoplift. You know that. And besides, cheerleading is good for me."

Like Mary Ellen, Olivia wanted to be Number One.

Her need wasn't quite as intense. She was willing to be a member of the Number One squad, rather than being the Number One girl. Olivia regarded Donny silently, and did not want him anyhow. Mary Ellen was attracted to Donny because he was important and not because she loved him. Well, everybody knew that, and nobody seemed to mind.

Nobody except Patrick Henley. Dark, strong, loving Patrick.

It blew Olivia's mind that Mary Ellen chose Donny instead of Patrick. Patrick literally offered himself to her and Mary Ellen turned her back. Over and over this happened, all year long. Amazing that Mary Ellen preferred others; even more amazing that Patrick kept adoring her in spite of the public hurts. But Mary Ellen was not going to date a boy who drove a garbage truck, even though it was his own. She wouldn't date him, even though he attracted her more than any boy — no matter how rich or how important — had.

Right now Mary Ellen had Donny by a thread. Not the noose Patrick was on. Just a slender thread. Perhaps it was a thread of hope, but Olivia didn't think so. Donny seemed very very interested in Mary Ellen.

Olivia forgot romance when she saw Garrison cheering.

They were so good!

Traditional — very, very traditional — but *good*.

It cut her to the core to hear Tarenton fans cheering Garrison girls. She put rage out of her mind, and jealousy and hurt. She analyzed the style, the appeal, the technique.

We can't dance like that, she realized. We have to capitalize on the strengths we've got, and dancing isn't one of them.

To prevent arguments with her mother, Olivia had toned down her own gymnastic routines. Now she knew that had been the wrong tactic. If you've got it, flaunt it. And Olivia had it. Her tiny, wiry body was light enough to catapult through the air, and she had tremendous strength in her thigh muscles. She could leave the ground as if gravity did not exist. And the squad was not making use of these abilities.

We will now, she thought grimly.

* * *

187

"It is time," Mary Ellen said, sagging with exhaustion, "for rubber wallpaper."

The Varsity Squad laughed in chorus.

Walt Manners said, "*You* may need a padded cell, Mary Ellen, but I personally thrive on this sort of thing."

Walt hugged all the girls. The most easy-going boy they had ever known, Walt was everybody's boyfriend and nobody's date. For years he'd half loved Mary Ellen, which he knew was crazy, because Melon loved exclusively on the basis of rank. Donny Parrish was currently number one, and therefore Mary Ellen loved Donny.

Walt had a pretty high score, due to his parents, rather than himself. They ran their own television talk show every morning. Walt had an eternal popularity from this, but he did not have enough on his own to get Mary Ellen.

In some ways Walt didn't mind. You had girl friends, you had problems.

Tarenton had lost to Garrison by three points. Walt knew the boys' locker room would be a scene of anger, shame, and hurt. Especially for Donny, who was expected to triumph at all times. Losing to Ben would not help his status. Donny was good, but Ben was better. It would be agony for Donny to realize that. Walt had a hunch, knowing Donny as he did, that Donny would blame everyone else for the loss — not for one minute would he entertain the possibility that he wasn't as good.

And the same went for Mary Ellen. She didn't date Number Two.

"What happens now?" Angie said in a ragged voice. She was actually crying. She wanted to win so much! She had cheered so hard, cared so deeply. Never once had she taken her attention off the game, never once had she thought of anything but victory.

Angie Poletti was really the backbone of the squad. She cheered because she loved to. She was loyal and honest, and when she was on the floor she was radiant.

And in spite of her wishes — her prayers, in fact — they lost.

Pres beat Walt to the comforting hug. With Angie and Angie only, Pres Tilford was brotherly. Any other time, Pres was the stud of the school. A girl here, a girl there.

Walt grinned, shaking his head. No, all that was changed now. Pres was in love. It was the funniest thing to see. Pres head over heels in love with a chubby little nothing sophomore named Kerry Elliot.

He marveled that Pres (a ten if ever there was one) would fall for a five. A boy with wealth and social position, brains and looks, whose father owned Tarenton Fabrication, was in love with a girl who had none of those. And Walt didn't think Kerry's appeal was willing sex, either. He was ninety percent sure they weren't going all the way. They just didn't have the look of two kids who knew each other that intimately. They were too dreamy. Too nervous and anxious with each other.

Walt liked Kerry. And the girls on the squad were nice to Kerry (they would not have dared be otherwise, because so much was done as a group) but they were confused by her. Kerry was so ordinary.

Pres was so special.

Walt shrugged. Love lives were other people's problems.

Nancy Goldstein was first out of the girls' locker room.

Her eyes traveled around the crowded halls, searching for her parents, but she didn't see them. Her throat was parched from all that shouting. How she would like lemonade. Not soda. Not anything carbonated. But orange juice, or lemonade. Cool and soothing.

Tarenton had vending machines in two places: the student lounge and the cafeteria corridor. It was the machine near the cafeteria that dispensed nutritious stuff: apples, boxes of raisins, beef broth, and fruit juices. Nancy walked slowly down the hall toward that one, feeling in her coat pocket for change.

The hall was dimly lit.

A red EXIT sign glowed at the far end, lending a rosy half light to the corridor. In front of her, Nancy's shadow lengthened, shivering and spreading out in dark, mystical patterns.

She was so tired. She had never cheered so hard, never struggled so much to keep a crowd from being too excited. Usually it was the squad's task to stir up excitement. Lately, it had been the reverse: keeping all that excitement in check.

She heaved a great sigh; pushing her thick, dark hair from her face; and felt marginally more alive.

In front of her, black shadows thickened and the faint light from behind was blocked out. The glimmer of the red EXIT sign shimmered ahead but cast no real light on the floor where she walked. She put out hesitant fingers and found the wall surface. Like a blind person she moved ahead.

There was a slithering sound behind her, and a creak.

Nancy's skin crawled.

She was completely removed from the chaos of the emptying school. As isolated as if she were down some dark, deserted alley. Once she turned this corner she would be out of sight and sound of everybody.

The body heat of overwork faded. Her palms grew damp.

This is ridiculous, she thought. This is ordinary, old Tarenton High. What am I afraid of? My locker is only fifty feet from here.

The darkness was complete.

It was as if doors had been shut on her, trapping her in dusty silence. Unmistakably she heard the soft, sinister sound of a person sneaking up on her. Terrified, Nancy whirled.

A pair of ghostly hands rose in her face.

Nancy tried to scream, but nothing came from her exhausted throat except a gurgle of fear.

No! she thought. *Oh, my God, no!*

CHAPTER

"**I**'m sorry. I'm *really* sorry. Don't have a heart attack," said a voice.

The body towered over her. Nancy sincerely tried not to have a heart attack. Her hands, up in front of her to protect herself, were caught by the hands of the man facing her.

"It's only me," he said.

"Only who?" she whispered. She was shivering with cold fear. What did I think he was going to do? she wondered.

"Ben Adamson," he said, and now she could make him out dimly: the hawk features, the bony lines. "I'm just getting orange juice from that vending machine. Isn't it back here somewhere? I can't quite remember from last year."

"You took two decades off my life," Nancy said furiously. "Creeping up on me like that! Do you realize I am now old enough to be your mother?"

Ben began laughing.

Nancy had never heard him laugh. In fact, she had not thought of him as the sort of person who knew *how* to laugh. She would have said Ben was too tough for laughter. He might glare, or snarl, but never laugh.

"You look familiar," Ben said, squinting at her.

He came from a very large high school. Probably one reason for the vicious rivalry was that Garrison had twice as many kids as Tarenton, and Garrison absolutely hated being beaten by the little guy.

At least I know he watched me cheer, she thought. Otherwise I wouldn't look familiar to him.

She was consumed with pleasure. Even if Ben didn't know it, his eyes had been drawn to Nancy Goldstein, just as hers had been drawn to him.

She took his hands in hers and lowered them to a more comfortable position. His fingers closed in that possessive, tough way he used throughout his life. She let him. She said, "You'd recognize me if I were wearing scarlet and white. I'm on the Tarenton cheerleading squad."

"Oh, no," said Ben and this time he grinned. In the darkness his teeth shone whitely. "I shouldn't be associating with a member of the opposite team."

"I have redeeming characteristics," Nancy said.

"You sure do." His voice was blatantly sexual. He was looking down, not at her face, but at her figure. It was the kind of thing her mother would hate. Normally Nancy would agree that she was not merely a sexual object. But Ben attracted her as no one had ever done, and she found herself posturing for him. With tacit cooperation, they moved on down the dark hall together, hands still touching, bodies apart, and turned the corner into utter darkness.

"We're never going to find the vending machine now," Ben said.

"We'll find it by the touch and feel system," Nancy said, leading him on.

Ben laughed deep in his throat. "That's my favorite system, anyhow."

It was a provocative remark. Nancy let the conversation continue in a flippant, sexual way. She could almost feel her mother standing there, eyes closed in distress. Nancy, Nancy, don't encourage this.

But she encouraged it.

He was Ben. The hawk of the opposite team.

They had reached the vending machine. "We'll have to guess at what we're taking," she said. "I think orange juice is on the far right. Press this." She held his fingers over a flat plastic square.

From his other hand she fished his change. The two quarters dropped into the vending machine with a muted thunk. A cup slithered down the chute and liquid whooshed into it.

"I just hope it isn't bouillon," Ben said. "What's your name, anyway?"

"Nancy Goldstein."

Ben's fingers released hers and swept over the vending machine, trying to find the opening where his drink would be sitting. Put your arms around me, she thought. But he didn't.

"It *is* orange juice," said Ben gratefully. "What a woman."

She got her own drink, moving her fingers over to the second button, and again her guess was right. The first sip was cool, sweet, tangy lemonade. Just right.

Very slowly, so as not to trip or spill their hard-won drinks, they moved back to the EXIT sign. When they turned the corner there was only the same dim light as before, but it felt like sunrise. They walked without talking to the front foyer where parents and fans still stood in knots. Policemen circulated, more relaxed than they had been an hour earlier, when they expected war to break out, but still on the lookout for sore losers or gloating victors.

Just as the two opposing basketball teams emerged from different dressing rooms, just as each boy schooled himself to remember his athletic manners, Ben and Nancy emerged from the darkness.

Ben: the boy who carried Garrison to its win.

Nancy: the girl who was supposed to cheer Tarenton to *its* win.

What a pair they made. Her lovely dark hair and narrow shoulders were framed against his huge body. Both protected themselves from the sudden light by looking sideways at each other.

The face of every single Tarenton basketball player tightened. Nancy Goldstein. *Their* cheerleader? Sneaking off into the dark to neck with the captain of the opposite team?

Smirks appeared on the faces of the Garrison boys. Not only could Ben steal the game from Tarenton — he could also steal the girls.

"Way to go, Ben," the co-captain said. "I like it when a victory is really complete."

Ben grinned arrogantly. You knew that Ben never settled for less than a complete victory. His eyes moved slowly across the foyer until they met Donny's, and Ben grinned even more widely. The hand that held the orange juice cup casually flicked it across the floor to the trash can. He didn't miss that basket any more than he had missed during the game. He put his hand on Nancy's shoulder.

Possessively.

The way he had owned the game, he seemed to own Nancy.

Cops and parents felt the instant furious change in atmosphere and moved uncertainly to stop things — but they weren't sure what they should be stopping.

The Tarenton Varsity Cheerleading Squad stared at their sixth member with horror and rage.

The Garrison Varsity Cheerleading Squad giggled. Their co-captain said, "Now Ben. Give poor old Tarenton a break. Let them keep *something* for themselves."

Nancy loathed scenes. She could not believe she was the center of one. Dozens of hostile eyes bored into her, silently calling her traitor.

But nothing happened! she thought. They have no right to look at me like that.

Ben Adamson loved a scene. Being the center of a fight was his life. For him, basketball was a fight, and later on in the year baseball would be another fight. He would never pass up a chance to start trouble.

Too much an actor to smile outwardly, Ben smiled inwardly. With his darkest expression, profile at its most hawklike, he said, "Saturday night, Nancy?"

She stared up at him.

"Good," he said. He leaned over — quite a distance, because Nancy was not tall — and kissed her mouth. Slowly, lingeringly.

There was an audible gasp from the Tarenton kids.

Nancy blushed.

People drew conclusions from the blush that would have shocked Nancy. Ben, satisfied by the hot red cheeks looking up at him, said calmly, "Seven-thirty." He thought, Look her up in the phone book. There can't be that many Goldsteins. Give her a call. She'll go. They all do.

He sauntered away from her to join his team. When he led the way to the team bus, he did not look back.

The Tarenton Wolves and the Tarenton Varsity Squad stared at Nancy Goldstein. She had no idea what to say to them. She couldn't begin to think. And she was furious that she had to say anything. It was all crazy! It —

"Nancy, it's time to go home.. We've been looking for you everywhere," her father said. His voice was scratchy and tired. Any other time she would have realized it was because he'd been cheering himself. Good news, when her father considered cheerleading the lowest possible activity for a liberated young girl.

But tonight she did not care whether he approved of cheerleading or not. She could think only of that kiss. A kiss she had never expected. Did not understand. Had no idea how to deal with.

Saturday night? she thought. Seven-thirty? Was he kidding?

A Tarenton girl muttered, "You couldn't find her because she was off making time with the enemy."

"I was not!" Nancy cried.

"At least don't be a hypocrite," Mary Ellen said coldly. "If you're going to be a traitor, admit it. That's the American tradition, isn't it? Benedict Arnold. . . ."

Her parents, who were paying no attention to this whatsoever, dragged her off to the car. The silent, angry stares of the kids Nancy cared about most pierced her back.

Too late now to laugh it off.

Too late to giggle and say, "Adamson, go drink your orange juice and stop bothering me."

Tomorrow there would be an important and very long practice. Mary Ellen and Olivia were determined to learn routines so impressive the world would fall off its axis. And when she, Nancy, walked in, they'd snarl at her. Because they thought she'd been necking with the captain of the opposite team.

I wish, Nancy thought, forgetting everything but the possibility of Saturday night.

Donny left Tarenton High without going near Mary Ellen.

Mary Ellen pretended that this was reasonable. She pretended that, given the shock of his loss, the exhaustion of such a long, difficult game, Donny had a right to slouch on home alone.

But *oh*, how she had counted on this evening!

She had seen them in the pizza parlor where

everybody went after a victory: laughter bubbling like the soda they poured from huge, cold pitchers, romance blooming like the artificial flowers that sat in the middle of the scarred tables beside the thick, sputtering candles.

Mary Ellen and Donny.

Number One and Number One.

She had wanted to hold Donny, and be held by him.

She wanted to see Donny, and be seen in his company.

And loss had ended that.

Angie — sweet gentle Angie — said, "It seems to me Donny shouldn't sulk. So we lost. He did his best. Why can't he come for pizza anyway? He's not acting his age."

"It wasn't his fault," Mary Ellen said fiercely. "It was —" she could never say that it was because Ben was better — "it was stupid referees."

"Even so," Angie said, "I don't like people who sulk. And Donny's sulking."

"The final touch was Nancy," Olivia said. "Could you *believe* Nancy, our *Nancy*, making time with Ben? Thirty seconds after we lose to them?"

Mary Ellen turned her anger to Nancy. Much easier, much more convenient to dislike Nancy instead of Donny. She went for pizza with the others and they spent much of the time saying terrible things about Nancy.

"Stop," Kerry said. "Stop it now. I can't stand it."

They all stared at her.

Kerry marveled at the courage she had gotten from dating Pres. She — dull, little nothing sophomore Kerry — could sit here and talk back to these shining stars: to Mary Ellen and Angie and the rest. She said, "So Nancy has a new boyfriend. We don't have to be spiteful."

The rest were silenced, considering. Nancy *was* their friend and fellow cheerleader.

After a while Mary Ellen said, "Still and all, if Nancy were to come down with a disfiguring disease, I wouldn't go hunting for the cure."

They giggled.

Pres, who was ready at any time to make wisecracks at anyone's expense, loved Kerry again for being nice.

Mary Ellen, for whom being nice sometimes took real effort, struggled to shrug about Nancy. She had never been able to shrug about any defeat. She did not see how she could shrug about this one. But they all had to work together the next day, and Nancy was as important to the squad as any other member.

Other people are naturally good, she thought. Look at Kerry. She really meant that. She really doesn't have any hard feelings. Me, I have to *coach* myself to be good. I have to memorize the *rules* in order to be good.

Five of the six Varsity members were having pizza. It was a loss not to have Nancy. We're a squad, Mary Ellen reminded herself. And I'm the captain. The squad comes first. I won't be angry with Nancy. No matter how much she deserves it.

CHAPTER

Nancy Goldstein missed the school bus, and ran down to the corner to flag a ride with her neighbor, only to see the car disappear around the bend. Oh, no! I can't be late, she thought. We've got that exam first period.

She ran home again, her books a dead weight in her arms, and raced in the door screaming, "Mom! Mom!"

Her mother, looking lovely in a cranberry red suit with a paisley-patterned silk blouse, was just slipping on a pair of shoes.

"Missed the bus, Mother. Can you drive me?"

Mrs. Goldstein glared at her daughter. "Honestly, Nancy. You've been up for an hour. How could you have possibly missed that bus? You know I work this morning. I don't have time to drive you."

Nancy had dawdled because of daydreams. Ben. The texture of the hands she had so briefly touched. The profile in the dim hall, the slight pressure of his unexpected kiss.

Wondering, over and over — did he mean it about Saturday? Do I want to have him mean it? What will it be like in school if I actually *do* date Ben Adamson?

"Mother, please? I have an exam first class. I've got to get there on time. I'm really, really sorry. Please drive me?"

Mrs. Goldstein gave in. She always did. She wanted to be stern and unyielding because it sounded like such a good way to parent, but Nancy was such a good daughter and a fine student that it was hard. Besides, they lived so far from Tarenton High it would take Nancy hours to walk there.

"All right, all right. Hurry up." Mrs. Goldstein reached for her coat and keys. They drove fast, Nancy's mother peering at her watch and worrying about being late herself. She was teaching an art history class in Garrison, and gave stern remarks to students who were late. She dreaded the thought of being late herself.

" 'Bye, Mom," Nancy said, leaping out of the car. She shouted thank you over her shoulder, but Mrs. Goldstein was already driving off.

Nancy ran into the huge lobby, her shoes clicking on the marble floor.

Nancy loved going into Tarenton High. Its design was a combination of formality and coziness that made her want to write to the long-dead architect and congratulate him. Just walking in was a good feeling. And it wasn't often that you felt that way about your school.

Except for a few kids rushing to homeroom late, the lobby was empty. A grundgy boy Nancy didn't know looked hard at her. "Oh. It's the little rah-rah," he said nastily. His voice frightened her. It was savage. Like a piece of violence left over from the game. "You having a good time being rotten, Goldstein?"

Nancy stopped walking, as stunned as if he'd hit her. Being rotten?

"Real wholesome bunch, you cheerleaders. Running around making time with the opposition. I like it, Goldstein. I really like it." He flicked a dirty sweatshirt in her direction. A sick taste rose in her mouth. Oh, please, no! she thought. Please don't let anybody else feel that way.

The boy left her alone. She walked unsteadily to her locker, down the very same hall she had last walked with Ben. Her palms were wet with apprehension. Was this how the whole school would react?

Taped to her locker was a little piece of paper. When Nancy read the words, she gasped and jumped backward, her hand over her mouth, her books cascading to the floor unnoticed. *Nobody would call me that! That's meant for someone else.*

She could scarcely bring herself to touch the locker, but she had to put her coat in and get out another notebook. Standing to the side, as if the horrid lettering could touch her, Nancy managed to retrieve her book. Ripping the paper off made her gag. She scrunched it up and threw it in the bottom of her locker. She'd throw it away somewhere else when she wasn't so upset. And didn't have an exam in ten seconds.

Who would write something like that? Vanessa? She *would* think being the daughter of the superintendent of schools would give her the right to do anything. But even Vanessa wouldn't print anything that ugly.

Running again, Nancy tried to fix her mind on advanced English literature. Never had this been so difficult.

She walked into class late. Being late always meant a brief flicker of embarrassment as eyes turned to assess the latecomer, but this time the thirty pairs of eyes seemed sharply judgmental. Nancy slid into a vacant seat at the back next to Mary Ellen. Melon, her friend and co-cheerleader, did not look at her.

Mary Ellen took every opportunity to smile. She had the finest teeth, the loveliest lips, and the fairest complexion in Tarenton, and she liked to show off the combination in a welcoming smile.

But she didn't even look up to greet Nancy.

Nobody looked up to greet Nancy.

She felt a chill as strong as if she'd walked into a restaurant freezer, and turned around to find no handle to get out by.

Misery engulfed Nancy. She had trouble with the test. She, who never had problems with anything printed. How she wanted everyone to like her! She had had to try so hard to win friends when she moved to Tarenton, and getting on the squad had seemed to solve it. Could she have ruined everything by something as silly as helping Ben get a cup of juice?

During passing period, she walked alone. Several people made remarks about Nancy dating the enemy. Several people made obscene gestures and one boy blocked her path threateningly. Nancy did not know what he might have done if Mrs. Oetjen, the principal, hadn't materialized at that moment.

It brought home to Nancy the enormity of the war between Tarenton and Garrison. This year people weren't kidding. It wasn't merely basketball. It was a battle. There *must* be victory. They *must* be Number One.

They were willing to spill blood to achieve it.

My blood? she thought.

The day passed without a single encouraging

word from anybody. Nancy fled to cheerleading practice and the five companions who had to work with her, and had to smile, because that's what cheerleading was — happy enthusiasm on the move.

Forty feet from the other five, Olivia stood for one moment in motionless preparation, gathering her muscles, planning her leap. She was clad in practice clothing: sweat shorts and a T-shirt that said *Cheerleaders make better lovers.* She had never tested the validity of this, but she liked pretending she knew the score.

She was shiny with perspiration. Her light-brown, fine hair clung limply to her forehead. Olivia was totally unaware of her looks at this moment. If someone had held up a mirror, she would not have seen the mirror, let alone the reflection of herself.

She was preparing to do the most daring jump she had ever attempted.

Pres Tilford stood tensely. He was sure of Olivia and he was sure of himself, but they had never practiced this. There was no way to rehearse, according to Olivia. They would start with the real thing. Nerves prickled on the back of his neck and the palms of his hands. The hands were cupped. He had taken off his ring.

Olivia drew herself together abruptly and began to run. Her remarkably strong legs and thighs propelled her along the gym floor at an astounding rate. It did not seem possible that she could achieve such a speed in such a short distance. Like an Olympic champion, Olivia leaped into the air, her right foot landing squarely in Pres's cupped hands. Pres thrust upward, adding height to her speed, and Olivia's slender, fragile body flew into the air.

The other four cheerleaders, lined up behind Pres, lifted their arms in a series of rotating fluid motions, as if they were tossing Olivia like feathers into the sky. Above their fingers, Olivia somersaulted, spread her legs, touched her toes, and landed perfectly: feet together, back arched, small breasts lifted, narrow waist in. She neither stumbled nor clutched the air, but simply stood there, as if she had strolled over to that position.

Mrs. Engborg, the coach, closed her eyes with relief.

If Olivia landed neck first from such a height at such a speed. . . . But it was better not to think of such things.

Ardith Engborg had never seen her squad like this. In all the years she had coached cheerleading, she'd never run into a year of such determination, such icy fury. The rivalry against Garrison had reached such proportions that even the cheerleading squads were pitted against each other.

Mary Ellen and Olivia had proclaimed that

the next time they appeared in public, they would be so spectacular that the entire gym would gasp when they performed. And perform they would. Not cheer. Not chant. Not clap. *Perform.*

"Olivia," Ardith Engborg said quietly, "that was magnificent."

Olivia nodded. She had that knowledge of her own ability that goes with being a truly fine athlete. Nervous, yes. Willing to practice for hours, yes. But confident. She *knew* she was good. She knew she was magnificent.

Pres Tilford thought, What if she'd missed my hands? What if I lifted too hard, and threw her to the side, or didn't lift enough and —

He stopped his thoughts.

Pres disliked thinking of failure. Success was everything to Pres. In some ways Pres was very much like his wealthy, social parents — he could not bear to be associated with anything or anyone but a winner.

Olivia's a winner, he thought, watching her objectively. He admired Olivia immensely, but his eyes went to the bleachers, where Kerry, whom he loved, sat with Patrick. The admirers: Kerry of Pres, Patrick of Mary Ellen. But Kerry did not have to admire from afar. Pres would gladly take her in his arms.

But Ardith pulled them back for the demonstration of a cheer Mary Ellen had devised. It was a very complex leap-frog maneuver. They flung themselves over each other's backs in a whipping tempo that would result in broken ribs for those whose timing was off.

When they finished that, they collapsed on the floor, gasping for air, passing the water bottle around and sucking eagerly on the clear plastic straw.

Angie said tentatively, "You know, these cheers are impressive, but they're not really *cheers*. This is like a gymnastics meet."

Mary Ellen was in no mood for dissension. "It'll make us Number One," she said flatly.

"But do we really want to be Number One?" Angie said wistfully. "I kind of like the old cheers. Clapping and shifting feet and . . . you know . . . plain old rhythms that everybody knows."

They stared at her as if tradition was a sin.

"Angie, those old cheers didn't get us anywhere," Olivia said. Olivia was incensed that Angie was not one hundred percent thrilled by her performance.

"They've gotten us championships for years," Angie pointed out.

"But this is not an ordinary year!" Olivia cried. "Don't you understand that Garrison is trying to whip us? They have that Ben Adamson" — she spoke his name like a curse — "and Ben might actually outplay Donny."

"Impossible," Mary Ellen said sharply. She had stayed up last night, hoping that Donny would call. Suggest a movie, a drive, a meal together. Talk about the game, about future games. But he had not called. She had no way of knowing if she had just been a passing fancy, or if he was just too busy or too hurt to do anything right now.

Her eyes went to Nancy at the mention of Ben Adamson, but Mary Ellen wrenched her thoughts away from that pair. She had promised herself not to think bad thoughts. Instead she looked up into the bleachers. Kerry and Patrick. She possessed Patrick. She knew it. But she didn't want Patrick. She wanted Donny. No, that wasn't true. She did want Patrick. If he had been Number One in anything, she would have loved him forever. As it was, in her most honest moments, face to face with herself, she knew she loved Patrick in a way she never had loved any other boy. She just wouldn't let the world know it . . . or Patrick.

Nancy decided to say nothing. Nothing had happened with Ben, despite what it had looked like, and she didn't know if anything would. Leave it alone.

But that was not anyone else's decision. Angie burst out, her school loyalty superceding her sweetness, "Nancy, how *could* you? I think the least a person loyal to Tarenton could do is to wait until after basketball season. Is that so much to ask? A cheerleader of *all* people shouldn't display a lack of loyalty in public."

Five sets of eyes bored into Nancy.

"Look," she said, trying not to cry, "Ben is

just a show-off. It was nothing. Nothing. I don't even know him."

They were uniformly skeptical.

"Really," she protested. "We were just going down the hall for lemonade and it was dark so we walked together."

"What were you doing in a dark hall all alone?" Angie asked. "I mean, when *I'm* with a terrific boy all alone in a dark hall —"

"He is *not* a terrific boy," Mary Ellen said fiercely. "He looks like a criminal. He probably pushes drugs. Steals cars. He's a creep."

"He is not!" Nancy cried. "You're just making that up. You're just jealous."

Immediately she knew she had made a terrible error.

Not only would the rest think she had a boy-friend to defend, but she had accused Mary Ellen of jealousy, saying without meaning to that Ben was better than Donny.

"Whether he's a creep or a teddy bear," Olivia said, "right now he's the enemy and I think it's pretty low of you to associate with him, Nancy."

I won't lose my temper. I won't cry, Nancy told herself. I'll get out of this and we'll all still be friends. "I'm not associating with him. I don't even know him. He was just there."

"Oh. That big kiss was brotherly?" Olivia snorted.

Walt Manners stood up, dusting himself off. "Listen, we've got to work on that cheer again," he said in a sparkling, cheerleader sort of voice. "Let's go, squad."

"Shut up, Walt," Olivia said.

"Now, listen," Walt protested.

"*You* listen," Olivia said. "I want to win. I don't care about anything but winning. And if I have to be a one-man band, I'm going to win. I'm going to show Garrison up so much they'll be laughed off the floor. We're going to put on the best display that Tarenton has ever seen." She was on her feet now, all five feet one inch of her, and her tiny foot stomped with a strength that proved her athletic ability, like a piston on an engine.

Walt shrugged. He detested arguments. He looked at Angie, who had not really meant to start anything. They all stood, ready to work again, letting the subject drop, letting Mary Ellen and Olivia run the show as they chose.

Pres steered clear of the whole thing. From this distance Kerry looked faintly blurry. She was a fluffy sort of girl anyway, with her hair ruffled and out of place, her soft collars and pink mohair sweaters adding to the look of fragility.

To Pres, she was exquisite.

He wanted to quit cheering and run over to her. Bound up the bleachers three at a time, fling Kerry into the air instead of Olivia, end with a passionate kiss instead of a cheer.

He could do that to Vanessa — dramatic, dark, violent Vanessa. Vanessa would have loved it, he would have loved it, the sparse audience would have loved it.

But Kerry was shy.

Much as she loved being seen in Pres's company, she did not like having attention drawn to her. She would hate that sort of trick on his part.

For Kerry's sake, Pres was revising his entire standard of behavior. Oddly enough, it wasn't hard. He had heard that personalities didn't change, but his was. Even his parents had commented on it. They were suspicious, to say the least, partly because Kerry was not what his mother had had in mind for her son's girl.

Kerry was too soft. Too quiet. Too unnoticeable.

Pres's mother was the most organized, elegant, impressive woman in Tarenton. A frequent guest on the Manners' talk show, Felicia Tilford was sharp enough to cut paper.

Pres did not want her cutting Kerry.

The squad began practicing again. It was an almost violent cheer. Angie stifled her complaints, although she wanted an entirely different kind of routine. But when Olivia did another dazzling gymnastic trick, complete with a circle of back flips and a breathtaking leap from Walt's shoulders to the floor, and off Nancy's back onto Pres's shoulders, Angie spoke up. "Cheerleaders lead cheers," she cried. "They don't perform suicidal leaps and —"

"It isn't suicidal," Olivia said. "Don't say that

word again. If my mother thought I was doing something suicidal she'd haul me out of the squad."

"She'd haul you out of the *state*," Walt said.

"Stop your chatter," Ardith Engborg said, "and *work*."

CHAPTER

They were always getting an audience, as if
if they were an episode on a favorite afternoon
soap opera. Kids drifted in, observed the cheerleading practice with half their attention, gos-
siped softly from the upper corner of the bleachers, and later drifted out. As long as they were
relatively quiet, Mrs. Engborg never complained.
The cheerleaders tried harder when they were
being watched, and it helped condition them to
an audience.

In fact the Varsity Squad had gotten so used
to the quiet traffic of kids waiting for late buses,
parents, or friends, that they rarely glanced at the
bleachers.

But when Donny Parrish walked in, things

were different and Donny knew it. Swaggering slightly, he walked slower than he had a year before, demanding attention even as he got attention without demanding it.

Even Ardith Engborg paused to admire the boy who was Tarenton's primary hope.

As for Mary Ellen Kirkwood, her heart stopped. Hot as she was from exercise, she felt a chill. Gravely, Donny saluted her. Not a wave, not a grin, but a serious martial salute.

He came here to see me, she thought, and all the confidence she had lost returned. She had a lovely smile and she knew it. As she smiled at Donny, she lifted her scarlet pompon, swirling it in a long, slow half circle around herself. Donny smiled back. Pure joy filled Mary Ellen. She could look even at Nancy with love. All was right with the world.

Donny Parrish had come into the gymnasium to see *her*, Mary Ellen Kirkwood.

Donny climbed the bleachers and sat down beside Patrick. Mary Ellen tried to ignore Patrick. On Donny's other side was Kerry. At last Mary Ellen had found something worthwhile in Kerry — no competition.

A wisp of understanding passed briefly through her mind. Perhaps Pres Tilford adored Kerry *because* she was no competition. But as soon as Mary Ellen had the idea, she forgot it. Donny consumed her, mind and body.

* * *

Only a month earlier, Kerry would have been destroyed by Donny's presence. Her tongue would have failed her. Her hands would have betrayed her, trembling and fidgeting. She would have lurched around, embarrassed, unable to cope with the presence of the star of the high school. She — a lowly, chubby sophomore — in the company of Donny Parrish.

But being Pres's girl had changed her more than she knew.

Pres impressed her so much that another boy could not impress her more. Sure, Donny was a high-scoring basketball player, but big deal. Look at all that her Pres was!

So she smiled comfortably at Donny. "Hi, there," she said. "The squad is coming up with some unbelievable new routines. You'll be amazed at what Olivia Evans can do. She's absolutely wonderful."

Donny nodded. "Actually," he said, "I came to watch Mary Ellen."

Kerry ached with happiness for Mary Ellen. She would quote Donny, and Mary Ellen would bask in the words. Kerry ached equally with pain for Patrick. She moved a little, to block Patrick from Donny, to give him a little privacy so he could absorb the rivalry without being watched.

Patrick leaned forward and watched Mary Ellen — the golden hair and long legs. He knew a lot about her. How she felt in his arms; how her mouth felt under his; and how she sighed when he kissed her. He knew she would come and go, but he could wait. He had something Mary Ellen always came back to. He counted on it.

I know how you feel, Patrick, Kerry thought. You're competing with the star. We all know which one Mary Ellen will choose.

She glanced at Patrick.

He smiled back.

"Life can be a pain," Kerry said to him.

"Agreed."

He knew she understood, and welcomed the understanding. No need for more words on such a painful topic.

Oh, Pres, thought Kerry. If what is between you and me were to end tonight, I've learned so much. I've learned to love. To be friendlier. To care more, enjoy more. Life is so much more intense than it was before I fell in love with you.

So much emotion in this room, she thought. So many of us tangled up with feelings we can't entirely deal with.

On the floor, Olivia and Pres went through their hurling routine again. Kerry quivered with fear as Olivia went so dangerously high above the ground. Her little body came down with such force! If they mistimed. . . .

"Wow," Donny said softly. "That's some leap."

The squad repeated the routine, and this time the sparse audience, perhaps a dozen at the moment, burst into applause. Impossible not to acknowledge the brilliance — the daring, dazzling brilliance — that Olivia displayed. Olivia turned to face them, an expression of triumph on her face.

This would wipe Garrison's squad off the map, and she knew it.

She thrust her arms up in a victorious jabbing motion that cut the air. The audience clapped harder.

"Two stars," Kerry commented. "You, Donny. And now Olivia."

Donny smiled. It was a quiet smile, but she knew that he loved being called a star. Who wouldn't, after all?

Patrick and Donny began talking casually about the yearbook, and the informal pictures now being taken. Donny was afraid the basketball team would get short shrift. Patrick assured Donny that the basketball team was the *last* group to get shafted.

"Shrifted, you mean," Donny said.

They argued about whether it was shafted, or shrifted. But they both knew they were arguing about Mary Ellen, vying for her.

And into the gymnasium came Ben Adamson.

Hulking, dark, beaky as Pike's Peak. Shoulders moving in opposing directions, as if he had enough muscle for two normal people.

The cheerleaders decorated the floor like so many cookies and glasses of milk. Pure wholesomeness. Clean-cut, all-round American youth.

Sweet smiles, happy gestures, pure thoughts. (Or so it looked.)

Ben. He truly looked like a criminal.

And he was. The most wanted criminal on the Tarenton High list.

It was unthinkable that Ben would saunter into their gym at a time when feelings were so high. All very well to say they were mature high school students who could handle their negative emotions — but they weren't . . . and they couldn't.

Ben was asking for a fight.

With Ben standing there, as if hewn from rock — granite — it was impossible to remember the existence of Donny Parrish. What was Donny but some guy sprawled on the top bleacher? Ben possessed the gymnasium floor like an explorer, the wilderness.

Donny knew it, and hated Ben Adamson.

Ben. Here. In his gym. On his turf.

I'll kill him in the next game, Donny thought. I'll plaster him to the walls. I'll destroy him.

But Ben never glanced his way. In that infuriating arrogant manner that so far surpassed Donny's own — because it was natural and Donny had *taught* himself how to be arrogant — Ben dominated the entire room.

The cheerleaders faltered and stared at Ben. Even when Donny had come into the gym, practice had not stopped, merely paused for a few seconds of recognition.

It's that worthless Nancy Goldstein, thought

Donny. He's actually come here, to my gym, to pick her up. They probably have some hot date somewhere. He turned his hatred equally on Nancy.

Ben's chin lifted fractionally. His cold stare sliced the atmosphere of the gym. The chin lifted to greet Nancy, and they all knew it.

Ardith Engborg cleared her throat noisily. "Squad," she said, "we'll work on the halftime show now, please."

She put the tape on. Blasting, pounding, throbbing rock music filled the large gym. The Varsity Squad spread out to begin an equally pounding, throbbing display.

Donny was blinded by rage. He could not even see Mary Ellen, gracefully taking center front. He thought, I'd like to see Ben take an icy curve too fast in the dark. Donny's jacket brushed Kerry's.

It seemed to Kerry she could feel his hatred right through the fabric. She sent Patrick a panicky look. Right now, because someone can toss little balls into a net a little better, Donny would probably kill.

She shuddered. Donny was unaware of her existence, let alone her shudder.

As for Patrick Henley, he felt the burden of a sense of duty. Whether it was duty to Mary Ellen or to Tarenton High, he did not know. He also had a maturity the others didn't have. Maybe it was because he had worked hard to get what he

224

wanted . . . his own truck. And next came Mary Ellen. He wanted her, too.

The girl he adored did not love him back. It was a terrible, painful nuisance. If he could have tossed his feelings for Mary Ellen aside, he would have done so immediately. Odd how easy it was to toss physical objects. Patrick, who owned his own garbage truck and had his own lucrative route in Tarenton, did more of that than any kid in the county. But emotions could not be tossed so readily. They had lives of their own.

He watched Mary Ellen now. Saw her slip, and mess up part of the routine because she was watching Donny, watching Ben, divided by a tumult of emotions that she could not control, any more than he could control his love for her.

Kerry murmured, "Patrick, what'll we do? Donny's going to explode. If he starts a fight, he'll be thrown off the team. And then we'll lose everything."

At last Ben glanced at them. His expressionless eyes met the smoldering hatred in Donny's eyes. And Ben was amused. He smiled at Donny, as if Donny were a child to be toyed with. Donny stood up, fists bunched.

Nancy was very, very grateful for all the hours of hard practice that had come before today. If she had not known her routines so thoroughly, she could never have kept going under the iron gaze of Ben Adamson.

For me, she thought, stunned. He's here for me. There can't be any other reason. *He can't wait until Saturday and he's come for me now!*

But what should she do? Walk over after practice ends? Hug him? Beam with pleasure? Pretend dismay that he'd interrupted an important practice?

But the only emotion to grip her was the thrill of being wanted. She didn't care how presumptuous Ben was.

It was like being wanted by a god. Lesser mortals would have to stand aside.

Patrick was not as tall as Ben — nobody was — but in his own way he, too, commanded attention. Ben had been designed for arrogance and game-playing, but Patrick was broader, and more real, and tougher beneath the surface than any of them.

With an easy grin, easy speech, easy manner, Patrick walked Ben off the floor and sat him down on the bottom bleacher in a less threatening posture. When Nancy joined them, twenty minutes later, Patrick escorted them to the door, blocking the astonished teenagers who wouldn't dare tangle with Patrick any more than with Ben.

My good deed for the day, Patrick thought wryly.

Saint, he told himself cynically.

He looked across the floor and his dark eyes met Mary Ellen's blues ones. She smiled at Patrick, a shy, odd smile for Mary Ellen. He never failed her, she couldn't help thinking. Patrick was always there for her. Their eyes clung and then Mary Ellen looked away.

Ardith Engborg watched the procession leaving the gym. She was no less astounded than the students that Ben Adamson had come to Tarenton to get Nancy. Ardith did not know Ben at all, but she knew one thing: Ben had not shown up because of a deep, abiding love for Nancy. He had shown up in order to show off.

That boy's name isn't Ben, thought the coach. It's Trouble.

CHAPTER

Kerry was knitting a sweater for Pres. Lopi wool: fat thick lambswool in undyed colors of deep brown, soft fisherman's ivory, and misty grey. It worked up quickly because the yarn was so fat and the circular needles so large. Kerry had never knit anything in the round before, and it was so easy. She could not imagine why anybody ever knit a sweater in four pieces when you could make it like this.

Pres did not know about the sweater. It was a surprise for his birthday. Sometimes Kerry day-dreamed about that day. His parents would do something spectacular, she knew. And she would be a central part of it.

Out on the court Pres was wearing a torn pair

of gym shorts and an old torn T-shirt in sweatshirt grey. His socks had no elastic left and his toes showed through the ripped sneakers. You would not have known that Pres could buy and sell every person in the gym.

Or, at least, his father could. Pres was on a slim allowance. His father said if Pres wanted more money, he could earn it at Tarenton Fabricators, working the loading dock. But Pres hated the thought of this and simply went without instead. Kerry actually had more spending money than the wealthy Pres!

She forget Ben as soon as Patrick seated him. For Kerry there was no male human being but Pres.

Even after weeks of dating Pres, Kerry felt flippy floppy when he talked to her. She still got flustered when he blew her a kiss in the halls, and tongue-tied when a knot of senior boys with Pres in the center stopped to talk to her for a few moments.

She knew they thought she was an odd choice. She knew they wondered just what there was about her that attracted Pres. What if, one dismal morning, Pres wondered that himself?

One reason Kerry had not told Pres about the sweater was her fear that he'd break up with her before his birthday and she'd never have a chance to give it to him. She hadn't even told her parents that the sweater was for Pres!

Icelandic sweaters were unisex. You just decided the chest size and started knitting. It was an outdoor sweater, meant to be worn over lots of clothing. She had a brother and a father who could enjoy the sweater, and she knew they half expected to be getting it themselves.

Every night that she wasn't out with Pres, Kerry stayed home, did her homework, and then went to the living room to watch TV and knit. She sat in the old wing chair, its upholstery half worn to threads where elbows and cats' claws had worked it over. Such a comfortable old chair. Perfect to curl up in with a long-term project.

And certainly a sweater was a long-term project. Kerry had never before known a boy she would have knit for. Knitting took hours and hours, night after night, week after week. You didn't knit a sweater for a boy unless you really and truly loved him.

She watched Pres cheer. Oh, Pres, I love you! she thought with delight and fear.

The practice ended. Everybody's attention followed the peculiar trio of Ben, Nancy, and Patrick out the door. Everybody's except Kerry's. Eyes glued to Pres, she walked down the bleachers — always tricky, always the fear she'd catch her ankle and trip and either kill herself (thus losing Pres forever) or make a fool of herself (she believed Pres would rather have her dead than be a fool).

Pres waved at her. "I'm too sweaty," he said.

230

"I'll take a shower and meet you in ten minutes, okay?"

"Okay," she said, smiling. He could do it, too. If she had to take a shower and meet him, she'd be forty-five minutes. He'd be ten. She sat on the bottom bleacher now and looked at the sweep hand on her watch, guessing exactly what he was doing every moment, imagining his body in the shower.

Wow, she thought, shaking her head to clear it. Think about knitting instead, Kerry old girl.

Pres charged into the gym, did a cartwheel over to her, and misjudged his timing, so that he skidded into her ankles and nearly knocked her skull into the wall. "Sorry about that," he said, and kissed her instead. She blushed and looked around, but there was nobody there. Pres took her arm with the eager affection that always knocked her off her feet, and they walked out into the hall and headed for the front foyer.

Pres was bouncing like a little kid.

"Where do you get all this energy?" she marveled. "You just went through the most grueling practice ever! I got so scared. Angie was right, you know. Some of Olivia's leaps really are suicidal."

Pres scoffed, in spite of the fact that he agreed. He was in a show-off mood. Usually Kerry's presence made him feel secure enough that he didn't have to show off. Today Ben's arrogance had set off a sort of eager anger: anger that any of them had been shown up, and eagerness to be sure that he still came first with Kerry.

"*Look* at that *wall!*" exclaimed Kerry. "Who on earth is *doing* all this?"

Pres looked at the wall in question.

Tarenton High had an anonymous vandal/athlete who had taken to leaving footprints on the walls. Whoever it was was agile. He could only achieve those black marks by racing up to the wall and actually running a pace or two on its vertical surface.

The unknown boy's favorite place of attack was the foyer. Flat white paint adorned its wide, high walls, and light streamed in the huge glass doors from the west-facing entrances. Tread marks were displayed to glorious advantage, and every single kid in the high school paused to admire or deplore the handiwork.

There were those who applauded every time the skidmarks appeared higher and higher on the walls.

There were those who thought it was disgusting vandalism, and helped paint over the offending black streaks each time.

Mrs. Oetjen, the principal, was out for blood. *Nothing* offended her more. Not drugs, not stealing from lockers, not academic failure, not basketball defeat. She had a thing about those white walls. The sparkling purity of that front foyer symbolized to Mrs. Oetjen a pride in learning and education. It was the first impression of the school that she ran, and she could not bear those stains.

Of course the marks didn't wash off. They were indelible, rubbery, had to be painted over, and sometimes bled through the paint, requiring another coat. Anyway, you could always tell where they'd been painted over because the paint itself made fresher, whiter streaks.

Pres said, "What do you think I should get my mother for her birthday?"

Hard to imagine beautiful Felicia Tilford getting older. Kerry doubted that the occasion was one for celebration on Felicia's part. "Well," she said, unable to think of a single item the wealthy, spoiled Felicia Tilford did not already have two of, "anybody with fingers and earlobes can always use rings and earrings."

Pres shook his head. "I've tried that. My taste is never good enough. She always tells me how *charming* they are, and how *thoughtful* I am, and then she puts the earrings back in the box and never wears them."

Kerry ached for him. Pres and his parents were endlessly getting on each other's nerves. Her own family was close in an easy, undemanding way, and she could not figure out why the three Tilfords were so irritable with each other.

"Presents are always a pain," Pres said glumly. "There was a Christmas when all I got was socks and batteries."

Kerry giggled. "Were you supposed to plug in your socks?"

"No. I guess they figured I had every battery-powered toy in the world, so all I needed were more batteries to keep them going. And I think I had so many clothes, they figured all I needed in that department was more socks."

Kerry squeezed his hand. "Bet they gave you something terrific as well. Like a Porsche."

"Nope. Got that when I turned sixteen. The year of the socks was thirteen."

They turned the corridor into the foyer. Strong sun poured in, half blinding them in the intensity of the angled setting sun. Framed like a silhouette on a white matte was a slim, dark figure with heavy black-soled shoes leaping into the air sideways, and leaving treadmarks so high they were nearly at the ceiling.

"Oh, wow!" Kerry breathed. "I hate those skidmarks, but that kid can really jump! Didn't he remind you of Olivia, leaping like that? You should have him on the cheerleading squad!"

Pres could not believe how much it hurt that Kerry thought there was somebody out there who could add to the squad. What could this kid do that he, Pres, could not do better? I'll show her! he thought. *I* can do anything, and do it *better*.

"I can leave skidmarks higher up than that," he said irritably.

"Oh, Pres, you cannot," she said.

Goaded, he left her side instantly, raced along-

234

side the wall, gathered speed and thigh muscles, and ran up the wall. He'd never tried it before, although all the boys did it occasionally in the locker rooms, but adrenalin and the need to prove himself to Kerry won.

He didn't get any higher than the boy before him, but he equaled it. He came down, delighted with himself, out of breath, leg muscles shaking, and bumped hard into the principal's wide, unyielding bosom.

"Preston Tilford!" screamed Mrs. Oetjen, grabbing his shoulders and shaking him. She was shorter than Pres, but fury lent her strength. He stood there and let himself be shaken. "So it's *you*! I am so disgusted with you! I cannot *believe* this. This makes me *sick*, Preston Tilford! I've been on that loudspeaker every single afternoon, asking that vandal to stop ruining our beautiful school, and it's *you*!"

She released him, stepped back, and glared at him with unparalleled rage. Anything else Pres had done in his school career had been mere mischief compared to this. Mrs. Oetjen was beside herself.

In normal circumstances, Pres laughed things off. He was not given to accepting much in the way of blame, or concerning himself much over incidents that upset other people. But he had never faced such pure fury.

She was like a hurricane, ready to rip him from his foundations.

"It wasn't Pres," Kerry said quickly. "Pres didn't —"

"Kerry Elliot!" Mrs. Oejten yelled. "I just *saw* him. *You* just saw him. How *dare* you attempt to lie to protect him? I thought better of you!"

"No, no!" cried Kerry. "I'm not lying. He did do it once, but it was only once, and it was my fault. The other times he —"

"You see?" she demanded. "*The other times!*"

Kerry subsided. She was making things worse. She was a little scared by the degree of anger the principal was displaying. She had never been in any kind of trouble in her life, and she didn't want to start now.

Mrs. Oetjen said a little more quietly, "Pres, I am so disappointed in you. I thought you were calming down at last. I was impressed by how much effort you were putting into the squad. You've pulled your grades up to where they should be and your classroom behavior by and large is acceptable. Now I realize it's because you were taking out all your hostility in another way. Pres, it's one thing to take risks, which you do every time you act stupidly. But it's another to force the entire school to suffer with you. I truly believe that defacing the school, week after week, is the most anti-social act a person is capable of. Come to my office. We'll call the police first, and then your father."

CHAPTER

Nancy knew they were attracting stares. Deep down she knew they were stares of anger and hostility. But she chose not to face that. She chose to consider the attention as admiration. The raw-boned, hawk-faced young man beside her made her weak with excitement.

Patrick left them at Ben's car. She remembered to murmur good-bye, but as she slid in with Ben, all else was forgotten.

Ben drove out of the parking lot and across Tarenton just the way she expected him to: with controlled but excessive speed. He wasn't endangering lives, but he wasn't obeying the rules either.

She debated locking her seat belt. If she put

it on, she'd be safer, of course. Ben seemed the type to require a safety net. On the other hand, she'd be fastened down at greater distance from Ben than she wanted. She did not know him at all. Should she sidle over on the upholstery and sit right up next to him?

Nancy could hardly even look at him, let alone touch him. Whenever she turned his way, he also turned, his dark, piercing stare giving her more troubling thoughts than the sum total of all the other boys she had ever dated.

After three exchanges like this — no talk, just charged stares — Nancy looked out her window instead. Gas station. Parking lot. Discount shoes. I can't believe I'm looking out the window, she thought. I am sitting next to heaven, and I'm studying the billboards advertising bank interest rates.

Ben Adamson got on the bypass, more so that he could drive fast than to save time, and congratulated himself. Going to Tarenton High gymnasium had been like a battle scene without the effort a real battle would demand. He'd had a victory, but been spared the fight. Poor Donny Parrish. Good enough in a small backwater town like Tarenton, but nothing to compare with a *real* basketball player. How Ben had loved sauntering into Donny's gym, and sauntering out with little Nancy on his arm. And Nancy was so obviously thrilled about it.

Ben loved thrilling girls. And did anything he could think of to thrill them.

He took Nancy for hamburgers. She barely ate hers. Ben took this as a compliment: She was either concerned that she should not gain weight and thus be less attractive for him, or she was so nervous in his presence that she couldn't eat.

Either way suited Ben Adamson perfectly.

He thought vaguely, I'll go out with her for basketball season. Stir things up a little. It's going to be such an easy victory for me this year, this'll add a little spice to it. Then after basketball's over, maybe that new girl, Wendy.

Wendy had just moved to Garrison. Willowy, distant, shy, and graceful, she didn't look like an easy mark. Ben thought it would be fun to prove to her that she *was* easy. Ben sat over his double cheeseburger and talked to Nancy, looked at Nancy, shared the condiments with Nancy — but throughout their meal, another girl was superimposed on Nancy's face: the elusive Wendy who Ben would go after next.

"Listen," Ben said, "how about breakfast tomorrow?"

Nancy was astonished and gratified. A boy so eager to see her that he not only couldn't wait until Saturday night for their first date — he wanted to drive all the way over from Garrison early in the morning, before school, and have breakfast with her?

She said, "Oh, I'd love that, Ben." Actually Nancy never ate breakfast. Her stomach was tight and unwilling in the morning. She knew breakfast was good for you and the most important meal of the day and all that, but it had no appeal for her. If she swallowed half a glass of orange juice it was a successful morning. However, for Ben, she was even willing to face pancakes and sausage.

"The Pancake House?" she guessed, because it was the only place in Tarenton that served decent breakfasts.

Ben simply laughed and shook his head.

Immediately she felt unsophisticated and ignorant. There must be some special place she didn't know about.

Ben lifted her hand, looked at it for a long moment, and kissed each finger, running his lips over her glossy, polished nails. She had been a hand lotion and nail polish addict for years. The final payoff, Nancy thought, half laughing. She glanced nervously around her, but nobody was looking. She considered lifting *his* hands to *her* mouth, but lost her courage. She just didn't know Ben. Imagine being able to make such carefree moves with a strange girl, without a quiver of worry that she'd be irritated, or put him down, or laugh in his face. She herself could never do the same. She'd have to date Ben for months before she reached his stage of confidence.

Date him for months, she thought giddily.

Ben swept the trash off their table and onto the brown plastic trays. Efficiently he dumped the trays into the trash cans and took her arm. Nothing he did was uncertain or insecure.

That's what being a star does to you, Nancy thought. I'm a little bit of a star from cheerleading, but he is *truly* a star.

They left, Ben confirming his star status by telling her about his latest college offer. "Yes," he said casually. "The coaches from State University were at that game where we creamed you guys."

Nancy did not enjoy that remark. They had not been creamed. They had put up a terrific fight and just barely lost. She looked away from Ben, wondering just what loyalty to Tarenton required her to say.

"I'm sorry," Ben said softly. "I wouldn't hurt your feelings for the world. But I can't help it that Donny Parrish just isn't in my league. You wouldn't want me to do a mediocre job at anything, would you?"

"No," she said. Impossible to imagine Ben participating in something mediocre.

"Now where do you live? I'll be getting you early in the morning, so I'd better learn the route now while it's still half light." He tucked her in his front seat like a package for the post office. His presumptuousness did not annoy Nancy. On the contrary, she found that she loved being a possession of Ben Adamson.

241

The minute this comparison crossed her mind, she knew she had the correct word. She was not Nancy Goldstein for this boy. She was simply his possession. He did not feel nervous because he knew he owned her.

And I don't even care, Nancy thought. What's happening to me? She said, "Where are we going tomorrow morning?"

"My surprise."

This was not said in a teasing voice, but matter of factly, brooking no discussion. In this relationship, Ben would make all decisions. Nancy was supposed to be happy about it. Period. She had a flicker of confusion, maybe even dismay, but it passed when Ben pulled into her driveway and took her in his arms. He wasn't tender or caring. Ben Adamson didn't know what tenderness was, but he expressed a passion that Nancy responded to.

If you counted them up, she had only known him for minutes. Minutes in a darkened hallway. Half an hour over a hamburger. And this kiss was more intense than some she and Alex had shared when they were going together for six months.

I like it, Nancy decided. I like a boy who knows what he's doing and where he's going and doesn't fool around getting there.

Ben smiled at her. Nancy was mesmerized by that smile, her head tilted up to absorb it, her thoughts caught on it. The smile vanished as fast as the sun behind a cloud and Ben kissed her another time. Fiercely. He did not give her any participation in this kiss. It was *his* kiss, but it excited her.

"Early," he said, leaning back. "About six." He turned on the ignition as a form of dismissal.

Six, Nancy thought. That meaning getting up at five to fix her hair and all. What a gruesome thought. "Fine," she said.

"Wear something nice," said Ben, as if she would ever have contemplated wearing something ugly. He leaned across her, opened the door from the inside handle, and waited for her to scoot out. She shut the door herself and he backed out of the driveway without glancing her way again. What a strange combination of business and flirtation he was!

All over Tarenton, people began getting ready for supper.

They were washing hands, peeling potatoes, putting water on to boil, setting tables, calling children in from play, and turning off the television.

Angie Poletti regretfully hung up the phone from talking to her darling Marc, still off at college, and unable to come home again this weekend.

Mary Ellen Kirkwood grated cheese for a macaroni casserole and wept because Donny had not spoken to her after practice.

Olivia Evans stood in her room in front of the

mirror, reliving the heady excitement of the applause she had heard during her most daring leap. Then she went downstairs to have another argument with her mother over whether she ought to be on the squad, or ought to stay home and get a good healthy rest.

Walt Manners did his homework alone over a frozen dinner, while his parents worked late on a tape of their morning show.

And in Mrs. Oetjen's office, Pres Tilford was begging. He had never begged for anything before. Never known the sick taste of being at someone's mercy. Never known the humiliation and agony of having to plead, and of knowing that he might lose.

And all this — in front of Kerry.

"It wasn't me," Pres said, trying to keep his voice from rising with anger and fear. Important to stay calm. If he screamed at Mrs. Oetjen, he would certainly never convince her. And above all, he'd better not throw anything. "I did do it that one time. I admit that. I was —" he took a deep breath. Only the truth could possibly work now. "I was showing off for Kerry. This boy up ahead of us was making shoe marks real high. Kerry was joking that we should catch him and draft him for the cheerleading squad, so we could make use of those unbelievable jumps. And it kind of irritated me that she didn't think *I* could jump like that, so I showed off. And you were there."

Mrs. Oetjen clearly did not believe a word of this.

Kerry said softly, "Please believe us. Really and truly this was the only time and it was my fault. I goaded him into it." Her voice trembled. The thought of the police coming, of Pres being charged with a crime, made her literally ill. She was afraid she was going to throw up, and she knew that Mrs. Oetjen felt nothing but contempt for her, with her trembly little voice and her shaky little hands.

And Pres — what did he feel? Resentment? Rage?

"So what did this other boy look like?" Mrs. Oetjen asked grimly.

Pres and Kerry exchanged hopeless looks. "Well," Pres said slowly, "we couldn't really see him. There was too much sun. He was just sort of a shape up ahead."

"Uh huh," the principal said skeptically. She picked up the telephone and started punching the little square buttons. Pres and Kerry watched with fatalistic silence.

If she calls the police, Pres thought, what am I going to do? My family will kill me. Kerry will dump me. I'll be thrown off the squad. I'll never get into a decent college, either, with a police record.

A record.

It chilled him to the marrow. And for something he hadn't even done! How unfair!

But he knew the number she was ringing, and it wasn't the police. It was Tarenton Fabricators. Pres didn't know but that the police would be preferable to dealing with his father. Preston Tilford II in a towering rage had always managed to terrify Preston Tilford III.

But he doubted if Mrs. Oetjen could get through to his father anyway. Tilford had a viciously protective secretary. She never let anybody talk to Mr. Tilford unless it was previously arranged.

Pres had not reckoned with Mrs. Oetjen's determination. She breezed past that secretary as if she were the President of the United States. "Mr. Tilford?" said Mrs. Oetjen sharply. And she began her version of the story. The high school was covered with black skid marks three, four, and five feet high off the floor. There were even some on the ceiling in the chemistry room, though she didn't know how Pres had done that.

"He didn't," Kerry murmured. "He isn't taking chemistry this year."

Mrs. Oetjen paid no attention to Kerry.

Pres, she informed the boy's father, had been caught in the act, but was nevertheless, in a very sneaky way, trying to get out of it.

Pres Tilford had many faults, but sneakiness was not one of them. More than anything else he hated that accusation. If I *were* doing it, he thought, I'd brag about it. I'd do it out front. I wouldn't sneak around, letting other people take the blame.

His father was so upset he was shouting into the phone. Pres and Kerry could hear his end of the conversation, as if he'd been in the room with them. "I understand the gravity of the situation, Mrs. Oetjen," said Mr. Tilford, "and I certainly thank you for calling me immediately. I am not asking for any special favors for my son, but would you hold off on calling the police until I have a chance to get to the school and talk to Pres myself?"

Pres held his breath.

Mrs. Oetjen agreed.

The three of them sat in her office as the sun set. There was nothing more to say. Pres was afraid if he talked again, he'd start swearing and that would definitely not help his case. Kerry was afraid if she started talking, she'd cry.

The phone rang.

Mrs. Oetjen answered in monosyllables and this time her eyes fixed with acid disgust on Kerry. "Your parents have been out looking for you for the last hour. Do you recall promising them to be home by five, so you could all drive to your aunt's house and go out for dinner?"

Kerry's heart sank. "Now I remember," she whispered.

"They will be here to pick you up at the front door. Kerry, I also thought more highly of *you*! Not only are you aiding and abetting in vandalism, but you are causing your family serious worry that something happened to you. Just so you could be in the company of a boy who clearly isn't worth it."

Kerry Elliot was not a stalwart soul. She took whatever any adult dished out. Shyness and insecurity kept her from ever talking back. But this she could not tolerate. She said without raising her voice, "Mrs. Oetjen, I think you are leaping to conclusions. I thought more highly of *you* also. You are so angry about the defacing of this school, that you're grabbing the first available scapegoat. Well, it isn't Pres doing this. We've both given you our word on that. You ought to know both Pres and me well enough to give us the benefit of the doubt. It hurts me that you won't even listen to us."

Pres was immeasurably touched. A testimony on his behalf. He knew what effort it took such a shy girl to speak like that, knew that she was trembling at the after effect, and took her hand. He squeezed it very lightly. It was cold and damp.

Mrs. Oetjen softened.

For a moment Pres thought they would clear it all up right then. That somehow it would all be okay, and he'd have gotten out of this mess without much problem after all.

But his father stalked into the room.

Mr. Tilford was tall, greying at the temples, wearing glasses that gave his expression an indefinable intensity. He wore a three-piece suit of dark grey, and a quietly patterned tie with a small clip. He looked utterly conservative, law-abiding, and upstanding. He also looked like the sort of man who would not tolerate a son like Pres. He did not so much as look at his son.

He said, "Mrs. Oetjen, I would like to suggest that I take on Pres's punishment myself. I will have him removed from the cheerleading squad. I will take away his Porsche, which we should never have given him in the first place, considering his lack of maturity. And we will ground him, so he won't be in the company of a girl who is such a bad influence."

Pres was on his feet in a shot. "Bad influence!" he shouted. "Kerry is the best influence in my life. How dare you say that about her! Kerry is good. She would never —" He was suddenly aware that he was advancing on his own father. That his fists were doubled and his muscles painfully tensed. It appalled him. Much as they argued in the Tilford household, nobody had ever thought of hitting.

But he was thinking of it now.

Kerry was up and tugging at him. "Pres, no. Don't. Just stay calm." Her soft, vulnerable features came between him and the implacable strength of his father. "He's upset," said Kerry, excusing the terrible remark. "It's natural he'd say things like that right now."

She's right, Pres thought. It is natural for my father to say rotten things.

249

"All of you please sit down," Mrs. Oetjen said crisply. You, too, Mr. Tilford."

The force of her personality was such that they all obeyed, however reluctantly, lowering themselves slowly into chairs, so that the wooden arms of the chairs kept them safely apart.

"Since my original call to you," Mrs. Oetjen said to Pres's father, "we have done a bit more talking. Kerry has had some sensible and thought-provoking things to say. I have decided to give Pres the benefit of the doubt. I do not see how we are going to test his guilt, or lack of it, because the boy doing this vandalism is very sneaky. If the marking stops, then probably it *is* Pres, unwilling to get caught a second time. If it continues, I still will not know who is doing it." She looked sadly at Pres and Kerry.

I've got to thank her, Pres thought, but he still felt so much like hitting that he did not dare utter a syllable or make a move.

Kerry said, "Thank you, Mrs. Oetjen." She thought, Terrific. Now Pres and I are going to have to catch this person who's really doing it, or be under suspicion for the rest of the school year.

"Nevertheless," Mr. Tilford said, "you are grounded, Pres. No dates. No cheerleading."

He had known it was coming. And he had known just how powerless he was to do anything about it. He could not cheerlead on the sly, because Ardith would be informed and have auditions to replace him. He could not date Kerry on the sly, because his father would call her parents and that would end that.

His rage grew.

Talk about a soap opera, Pres thought. Calm down, Pres old boy. Calm down.

Kerry's cool fingers rested on his taut muscles. Lightly, ever so lightly, she massaged them, saying the same thing with her touch, but more effectively, more lovingly: *Stay calm.*

Mrs. Oetjen said, "I believe that if we give the benefit of the doubt in one way, we should do it in all ways, Mr. Tilford. I would be against denying them each other's company and equally against taking Pres off the squad. If they are given a chance, it must be a whole chance, not a fractional chance."

She was like a block of granite. Kerry was filled with admiration for her obstinance. She could not know that Mr. Tilford looked at this woman with even more admiration.

Like to have her working for Tarenton Fabricators, he thought. She's wasted at a school. She should be in manufacturing, a strong woman like that. He accepted her decision. "Pres," he said to his son, "you are a very fortunate boy."

The office door slammed open and Kerry's mother and father burst into the room.

"Oh, no," Kerry cried. "I forgot *again*. I was supposed to meet you outside. Mom, I'm really sorry." She stood up fast, and Pres stood up right beside her, so they were a team giving each other support.

"Kerry," her mother said, tense and exasperated, "I am seriously thinking of grounding you."

Mrs. Oetjen laughed, Mr. Tilford laughed, and the surprise of their laughter was so great that Pres and Kerry giggled, too. "We just dismissed that as a possibility," Mrs. Oetjen said, smiling at the Elliots and giving them a fuller explanation. "Let's let these two sort out their own problems. As for the vandalism, I'll have to find another way to deal with it."

She turned to Pres, with a heaviness in her manner that chilled him a second time. "If you *are* doing this, Preston," she said quietly, "it will be the police we call and not your family. I will bring criminal charges against you. Do you understand?"

CHAPTER

7

Mary Ellen wept over Donny until quarter to eight. She stopped not because of homework that had to be done, but because the sobbing was giving her a terrible headache.

How could there be such perfection in life one day, and such misery the next?

How *could* Ben have done such a thing?

Mary Ellen raged at Ben . . . and at Donny.

Who was Donny, to let Ben take control like that? Patrick stood up to Ben. Patrick kept Tarenton's honor. Donny just sat there, taking it. Letting Ben own the Tarenton gym.

Don't think about Patrick, she told herself. Forget about Patrick. If you *can*, a small voice said.

At quarter to eight, Mary Ellen pressed a cold, wet washcloth to her forehead and began her English homework. Shakespeare. Mary Ellen had not told anybody, but she truly loved Shakespeare. She loved to whisper the lines, hearing their symmetry and their style. This was the fourth play they'd studied in high school: *Macbeth*.

Such tough, determined people. The characters in *Macbeth* knew what they wanted, and they went out and got it.

Amoral, maybe. But achievers. Mary Ellen respected achievers.

Would I rather be one of the witches, she thought, or Lady Macbeth?

Right now she felt witchy. She felt like bending over a great bubbling cauldron, coming up with vicious spells and cruel concoctions. She saw herself: dark and dank and stringy and mean. Casting a spell on Nancy, who had brought Ben into their lives and taken the glow off Donny.

The phone rang.

I come, Greymalkin, Mary Ellen thought. *Fair is foul and foul is fair.* "Hello," she said sweetly.

"Hello." It was a heavy, masculine voice. She knew the speaker, but she couldn't quite place him. After a moment of confusion, she said, "How are you?" which seemed safe.

"Okay."

Two syllables. No clues. But if the call had been for Gemma or her parents, the voice would have said so. It was her call. "I'm doing my Shakespeare," she said.

"What a horrible thought."

Donny. Was it Donny? She could not tell. She had talked to Donny only once on the telephone. Stupid as it seemed, she could not absolutely recognize his voice. Once, months ago, Mary Ellen had publicly mistaken Patrick for Pres, making a total fool of herself. She would not address this boy by name until she was one hundred percent sure.

"I love Shakespeare," he confided.

"You're kidding."

"What can I say? I like older men."

A shout of laughter.

So it was Donny, definitely Donny. His laughter was most unusual, a true shout. Literally gales of laughter. She loved Donny's laugh. How wonderful to hear it now, and know that she had brought it to him! That he'd called in spite of the afternoon's fiasco. She would willingly have hugged a porcupine, she was so pleased. The world that had rated dark tears became a world of sunshine.

"I hate Shakespeare," Donny said. In emphatic detail, he told Mary Ellen what he held against Shakespeare. Poor Shakespeare, thought Mary Ellen.

She held the phone with her left hand, scribbled her analysis with her right, and chatted happily with Donny for an hour.

255

Gemma, her younger sister, sat in the kitchen. She had heard the phone ring, heard the delighted peal of laughter, knew that there was an admiring boy on the phone.

Cheerleading was supposed to make Mary Ellen's life terrific, Gemma mused. I guess it does, sometimes. But sometimes it seems to me that the closer Mary Ellen gets to Number One, the harder she has to struggle to stay there.

Much as she idolized her sister, Gemma wondered if she would want to be on Varsity when she was old enough to try out.

But Mary Ellen Kirkwood had no such qualms. She had a great capacity to enjoy the moment — and this moment was *hers*.

Very early the following morning, Ben Adamson pulled into the Goldstein driveway and tapped lightly on the horn. He made no move to come to the door. Nancy waved through the window that she had seen him and was coming. As she gathered her books, Mrs. Goldstein remarked, "Always be careful of a boy who expects *you* to go to *him*."

"It wouldn't be efficient for him to stop the engine and walk up to the door when I'm on my way out," Nancy said.

"Boyfriends shouldn't worry about efficiency," her mother said.

Nancy chose not to pay attention. She zipped her heavy jacket and took a final glance in the mirror. The scarlet of her jacket set off her dark, thick hair beautifully. She looked just the way she wanted to look. Lovely.

They were going somewhere for breakfast, she would have a wonderful time, and Ben would have something grand planned for Saturday night. The fact that in one short week there'd be a tough, angry grudge match against Garrison, with her cheering Donny and not Ben, was something Nancy could not deal with right now.

Her mother said softly, "Nanny, honey, I'm not sure about this arrangement."

Her mother had not called her Nanny in ages. Nancy said, "Mother, really. Everything's fine. I can handle it."

"I'm not so sure," Mrs. Goldstein said, but she did nothing to interfere. Nancy left quickly and got into the car with Ben.

He literally filled the front seat. She had never felt so dwarfed, or so happy, or so tense. She wanted to snuggle up against him, but he made no move toward her. He just drove. She sat on her side, feeling like a mouse next to him. She could not take her eyes off him.

It was not that he was good looking. It was that he had so much personality, you were forced to look at him.

"Where are we going?" Nancy asked.

She generally had some breakfast at school. The junior class sold donuts, Danish, coffee, and orange juice, and kept the profits for their dances and activities, and it was infinitely more fun to breakfast there (on her pitiful glass of orange juice) in good company than to bother with it at home. She knew she'd never run into any high school kids this morning because if they had breakfast out, they'd have it at school.

A breakfast date, she thought. Not very romantic.

It was very cold, but Ben wasn't wearing much. A sleeveless ski vest over a wool plaid shirt. On another boy, thinner and less impressive, this would have been an attempt to be macho. But Ben was the living definition of macho. On him it was real. Compared to Ben, all boys Nancy had ever known seemed wimpy.

Ben turned north and headed into the deep woods. Nancy was startled. There weren't any towns out this way. There wasn't much of anything out this way except trees, forests, lakes, and narrow logging roads.

Ben said, "I'm going to be on television."

Nancy gasped. "You *are*! Tell me about it!"

"You know the Manners' show?"

Of course she did. Aside from the fact that Walt's parents *were* "Breakfast at Home," she'd watched it nearly every weekday morning since moving to Tarenton. She loved the whole format, and so did her mother and father.

"Well," Ben said, "they're doing a segment on sought-after high school athletes. College scholarships. That kind of thing." Thick pride was in his voice.

She wondered how she was going to see this through. How she was going to face Walt, when she was with Ben. How did this happen to me? she cried silently.

Nancy said thickly, "That's exciting. I guess there was nobody to interview but you, Ben."

Immediately she felt like a genuine traitor. There was Donny Parrish. He was pretty darn sought after. Flushing slightly, imagining her Varsity Squad listening to this conversation, Nancy stared out the window. Trees. Endless trees of the North Woods. The road seemed vaguely familiar, though.

"Tell me about your offers," she said.

"You aren't a spy for Tarenton, are you?" he asked teasingly.

Nancy protested, "Ben, I am one hundred per-cent on your team." The words did not gag her. They came out easily. They shocked her, though. How can I, Nancy Goldstein, Tarenton Varsity cheerleader, tell this boy I'm one hundred per-cent for the opposite team? she wondered.

Ben grinned inwardly. He had made a con-quest here, that was for sure. How far would this Nancy go to prove she liked him? Well, he would find out Saturday night. He would arrange things so that if she proved the least bit willing, they could go all the way.

259

* * *

Three years ago, Walt Manners' mother, sick
and tired of the same old wallpaper in the family
room, stripped it off. It was a laborious task that
took her long hours over several sweaty days.
Eventually she was down to the plaster of the old
walls in the log cabin area of the house. They
did not film there, but guests, awaiting their
turns, relaxed in this room, adjacent to the
kitchen.

What with one thing and another, Mrs. Manners never got around to repapering. Since they
expected to cover the wall shortly, they began
writing their telephone messages, grocery lists,
and family reminders right on the plaster because
it was such a large and useful white space next
to the phone. Before long, a famous guest happened to jot a message from a still more famous
person right there on the wall. Another important guest, impressed by such names, added a
little graffiti of his own. Still another drew doodles
that had a certain grace and appeal, and these
were later included in a huge, penciled cartoon
by a famous cartoonist.

The wall became one of the household's most
beloved possessions. If you did not like something, you could erase it. Meanwhile, the graffiti
collection grew, spreading across the family room
and pushing toward the kitchen.

Guests on the "Breakfast at Home" show
made references to the wall when they were on

260

the air, and locally it became quite famous. People were always flattered to be asked to sign the wall. The wall was often referred to in conversation. ("I wrote my name over next to the governor's, of course.")

Until the morning that Ben Adamson was the guest on his parents' television show, Walt had no feelings whatsoever about the wall.

He had not known about Ben.

Frequently he had no idea what was going on in the show. When school was demanding, when basketball was in season, when the winter sports he loved were being played, Walt barely noticed his parents. Mr. and Mrs. Manners rose very early in the morning to prepare for the taping. Walt rarely saw them in the morning.

He didn't even tend to watch when he had breakfast. He chose to have his English muffin in peace in the kitchen, away from the action. If he had the kitchen TV on at all, it was usually tuned to cartoons, which he loved.

He paid no attention to his mother's aide, who was setting out freshly perked coffee, juice, and donuts for this morning's guest. He took a donut, wishing it could be chocolate. But they never set out anything sticky. You didn't want a guest with chocolate or cinnamon sugar on his face.

He ate the first donut standing up, staring vaguely out the kitchen window, watching a light snow fall. His parents would be delighted about the snow. The viewers would see it through the great glass windows that faced the woods, and it would lend a real down-home backdrop to the interview.

"Hi, Walt," said a familiar soft voice.

Mouth full of English muffin, jam on his fingers, Walt turned to see Nancy Goldstein looking at him.

He was used to strangers dropping in, but he was not used to friends. The house was much too far off the beaten track for kids to drop in. He felt very self-conscious sucking the jam off his fingers while Nancy stared at him. He felt weird, standing in his kitchen with her there — no explanation, just there.

"I'm here with Ben," she said nervously. "He's going to be interviewed by your parents. He and his coach. He's gotten all those terrific college athletic offers, you know, and there are so many places trying to sign Ben up, so your mother and father are interviewing him."

Nancy looked at Walt, pleadingly. "Look, I didn't know we were coming here. He didn't tell me, until we were on the way. I couldn't. . . ."

Walt couldn't believe it.

Bad enough that his parents were interviewing the star of some other high school, but that Nancy — his co-cheerleader, Nancy — should have come along was like treason. His parents he had to forgive: The show covered a dozen area towns, of which Tarenton was the smallest, and Garrison, in fact, the most important.

But Tarenton was — *had* to be — the most important for Nancy and Walt.

Nancy reached a hand out to touch Walt's arm, asking to be forgiven.

Walt turned away from her and forcefully shoved down the knob on the toaster for his second English muffin.

Ben Adamson entered the kitchen. He had to stoop to come in, the low threshold an obstacle. Stooping made Ben appear even larger, formidable, unbeatable. There were no air spaces around Ben, no glimpse of the room beyond. There was just Ben, and Ben's shoulders. And Ben's condescending smile.

Walt, who was not small, felt small.

If he had felt awkward and irritable with Nancy, he felt deeply trespassed upon by Ben. Guests were not invited into the kitchen. They were supposed to stop at the door, where the aide handed them a donut and a Styrofoam cup of coffee.

Ben sauntered on in, keeping his head low, as if even in the kitchen he would not fit, he being a superstar who needed extra space.

Never had it been so hard for Walt to keep from shouting. As calmly as he could, he said, "Guests normally wait in the other room, Ben."

Ben looked gratified. "You know who I am?" he said. "From basketball, I take it?"

Walt managed not to tell Ben where to take it. He chewed hard on his muffin instead. Nancy stood there, tears gathering in her eyes.

Ben extended a hand to shake.

What timing, Walt thought. I've got butter and jam on my hands. Then he thought, What better person to get a little stickiness and grease on? He shook hands eagerly, and smiled to himself as Ben realized he now had a very messy hand and nothing to wipe it on.

Won that round, Walt thought with satisfaction.

"Walt's a cheerleader with me," Nancy said, trying to ease the tension.

Ben laughed. Actually *laughed*. Clearly the thought of a boy cheerleader was comical to Ben.

I will not hit him, Walt thought.

Ben began reading the wall graffiti out loud. Naturally he picked the supremely stupid ones. "Call plumber to take out toilet before linoleum goes down," Ben said, laughing again. "You people immortalize all the really important things, don't you?"

I could dismember him, Walt thought. But Mom wouldn't like blood all over the floor.

Ben's bleak face held its contained but deep amusement. Amusement at Walt's expense. Then Ben laughed *again*, that ragged, rough laugh that made Walt feel furious and made Nancy giggle in panic. "I can't believe what you're watching on this television," Ben said.

"What's he watching?" Nancy asked.

"Mighty Mouse cartoons." Ben doubled over with laughter. Ben doubled over took up all the free space in the entire kitchen.

Walt did not know what he might have done if his mother hadn't appeared in the doorway. She was wearing a soft wool dress, smelling of lilac perfume and looked pretty, warm, and welcoming. "So this is Ben Adamson," she said in her throaty voice. "I've heard *so* much about you." She extended a hand and did not flinch or comment on the jam and butter that were now passed to her. She was far too poised. She explained just how the filming would go: where Ben would sit, where his coach would sit, the sort of questions they would be asked, where to direct their gazes during the interview. Ben listened intently. There would be no flubs in his first TV appearance. Ben was not the type to get flustered under pressure. He thrived on it.

Probably get offered a job as an anchor as well as a full scholarship to college, Walt thought morosely. He thought if Nancy said one more word of explanation, he would shove her into the toaster.

Mrs. Manners took Ben into the living room, shutting the thick kitchen door tightly behind her. Quickly Walt changed TV stations so they'd be tuned to the Manners' show.

"You can watch Mighty Mouse," Nancy said.

Walt's mother came into focus. The camera turned to Ben. "I *am* watching Mighty Mouse," Walt said.

"Oh, Walt, if I'd known. . . ."

"I think it's the perfect name." Walt said, ignoring Nancy. He hoped Ben would be awful. His mother would say, "And were you surprised to win by such a wide margin?" and Ben would say, "Unhhh, dduuhhh, welll, guess not, uhhhh."

But no such luck. Mighty Mouse chatted away like somebody up for a professorship. Then his mother did it to him. She said, smiling sweetly, "And what are your biggest plans for the moment, Ben?"

A sharp smile decorated the hawklike face. "Whipping Tarenton. But it won't be hard. They don't have much to offer."

CHAPTER

It wasn't so much that the Tarenton High students were rude to Nancy. In the short time she'd lived in Tarenton, she had proved herself a good kid and a good friend. They just didn't bother with her at all. She wasn't included in the chatter and she wasn't in on the jokes. She was just there on the sidelines, watching.

It was like being new in school all over again. Unnoticed. Unwanted.

Except for Vanessa Barlow. Vanessa never let a chance to attack Nancy go by. She did it blatantly, not trying to be clever. She simply let Nancy know, in every way she could, that she thought Nancy was a traitor.

Walt managed to get out of any blame for his

267

parents' interview by referring to Ben Adamson as Mighty Mouse. Tarenton loved it. The nickname was picked up instantly. "Did you hear what Mighty Mouse said?" went the talk up and down the halls. "Mighty Mouse doesn't think we have anything to offer."

Mary Ellen said firmly to Donny, "We'll show Mighty Mouse, won't we?"

Olivia said to Mary Ellen, "Wait till Mighty Mouse sees the new routine we've got. We can cream Garrison any *place*, any *time*."

Nobody said anything to Nancy Goldstein.

She did not know what to do about her divided feelings. Of course she didn't want Tarenton beaten! But neither did she want Ben beaten, not when he was on this fabulous winning streak. And, maybe, herself beside him.

During English, she paid no attention to the lecture on Shakespeare. She made a mental ledger and weighed having Ben against not having Ben. As long as her name was linked with his, even a little bit, she had no friends, no companionship, no shared laughter. But she did have the hope of being Ben's girl, and never, *never*, had she met a more exciting boy.

It was not a good day for her.

But like all days, it ended eventually. She went to cheerleading practice, grateful to be with the only group that had any use for her.

But today was different.

Today she was the traitor in their midst, and

they resented having to use her at all. When Nancy spoke, they said, "Listen, Goldstein, we'll do it our way. Play games with Mighty Mouse if you don't like it."

When Nancy got tired, they said, "What's your problem? You trying to sabotage our practice? Throw the ball to Mighty Mouse, maybe? Keep working, Nancy."

I can't do it, Nancy thought. I'm not strong enough. I can't stand up to them.

But then she remembered Ben, who could stand up to anybody, and it gave her strength. She shrugged off their attitudes and kept working on Tarenton cheers, thinking of a Garrison boy.

Mrs. Evans rumbled into the gym on Thursday afternoon. They had been practicing for a hour and they were tired, sweaty, disheveled, and snapping at each other. Carrying her own chair, she marched in, thrust the folding metal chair with its padded seat into the floor as if it were a stake at which someone would burn, and said harshly, "Olivia? What are you doing? That looks very dangerous to me."

"Oh, no, Mother," said Olivia. "It's quite ordinary."

Nobody met anybody else's eyes. Mrs. Evans was totally right. It was a dangerous routine. "In fact, I think we'll do it again," Olivia said brightly. She turned to the squad, her whole posture one of daring, of *I'll show my mother a thing or two.* In rhythm, she yelled, "Are you *ready?*"

They rose to the occasion. "We're *ready.*"

"Roadway, runway, *rail*way," Olivia led the cheer. They began their new motions.

"Make this game our vict'ry day!"

Olivia pirouetted dramatically back beyond the rest of the squad. In perfect symmetry, their arms at precisely the same height, their legs lifted in kicks, their feet smacking the gym floor for noisy emphasis, the other five took new positions. "*Allllll the way!*" they screamed. "*Allllll the way!*"

Olivia ran. Hurtling through the air, she leaped, her right foot touching Pres's cupped palms lightly. He thrust up, and this time Olivia flipped over the outstretched fingertips of the girls, landing by a crouching Walt, and flipped over him, to end in a somersault, then a split. The girls moved forward flashing their scarlet and white pompons like a bouquet of flowers, and Walt and Pres leaped up on the sides and came down in matching poses opposite Olivia.

Wow, Pres thought. He didn't suppose he'd ever get used to that cheer. It scared him that he might foul up and it would end with Olivia getting hurt.

He wished his parents would come to the game Friday against Grove Hill. Grove Hill wasn't much of a team and it would be an easy win, as long as Tarenton didn't get cocky. But it was a time to practice their spectacular routines, the ones that would help in the downfall of Mighty Mouse.

But his mother had gone to Scotland for ten days and was due back tonight. She would still be too tired to attend a school basketball game. Actually, the Tilfords were too tired to attend any game where their son humiliated them by cheering, but Pres chose not to think of that at this moment. He just hoped she'd come back from Scotland in a better mood than she'd left.

"I won't have it!" Mrs. Evans screamed. "Won't have what?" Ardith said innocently.

"Won't have my little girl risking her life like this!"

"I'm not risking my life, Mother. I'm just showing off the skills *you* gave me, Mother, when you paid for those gymnastics and fencing lessons all these years."

"This is not what I had in mind!" Mrs. Evans said.

"But it *is* what I have in mind," Olivia answered.

They were stalemated. Mrs. Evans, woman of steel, had inadvertently raised a daughter of steel.

Ardith said meekly, "I wouldn't allow Olivia to do this if I really thought she could hurt herself, Mrs. Evans."

"Then you aren't really watching," Olivia's mother said. "I cannot believe you are encouraging this sort of maneuver. Whatever happened to the nice cheers? The sweet friendly ones, like 'Go Get 'em'?"

"*Go Get 'em*" was the least sweet cheer imaginable, with a final line describing the blood and guts that would spill before the game was out, but nobody felt like arguing with Mrs. Evans. Ardith walked her toward the door. Olivia muttered, "Let's get out of here while the getting's good."

"You can't leave," Angie objected. "Your mother will kill you."

"I'm going," Olivia said. "Who volunteers to give me a ride home?"

"None of us wants to tangle with your mother," Pres said. "Especially me. I've got my own mother to cope with tonight."

"I thought your mother was away," Mary Ellen said.

"Yes, but she's coming back." Pres made it sound like the second eruption of a volcano.

Mary Ellen was in a very expansive mood. The world was going her way again. Ben had been reduced effectively to a cartoon mouse; Donny had called her, sat with her at lunch; Nancy was nothing but a trespasser instead of a threat; and the squad had done so wonderfully during practice that *nobody* could ever call them second best again. She said, "Olivia, I'll ride home with you so that your mother can yell at me instead of you."

"Mary Ellen," Olivia said, "you are a true saint."

"Well, for a minute or two anyway," Mary Ellen said honestly, laughing.

"You aren't riding home with Olivia," Donny Parrish said, appearing from nowhere, grinning down at them all. "Olivia's riding with us. I'll drop her off on our way to get a bite to eat before I take you home."

All eyes inspected Donny. It was partly for him they were going through such effort. If Donny were less of a player, or less of a person, they would surrender to the inevitable and let Ben Adamson and Garrison take the championship.

Donny satisfied them.

Tall, rangy, broad, and competent, he looked the way a good basketball player ought to look. A nice, wholesome grin decorated a nice — Mary Ellen caught the word *bland* going through her mind and killed it — face. *Handsome*, she told herself. Future ahead. Going places.

Mary Ellen and Olivia went off on either side of Donny, and he escorted them as if it were his honor.

Standing behind, Pres murmured to Walt, "The trouble is that Ben will be showing off for our Nancy. Ben's going to try harder just because of Nancy."

"Nancy is welcome to move back to Ohio this afternoon," Walt said.

"Women are nothing but trouble," Pres said, thinking of Nancy and his mother.

Kerry walked into the gym and Pres said, "But there are exceptions."

He and Walt laughed.

The afternoon with Kerry put Pres in a wonderful frame of mind. He even thought of it as an entire afternoon with her, although it had been less than three quarters of an hour, really. The practice dwindled in his mind and the moments with Kerry expanded, and his thoughts dwelled on the kisses they had shared and the closeness of their thoughts instead of the strife at school.

Because of Kerry he met his mother at the airport cheerfully, and gave her a genuine kiss and listened to her chatter about Scotland.

That night, after a late dinner, the three Tilfords were sitting in the most elegant room in the huge old Victorian mansion. Furnished with his great-grandmother's belongings, it was red velvet, ornate walnut, and scrolled chair legs. By the firelight his mother sparkled.

She began handing out the presents she had brought them. She had actually brought a kilt for his father. Pres tried to imagine his father in a kilt and failed.

"I hope you've brought a kilt for our son, too," Mr. Tilford said. His voice was cutting, but Felicia was too happy to hear it. Pres picked it up immediately and waited for the sniping to begin.

"So what did you bring me, Mom?" Pres asked.

"It's something for you to wear," she said. "And I want you to promise me you'll wear it to school tomorrow."

"If it's a kilt," said Pres, "I will never even unpack it."

"It's not a kilt," she promised, and she handed him a large package.

CHAPTER

Kerry Elliot's life was built upon tiny glimpses of Pres. She cherished every conversation they ever had. At night, lying snuggled under layers of quilts, she would run through the conversations again until she had them by memory, like so many hit songs.

In school, having memorized his schedule and his habits, she had found ways to see him in the distance. She had told nobody — not even Pres — that she was doing this. It was her private joy, to spot Pres when he was unaware of her. To know that this fabulous boy was hers, that that wonderful young man sauntering around the corner would drive her home in his red Porsche that very day.

Each day she ran the long way between biology and English, because if she was lucky, she'd see Pres and Troy and Donny together, going from their gym class to Spanish.

The three walked in that space-taking manner important boys had, and the momentary glimpse of Pres's dark-blond head laughing next to Donny's kept Kerry buoyed with happiness for the next two classes, before she sat with him at lunch.

Today Kerry felt wonderful.

She was no longer worried about the vandalism. It was still going on. In fact, there were new shoe marks in the foyer that very morning.

And the sweater was almost done. Kerry was so excited by being so close to the finished product. All those hours! Every stitch a stitch for Pres.

Kerry decided not to wait for Pres's birthday. Too far off.

Besides, the weather was cold right now. He *needed* her sweater. She'd give it to him hot off the needles, so to speak. Maybe Saturday night? At the celebration when they whipped Garrison? (Or the funeral if Garrison whipped them.)

Kerry rushed from biology to get to the west wing in time to spot the boys. She arrived just as Donny appeared, a head taller than the others, but not, to Kerry's eyes, nearly as appealing. Too ordinary, which was an odd thing to think of a star like Donny Parrish. And yet, that's what

Donny was. Bland. Troy followed Donny, and then Kerry saw —

Her sweater.

Her wool.

Her design.

On Pres.

Kerry felt as if she had been hit by a truck.

Hours . . . hours . . . *hours* of love, and the offering was ruined.

Pres had not gone to her house, sneaked into her bedroom, gotten the all-but-one-inch finished sweater out of its tote bag, finished the neckband himself, and worn it to surprise her. Somebody else had given it to him.

It could only be his mother. His mother who arrived back from Scotland last night. Scotland, where you could buy wonderful handknits.

Tears rose in Kerry's eyes. No, the pattern wasn't identical, but the style and weight of the yarn was. How much thrill would there be in her gift now? She could not speak. A hot, thick lump blocked her throat. Don't see me, Pres, she prayed. It was the reverse of her usual prayer: *See me, Pres*, see me.

She was going to cry. She knew it. Kerry loathed crying. It took her like a virus: an implacable, destructive illness that, once it took hold, could wipe her away. Once her tear ducts opened, they stayed open for days.

I cannot give in, she thought. If so much as

one tear overflows, I will weep all day, through every class.

"Kerry?" said a friend of hers. "Did you get that math problem on the second page?"

Kerry could not even focus on the friend to identify her. She nodded blindly. Math rarely troubled her.

"I didn't understand a single problem," another girl said glumly. "I hate math. Why do we have to study it anyhow? We can use calculators whenever we need to know something."

"It's good for us," the first girl said. "Builds our characters."

This is good for me, Kerry told herself. It's going to build my character. Isn't that wonderful? Isn't it great to know how strong I'm going to be, because I had my heart set on giving Pres the sweater of his life? Isn't it terrific to know that I, Kerry Elliot, spent dozens and dozens of hours for no purpose except to strengthen my character?

Kerry willed her tears away.

It was a sweater, nothing more. A little wool, a little time killed. She could give it to Pres anyhow. At least he'd know she made the effort. Or she could give it to her father or brother, who both yearned for it.

Or she could lie down here on the math room floor, wailing and gnashing her teeth and beating her fists. Kerry estimated how many calories she

279

would use up having the temper tantrum of the century. Enough to lose the weight she would like to take off? There should be a silver lining in every cloud; maybe this would be the silver lining.

Five minutes before the bell rang, just as she was congratulating herself on self-control, the kind she deserved a gold medal for, the teacher announced a surprise quiz.

The class looked at him in disgust. Quizzes were rotten enough, but surprise quizzes?

Like doom, the teacher passed out mimeographed sheets — half sheets actually — with six problems. When there were so few problems, you knew they would all be terrible. On the other hand, there were only five minutes left in the class. How terrible could they be with so little time to work them out?

Kerry lifted her pencil and that tiny act brought memory flooding over her. A day one month ago . . . sitting in Pres's kitchen . . . Pres running upstairs to get something for his mother. . . . Mrs. Tilford, who was no fan of Kerry's, asking why Kerry was leafing through a book of sweater patterns . . . Kerry flipping to the page where she was using a pencil stub for a marker and showing her the sweater she was knitting for Pres . . . Mrs. Tilford saying nothing good or bad about the idea . . . Kerry swiftly shutting the book and saying nothing herself because Pres was thundering down the stairs again and whirling into the kitchen.

She did it on purpose, Kerry thought.

Pres's mother did that on purpose! She went out and bought a sweater just like the one I was knitting for him. She wouldn't let some dull little chubby sophomore give her precious son something special.

Kerry's pencil moved independently, solving the problems on the math quiz, checking answers, doing proofs.

Kerry's eyes saw Felicia Tilford. Beautiful, oh so beautiful. But shallow. And perhaps not very nice. Whenever Pres said bad things about his parents, Kerry always stood up for them. Maybe she was wrong. Maybe they didn't deserve her support.

Maybe Felicia Tilford was truly capable of treachery.

Kerry shook herself and the pencil made a long, black, stabbing line across the half page. Treachery was much too strong a word. It was just a sweater, after all.

She had gotten into the habit of exaggerating because of the anger over Garrison, over Ben Adamson, over Nancy Goldstein. They were calling all three The Enemy now. Poor Nancy.

You couldn't help who you fell in love with.

I suppose, Kerry thought, passing in her paper without noticing, I can't help it that I love Pres, and Mrs. Tilford can't help it that she doesn't like me.

So now what do I do? she thought, changing

classes, calling hello to her friends, waving at the people she knew, smiling at those she didn't. Did she tell Pres what his mother had done? Would he believe her? Did she want Pres to know a bad thing about his mother? Would he think Kerry was crazy to get all worked up over some dumb sweater?

Maybe it would be best for Pres to wear his mother's sweater happily, glad that this gift was not flashlight batteries and socks, proud that she had bothered to think of him when she was abroad.

Why, after all, should Pres know that mixed up in his gift was anger and resentment toward Kerry, and toward them both as a couple?

In the front foyer a tall, slim, dark boy, wearing cheap shoes with heavy black rubbery soles, walked silently. Sun splashed across the foyer with a glaring intensity. Clear on the foyer walls were wide streaks of fresh white paint, blotches covering the shoe marks of the week before.

He was not a bad person. He would not hit somebody, or steal, or peddle drugs, or even say vicious things. He had never done anything against school rules. In fact, he had never done anything at all.

He had little personality and fewer skills. Never gotten a high mark. Never made a team. Never been told a paper was excellent. Never had his artwork hung on the wall.

And suddenly, all he had to do was run down a hall, leap into the air while still running, leave a footprint, and the entire school was talking about him. Principals were after his skin. Kids admired his anonymous ability to jump high. And now, indelibly, his artwork was on the walls.

He liked sneaking. Nobody knew. Nobody suspected. He liked that. It was a secret to hug to himself: dark and wrong and successful.

To think that Mrs. Oetjen suspected Pres Tilford. It was comical really. Pres, of wealth and good looks, sophistication and beautiful girls. Pres, who could get away with anything because of who he was. Preston Tilford III. In deep and serious trouble.

An extra dose of vandalism. First the walls. Then Pres. He had vandalized Pres. Pulled him in, pulled him down, and Pres had no choice. Pres, who could make any choice, had no choice at all.

The boy thought, I'll leave the walls alone until after cheerleading practice. Nobody notices me. They won't remember I've been hanging around. The moment Varsity leaves the gym, but before Pres can go out to that Porsche of his, I'll do it.

He would never own a Porsche.

But he could get Pres in enough trouble that Pres would lose the Porsche.

Heady thought, all that power. The boy laughed to himself, and put a hand over his mouth to hide the amusement, lest somebody suspect, and think, and draw conclusions.

TGIF, Nancy Goldstein said, eight hundred times.

She even made it into a cheer inside her head. Thank God it's Friday. Yea, rah-rah, *Friday*!

School, which she normally loved, would be over. In the brief time she'd known Ben, school had become a silent torture.

Tonight she would go out with Ben. And Saturday, too.

The weekend seemed complex beyond all imagining. Nancy couldn't see how she was going to cope.

The game against Grove Hill would be their first time showing off the brilliant, daring cheers that made her so anxious. And post-game celebrations would not exactly be a source of relaxation either.

She had agreed to meet Ben at the Tarenton Burger House after the game. He would be coming from (presumably) *his* basketball victory game in Garrison, and she would be coming from (she hoped) *her* victory. And then what? Would they sit there, just the two of them, pretending they hadn't noticed that they were on opposite teams?

She could hardly invite him to Pres's party. He'd be killed.

There were unexpected advantages to having

Pres date Kerry. It had made Pres a host. Nancy wasn't sure why. Perhaps Pres had not wanted sharp, hard Vanessa or glossy, demanding Mary Ellen on his home territory, but once he had Kerry at his side, he could welcome the world.

And it pretty much *would* be their world. The basketball team and their dates, the Varsity Squad and their dates, plus assorted friends nobody could party without. Nancy could not bear missing it. Parties like that were half the reason she tried out for cheerleading to start with. But to bring Ben was unthinkable. And meeting a boy like Ben was the other half of her reason for being a cheerleader, and she wasn't about to give him up either.

But Friday night was a mere nothing compared to Saturday.

Nancy's head ached whenever she contemplated Saturday. Ben would play against Donny. She would cheer for Donny. She would participate in those terrifying leaps and precisely timed moves for Donny's sake, while Ben — tall, rugged Ben — would be right there. And everyone on the Tarenton side of the gym would watch her to see how she handled it.

Maybe I'll just get sick, Nancy thought.

Back in Ohio, Nancy had found getting sick to be an excellent way of removing herself from unpleasant situations. But it wouldn't work now. She was too old. A ten-year-old could play games like that, but Nancy couldn't. Furthermore, she was a squad member, and she had no right to damage Varsity just because of her discomfort.

And what would happen after the game?

If Tarenton lost (it was beyond bearing — they *had* to win!) would she really have the guts to go out with Ben Adamson and celebrate a Garrison win?

And if Tarenton won (they'd better!) would Ben still be willing to cart her along to whatever miserable excuse for a party his bitterly disappointed team would have? Or not have?

Nancy pressed her hands to a throbbing forehead. How could this have happened to her? Why couldn't you just fall peacefully in love with somebody suitable and go your own private way, making your own private decisions?

School had never seemed like such an imposition. Who could be expected to pay attention to dull things like history and math when they were faced with the kind of decisions Nancy Goldstein had to make this afternoon?

At lunch, Kerry would have preferred not to see Pres. She had the tears under control — but barely. Once she got close to that sweater (and she saw, she was sure, the perfection of its workmanship, the beauty of its pattern, whereas her efforts were just that — efforts), she would crack up.

Kerry would have skipped lunch if her girl friends hadn't linked arms with her and all, unknowingly, dragged her downstairs to the cafeteria. They loved Kerry dating Pres as much as Kerry did. They all hoped they, too, would be noticed by these shining senior boys and asked out. Be able to live in a dream, like Kerry.

Little did they know that the dream could get pretty frayed around the edges.

All cafeteria talk was of basketball games.

"Grove Hill tonight."

"No prob. We'll whip them like cream."

"I'm not even going. I'm saving my throat for Saturday."

"It's going to take more than your screams to knock Ben Adamson out of the game."

"Did you hear that Nancy Goldstein is going out with him?"

"Nancy Goldstein? *Our* Nancy Goldstein?"

"Yes. Isn't that disgusting?"

"And she calls herself a cheerleader. Honestly. If that's the kind of girl they put on Varsity, who needs it?"

"I just hope we don't have to be ashamed of the squad again this week. It was pitiful the way those Garrison cheerleaders showed us up."

Across the cafeteria, Donny and Troy waved at her. Pres wasn't there yet, but they had saved her a place. On other days, Kerry was thrilled with it all — catching signals from boys like that! Today she sagged. Reluctantly she left the safety of her friends and sat with Donny and Troy. Mary Ellen breezed in, looking her goldengirl self. Kerry felt chunky and worthless. Tears attacked the back of her eyes.

Pres walked in. Broad shouldered and oh, so handsome in his new sweater. The first thing he said was, "Like my new sweater, Ker?" He kissed her, which had a ripple effect, because Donny then kissed Mary Ellen and Troy kissed the senior girl who was with him. Kerry didn't even know her.

"My mom brought it from Scotland," Pres said happily. "I was afraid she would bring me a kilt, but she brought me this. Isn't it great? I always wanted a handknit sweater like this."

So that's what it means to rub salt in the open wound, Kerry thought, wincing. She smiled at Pres, but didn't speak. One syllable would have broken her voice and spirit and she'd cry for the next hour. She could never do that in front of Pres, but she could *really* never do that in front of Mary Ellen.

In some ways, Melon was an Iron Maiden. Never would Mary Ellen show what bothered her. Kerry had never seen Mary Ellen flustered, let alone weeping. Melon was above the common run of human emotion. Usually Kerry did not know whether to envy this or not. Today she envied. Would that she could stalk through life without being upset by anything!

The boys talked exclusively of basketball.

Kerry had lost interest in the entire sport. In her opinion the season was too long. How nice that nobody cheered for baseball. Pres would be at rest, and she and Pres could concentrate on each other instead of school sports. With her luck, though, Pres would decide to go out for baseball, and she'd spend the entire spring clapping when he made a run and commiserating when he didn't. She felt dishonest at times, dishonest to herself, but she ignored the feeling and played the game Pres wanted.

Sports. Yuk, she thought dismally.

The sweater was as lovely as she had known it would be. Would Felicia Tilford buy something ugly? Of course not.

Rotten, rotten woman, Kerry thought. She said to Pres, "It's beautiful, Pres. You can't say you never get anything but socks and batteries. Not when your mother does something as thoughtful as this. And it fits you perfectly."

I am a saint, she told herself. Kerry, the Pure and Good.

Pres beamed, abandoning the topic of sweaters and going back to basketball.

So Kerry had made her choice. To keep peace in the Tilford family rather than tell Pres the ugly truth: The purchase of that sweater was not a gift for Pres. It was a slap for Kerry.

She felt curiously peaceful.

She had done the right thing. It wasn't fun. It wouldn't become fun. Especially tonight when she would look at the all-but-done-sweater in her bedroom. But she felt good about herself for doing it.

Ardith Engborg had been sitting with Mrs. Evans for twenty-five minutes, but it felt like two lifetimes. It was a miracle that Olivia had grown up sane. With a mother like this, a father who never spoke up, and all those earlier health problems, how had Olivia become such a fine girl?

Ardith said, "Mrs. Evans, if I thought for one minute that Olivia was endangering her life, I would not allow the cheers to be choreographed like that. I agree that these cheers are dangerous in comparison to ordinary sideline cheers, but they are not life-threatening."

"I am taking Olivia off the squad unless these dangerous stunts are eliminated," Mrs. Evans said implacably.

Ardith could argue no more. She had repeated herself enough. Mrs. Evans had the right and Ardith could not stop her. So on the final two games, the most important two games, there would be not six but five Varsity members. Nothing could be done but the most ordinary of cheers, because every single good routine required the perfect placement of each of the six, and each worked in precision with the others — depending on them, needing them.

All they'll be able to do is stand there and yell go, team, go, and wave a pompon or two, Ardith thought miserably.

Of course, there was a way out. She could agree to Mrs. Evans' terms. The kids would have to skip the spectacular routines Olivia and Mary Ellen had designed.

Which meant Garrison would outshine them totally.

Here they had raised the spirit of the entire school with carefully circulated rumors about how fantastic their cheers were going to be . . . and they would be depressingly, appallingly ordinary.

Ardith hated to lose as much as any high school kid.

Most of all, she did not want to be known as the coach of a *formerly* good squad.

They'll be destroyed, Ardith thought. They can't survive any more scorn. This, on top of Nancy's defection! How will my kids deal with it?

"All right," she told Mrs. Evans. "But you must come to the practice after school and tell the squad yourself."

If Ardith hoped this would deter Mrs. Evans, she was mistaken. Mrs. Evans relished the opportunity of telling those silly cheerleaders her daughter was associating with just what she thought of their so-called sport.

That afternoon, six kids gathered.

Pres was in a better mood than usual. It was rare for him to be on good terms with his parents and it made him lighthearted. He had no idea his emotions were a gift from Kerry.

Mary Ellen, having stayed in the hall until the last second — embracing Donny, stroking his lovely hair, posturing next to his large fine body — was soaring with pleasure. Angie was her usual sweet, distracted self. Walt was quiet, but seemingly happy, though one never knew anything about Walt's feelings. Nancy was hesitant, unsure — as well she might be, Ardith thought grimly. She did not know who she was angrier at right now — Mrs. Evans or Nancy.

And then there was Olivia.

Frozen in space. Fury and apprehension destroying the pretty features. Olivia knew better than anybody what her mother was capable of, and one look at the smug expresion on her mother's face had told her the bad news.

Ardith wished she'd taken two aspirin. But then, she thought, I wouldn't feel good now even if I could be comatose through this whole weekend.

The six began their warm-ups. Each had a favorite series and each worked quietly without fanfare. Limbering up. Relaxing their muscles. Getting ready for the long afternoon. Not too long — they didn't want to exhaust themselves before the game.

Little did they know there was no worry about exhaustion. Once they obeyed Mrs. Evans, they would have precious few things to do anyhow.

Ardith could have wept.

Her beautiful, hard-working, kids!

Ardith blew her whistle. The six stopped their exercising and walked over to her. At the same moment, the gym doors opened. Donny Parrish walked in, crossing this gym on his way to the lockers for the final practice his basketball team would have. He was closely followed by Troy and by a group of girls including Kerry, who climbed quietly up the bleachers to watch. Donny waved at Mary Ellen, who beamed at him. Nobody paid attention to Nancy. Nancy stared at her sneakers.

Perhaps an audience would slow Mrs. Evans down.

But Mrs. Evans looked delighted. More people to listen to her low opinion of cheerleading.

"Mrs. Evans has something she would like to say to the squad," Ardith said. She stepped back, removing herself from whatever Mrs. Evans chose to announce.

Five kids sat Indian-style on the floor, patiently waiting. They looked like kids expecting a party to be announced, or special prizes, or perhaps monetary awards.

Olivia did not sit. She stood among the others, her small wiry body as tight as a fist. When she spoke, her words came out brittle and hard. She almost whispered, and it was like a hiss of rage.

"I won't have it!"

Nobody beyond the squad could have heard a

sound. But the squad could hear, and was shocked by the rage in Olivia's voice. None of them, not even Pres, would have addressed a parent like that.

"You've tried to run my life since I was a child," Olivia hissed at her mother. "Well, you can't any longer. This is *my* life. If I want to risk breaking an ankle, it's my choice. All sports have a degree of danger. Soccer, football, gymnastics, and cheerleading. Everything good contains risk. And you're not ruining this for us, Mother. *You are not!*"

Mrs. Evans stared at her daughter, then she turned and left the gym. The squad watched her go. Olivia shrugged. "Don't think that means she's given up. She'll be back."

CHAPTER

P res Tilford had had stage fright before, but
nothing compared to this! His nerves rippled as
if they were flexing their muscles. He ran through
in his mind the routine he and Olivia were about
to execute. He had to have just the right force
behind the lift. Just the same stance as at practice. (Practice! Wow, that Evans woman was
something. And he thought *he* had family problems. You had to admire Olivia settling things
like that. Still, Pres didn't like the thought of
Mrs. Evans seated directly behind Mary Ellen.
What sort of depressing, frightening things might
she be muttering in Mary Ellen's ear?)

If we don't do that first routine soon, I'm going
to flip out, Pres thought. He tried to glare at

Mary Ellen, but cheerleaders don't glare, and standing in a row the way they were, leading an ordinary sideline cheer that kept Angie happy but irritated everybody else, it was impossible to catch Melon's eye.

The game was hardly worth glancing at. It was only Grove Hill. Grove Hill was a soccer town. That Tarenton would cream them in basketball was undisputed. But people had not particularly come for the basketball tonight. They had come to see the honor of Varsity cheerleading restored. The whole school knew about the new routines. Every kid who'd watched even a minute of practice had reported with awe what Olivia and Mary Ellen had worked up.

"Time-out!" The ref's whistle was immediately followed by the piercing electronic bullhorn, and the teams quit playing and ran to the bench.

Pres tensed, ready to run out.

Mary Ellen did nothing.

Nothing.

Grove Hill cheerleaders danced out, taking the empty floor, and proceeded to spend a long, fruitful time-out with *their* best cheer!

The fans on the Tarenton side looked resentfully at their squad.

Walt muttered to Pres, "What's going on here? Did Mrs. Evans pay off Mary Ellen?"

"I think adoration of Donny fried her brains," Pres said.

Olivia's mother looked happy. She was the

only one. Nobody could imagine what was going on. A second time-out came (basketball was sometimes an infuriating game for cheerleaders — you never knew when, or if, you could get on the court, and you had to take advantage of openings quickly) and *again* Mary Ellen let Grove Hill seize the opportunity.

"Listen to me," Olivia hissed. "We practiced a jillion hours in order to make a display out here, Mary Ellen. What is your problem? Why aren't you doing anything? What kind of captain are you, anyway?"

Ardith Engborg did not interfere. She sensed in Mary Ellen a fine control that the squad did not see. Mary Ellen had something up her sleeve, though what it could be, Ardith had no idea.

Mary Ellen simply ignored her squad. The action began again, and again they began their rather ordinary, familiar sideline cheers.

A *third* opportunity — and a *third* time Mary Ellen did nothing.

Even Angie was upset now, and it took a lot to get her angry. "Their captain even waited for you, Mary Ellen," she protested. "She knew it was our turn. She only went out when it was perfectly clear that you weren't going to make a move."

"This is not a game tonight," Mary Ellen said. "This is war. And this is my strategy."

"Some strategy," Olivia snorted. "We never do it at all. I love it, Mary Ellen. It's really exciting."

Mary Ellen tossed her lovely blonde hair. Before the game she had sprayed sparkle into the curls. It seemed that her whole personality glittered like her hair. She was unsurpassably lovely.

She caught even Donny's eye, as he waited for a Grove Hill player to attempt a foul shot.

Mary Ellen thought, How wonderful — his eyes are on me.

The crowd thought, How awful. He's putting romance ahead of the game he has to win. What if he does this tomorrow night against Ben Adamson and Garrison?

And Patrick, seeing Donny look at Mary Ellen, felt his heart turn over.

Mary Ellen said quietly, "We let Grove Hill go out there three times. Three times they do acceptable, ordinary routines. Then we go out. And we knock 'em dead. This gym is going to give us a standing ovation. You wait and see."

Nancy Goldstein had never heard of a standing ovation for cheerleaders. Or one at any kind of ball game. It seemed to her standing ovations were confined to musical concerts, or maybe Presidential candidates. But not cheerleaders at Grove Hill basketball games. However, Mary Ellen's strategy did sound reasonable.

Nancy wondered how Ben was doing in his game. She wondered what she was going to do tonight. Tomorrow night. And all the nights that stretched out there, filled with painful decisions.

* * *

In the bleachers, Kerry Elliot sat with two girl friends. During the third time-out when Grove Hill cheerleaders were once more boring everybody, and Mary Ellen once more enraging everybody, Kerry climbed over laps, legs, overcoats, and toddlers, down four rows and across twenty bodies, to where Mr. and Mrs. Tilford were sitting.

It was rare for Pres's parents to come to games. And this was a game against a weak team. Kerry did not know what had brought on this loyalty. Had Scotland wrought a change of heart in Mrs. Tilford? Had Pres begged them to come see him in the new routines?

Kerry sat down next to Mrs. Tilford and said gaily, "Hi, there! Isn't the game exciting?"

It was not exciting. Grove Hill was being beaten so solidly it was almost embarrassing.

"I'm no judge of basketball," Mrs. Tilford said, hardly glancing at Kerry.

"If this is typical opposition," Mr. Tilford said, looking with boredom at his watch, and then the scoreboard clock, "no wonder Tarenton is the reigning champion. How come our cheerleaders haven't done much of anything?"

"They're saving themselves," Kerry said.

"For what?" Mr. Tilford said irritably.

"Wait till you see Pres," Kerry said. "He's fantastic."

Mrs. Tilford looked uncomfortable.

Kerry could not hold back any longer. She had to find out. She said, "That was an absolutely lovely sweater you brought Pres, Mrs. Tilford." She looked right into Mrs. Tilford's eyes and smiled her sweetest smile.

Felicia Tilford flushed hotly.

I was right, Kerry thought. She did do it on purpose.

A scream rose up from the court. Grove Hill stole the ball, and proceeded to make one basket after another, until they were a mere two points behind. Tarenton, shocked out of its complacency, was going to have to fight after all! The game picked up in intensity. Fans began screaming. The Pompon Squad waved scarlet-and-white clouds of fluff and Varsity led the crowd in several throat-ruining cheers.

Kerry said, "We're all looking forward to the party tonight."

Mrs. Tilford shuddered. "I just hope there isn't any damage. I thought this party was just for the squad, but Pres informs me all those basketball players and their girl friends and all these other kids will be there. They look like a rowdy bunch to me."

"Don't worry about them," Kerry said. "I'll make sure nobody does a thing. All they want to do is stand around and eat and tell each other how brilliantly they all did, anyhow."

Mrs. Tilford made no comment.

Kerry had to decide if she really wanted to

win Pres's parents over, or if she wanted to join Mrs. Tilford in some sort of backstage play of being rude to each other. Mrs. Tilford isn't very grown-up, Kerry thought.

She went back to her girl friends.

Halftime.

The score was Tarenton, thirty-three; Grove Hill, thirty-one.

The basketball teams trotted off to their locker rooms.

Fans began to think in terms of Coke and Pepsi, popcorn and hot dogs.

Ardith Engborg put a loud, rhythmic rock tape on the loudspeaker system.

Mary Ellen led the Varsity Squad out for the halftime display.

People were getting up to go outdoors and have a cigarette. Little children were begging for money to buy snacks. Friends were shouting across rows of people to greet each other. Mittens and scarves were falling under the bleachers and nine-year-old boys were scrambling underneath to rescue them.

People watched with half an eye as the squad lined up. Halftime was background. Like piped-in music in an elevator. Action to gossip by, or sip a cold drink by. It was filler before the game began again.

And then the new routine started.

Vibrant, demanding splashes of scarlet and white.

Strong leg movements, sharp geometric arm movements.

The fine smiles on six handsome faces.

The swirl of pompons, the grace of flared skirts, the strength of the boys' lifts.

The crowd quieted. The flow to the exits ceased.

Mary Ellen had the crowd in the palm of her hand. Her timing was perfect. Just when they had hundreds of eyes upon them, they would move into the spectacular part of Olivia's design. The music throbbed. The beat intensified. This routine had no words, no actual cheering — it was a *display*.

And display they did.

Olivia leaped in front of the squad, and swerved dramatically in a series of eye-catching movements. The other five slipped gracefully to new positions. Olivia ran to the far end of the gym, her small, light body the picture of feminine strength and beauty.

Pres's throat tightened. He bent slightly and cupped his hands. He forgot Kerry, his parents, the crowd. He thought of nothing but the motion to come, which had to be exactly right.

Olivia straightened, holding herself dramatically. Hundreds of people frowned slightly, not sure what to expect, but sure that it was something special. They knew by the way this little girl stood, by her confidence and excited features. Olivia ran. With breathtaking speed she launched herself at Pres, landing with one slender foot in his cupped hands, her fingertips grazing his shoulder for support as she rose. He thrust her into the air. She spun like a nymph over the heads of the other cheerleaders, landing effortlessly yards beyond them. The crowd gasped. Before they could think of clapping, the squad reversed positions and repeated the maneuver from the opposite side.

Then Mary Ellen and Olivia both burst out from the squad, like matching bombshells — except that one was small and wiry, the other golden and sparkling. They exploded in a series of cartwheels and flips that brought the crowd to its feet. Just as Mary Ellen and Olivia landed in front of the others, Pres and Walt lifted Nancy to their shoulders. Nancy flung out a pair of huge fluffy pompons and laughed at the skylights. Angie leaped with arched back and neatly curved legs to land in front of them all, the most angelic smile in Tarenton decorating the squad like a star in the sky.

For one moment the Varsity Squad remained there: frozen in time. And then the crowd began to clap — wild, thunderous clapping and foot stomping and cheering. Whistles came from the boys in the back who could pierce eardrums with their pursed lips.

"Tarenton! Tarenton! Tarenton!" they screamed over and over.

Mary Ellen broke formation first, and the others followed her lead. They had never practiced such a thing, but when Mary Ellen made a sudden sweeping bow, the others did, too, and the applause rose to even greater heights. Hands resting lightly on their waists, the squad ran lightly off the floor, as if they had never exercised at all. They reached their bench at the exact moment that the teams emerged from their locker rooms for the warm-ups.

Patrick and Kerry felt the same emotions as they looked at Mary Ellen and Pres: pride and excitement and overwhelming love. Vanessa Barlow narrowed her eyes as she stared at the squad, and felt that she had never hated six people so much in all her life . . . and Vanessa knew what hatred was.

Mrs. Evans let out a long breath. She felt as if she had not breathed in hours. She had been suspended in the space of her anxiety.

But Olivia is wonderful! she thought, astonished. I knew she was wonderful, of course. She's my daughter. But I didn't know she was *that* wonderful.

Nancy Goldstein was so tired she could hardly sit up straight. And so proud she could burst. *We did it!* We showed them. Mary Ellen said we would and she was right!

"Olivia, you were so perfect," Mary Ellen whispered, hugging Olivia fiercely.

Olivia was not good at accepting praise. "There's no such thing as *so* perfect," she scolded. "Either you're perfect or you're not."

"You are," Pres said, and he kissed her forehead. Now that they had done the routine in public once, his fears were gone. Tomorrow night against Garrison he'd be tense, but not terrified.

Mary Ellen really was an excellent captain. Pres hadn't realized it until now. She was calm, calculating, like a general at war. And she'd won.

He looked past the squad, searching the bleachers for Kerry. He spotted her at last, directly behind him, up six rows. She was smiling that cherished smile that made him feel so good. Kerry saluted him to tell him how well he'd done.

He could hardly wait for the party. He waved to her once more and turned his attention to the upcoming second half. He did not look for his parents. It had not occurred to him that they would have come.

Angie hugged Mary Ellen, hugged Olivia, hugged Nancy and Walt and Pres. Nancy hugged everybody right back. *Never* had she felt so important, so much a part of a truly fine piece of work.

From behind them the Tarenton fans called out praise. For this moment, the crowd was not composed of basketball fans — but of cheerleading fans. Nancy thought she would burst with pride.

And then she thought of Ben.

And anxiety gripped her as fiercely as the joy of a moment before. She was part of a wonderful group, and they gave her a lot, as she gave to them. What did Ben have to equal that?

CHAPTER

Rarely had Tarenton High emptied so fast. Exhilarated by their victory and the sight of their wonderful cheerleaders, Tarenton kids abandoned the building for their various celebrations. There was the Burger House crowd, the Pizza Parlor crowd, the going-home-and-lonely crowd, and there was the partying-at-Pres-Tilford's crowd.

Nancy was not a member of any.

The thrill of success vanished in quivers of nervousness. The joy of the teenagers around her — the pummeling and shouting and congratulating — seemed to have nothing to do with her. *What am I doing?* she thought. *Why am I standing here alone?*

I'm doing this for Ben.

Sometimes the face you most want to picture is the most elusive. Nancy tried to summon up an image of Ben, to comfort herself that she was doing what was important to her. But she could not seem to remember Ben. She had a vague sense of his bulk, and that was all. She could not feel his personality, recall his looks.

Nancy could not make herself go out on the front steps of the school and find her parents, who were driving her over to the Burger House to meet Ben. It seemed an irrevocable step, which would lead to terrifying things, painful things, lonely things.

She pretended to herself that she had forgotten something in the girls' locker room, and walked swiftly back, trying to look purposeful. Several faces studied her, and she thought the looks were ones of scorn and dislike: that they knew all about her, traitor that she was, and a sick taste rose in her throat.

Mary Ellen was brushing her hair. Tiny sparklets of gold and silver shivered momentarily in the air as the stiff bristles pulled through her thick, lovely blonde hair. Mary Ellen stood in her pale blue bra and pants in front of the full-length mirror and admired herself. She kept tossing her head lightly, so that the shining hair trembled on her shoulders and slipped across her soft skin. She thought of Donny, and how brilliant he had been tonight, and would be in the future, and she thought of herself at his side. And then she thought of Patrick. She tried not to compare Donny to him, knowing which one would sweep through her heart. Mary Ellen, she thought, why are you so superficial?

She slipped into a pair of deep green, almost black, cords and belted them with a leather sash. Then three layers of shirting, deftly tugging the collar and cuffs of each layer, running her fingers under her hair and flicking it up and out. It fell back on her shoulders, glistening.

And now the party. Pres's house. The mansion on the lake, with all its wonderful large, dark rooms and their deep, imperious colors. What a house for romance! She saw herself falling onto one of the plush velvet sofas under the ancestral portraits with their intricate gold frames, lying there with Donny.

And then, in the mirror, she saw Nancy Goldstein.

Mary Ellen's lips tightened with annoyance.

Nancy was making a big mistake. Pretty soon Nancy would destroy her Tarenton existence and what would she have to show for it? Not much: a hulking basketball star who would graduate and go on to other things that wouldn't include Nancy.

Well, if she acted like that, Nancy didn't deserve anything good anyhow. True, Nancy had worked wonderfully tonight, as hard as the rest. Varsity had been six people as one, and Mary Ellen was proud of her squad. But that did not cancel the fact that Nancy was going to go out with Ben Adamson.

Nancy was silent, and Mary Ellen did not speak to her. Two girls who worked intimately every single day, for the same cause, and neither acknowledged the other's presence.

Mary Ellen's faith in her own beauty was marred. Nancy was so lovely in such a different way: dark, mysterious, curvaceous. Right now clad in a dark crimson sweater the color of Pres's formal parlor.

I hate her, Mary Ellen thought. She left the locker room without talking to Nancy, and so did everybody else there. Only Angie whispered, in a flute-like voice, "Bye, Nance."

Nancy's chin quivered.

Good, Mary Ellen thought. I hope she cries, and her mascara runs and her eyes get red and her cheeks get all blotchy. Traitor.

"We'll miss you at Pres's," Angie said gently.

We will not, Mary Ellen thought.

Donny had showered and changed faster than Mary Ellen, which came as no surprise. Almost anybody on earth could shower and change faster than Mary Ellen Kirkwood. Of course, most people didn't have as much fun looking in the mirror, either. Furthermore, Mary Ellen loved to make people wait for her. It made her feel powerful. And it was so much more fun to walk into waiting arms, rather than leaning on a wall waiting for the body to emerge.

They were the focus of all eyes. There was nothing — *nothing* — that Mary Ellen loved more than to be watched when she looked her very best. Against her will, she found herself looking surreptitiously beyond Donny to see if Patrick was also watching.

And there he was, true to form, standing in the back of the press of kids. Their eyes met. Patrick was calm, a small, knowing smile on his face. Mary Ellen swept her lashes in her sexiest way. Donny thought the message was for him. Carefully Mary Ellen did not look Patrick's way again, but that one moment when their eyes had locked had rocked her. She left the school with Donny, casually offering Angie a ride to Pres's with them.

Angie accepted with a sigh.

Pain at seeing the affection between Donny and Mary Ellen chewed at Angie. She had a much deeper affection for Marc than Mary Ellen had ever had for *any* boy, but Marc was not there. She was beginning to wonder if he would ever be there again. College was much harder for him this semester and Marc was broke and having to work extra hours, with the result that Angie rarely saw him. At times her life was painfully lonely, which was absurd, because Angie was more in love than any of them. All very well to have a wonderful boyfriend, but an absentee boyfriend could be an equal agony to not having one at all.

But it was not in Angie to complain.

Cheerfully she greeted Donny, congratulating

him, careful to remember each of his spectacular baskets and steals. She got in the backseat alone, grateful that the ride to Pres's house was short.

Nancy Goldstein was left alone in the locker room.

She straightened her collar several times and questioned the wisdom of wearing that particular necklace. But there was no jewelry box here in the locker room. She was stuck with what she'd chosen. Was she too dressy? Such vivid colors! Nancy looked her best in bright things, but now she felt as conspicuous as fireworks on a black night.

She left the locker room shaking, but there was no need. Her friends and fellow students had left several moments before, and the hallways were almost deserted. She did not have to face the questioning looks of a single person. Her parents were waiting by the door and it was just a question of walking in the dark to their car.

Kerry could not imagine what was taking Pres so long. As usual, the two boy cheerleaders used the same locker room as the basketball team. (They could hardly go into the girls' locker room with Nancy, Angie, Olivia, and Mary Ellen, although they generally asked to do so!) But Pres was the swiftest of dressers. Much to his mother's disgust, Pres took few pains with his appearance. He was sufficiently good-looking to get away with this, tugging on old jeans, half buttoning an old

312

shirt (skipping the buttons that didn't show), and pulling on a sweater that more than likely had torn elbows. Then he'd run a comb through his dark-blond hair and call it quits. Sixty seconds max.

Sighing, Kerry walked in a circuit of the front halls, wondering where Pres could be. Most of the team had already left for his house, and Mr. and Mrs. Tilford had left literally before the game was over. They'd taken a position at the door and when it was clear that Tarenton really would win, had walked out, missing the final cheers and screaming. They were obviously nervous over this party. Probably had visions of drunken kids hanging from the chandeliers. There were a few who would do that, given the chance but since everybody wanted Pres to give another party, they were going to be careful at this one. Very careful. Even Pres would be careful.

Kerry was not exactly annoyed that Pres hadn't come out. It took a lot to annoy Kerry. She did wish, however, that he would hurry up. He was probably telling silly locker room jokes to the other boys. He'd want to wrap that up before he joined her. He was meticulously careful to speak and behave in a gentlemanly fashion around Kerry. If Mrs. Tilford had liked Kerry, Kerry would have shared the joke with her. Kerry told plenty of locker room jokes with the girls, but she was equally carefully to maintain a pristine, pure front for Pres! It was funny, really.

313

When Pres still hadn't come out five minutes later, Kerry was so restless she hiked down another corridor. This is just what Nancy Goldstein did, Kerry thought, giggling to herself. And look what happened to her! A sex god caught up to her.

Well, Kerry already had a sex god in her life, and he'd better catch up to her or he was going to be a sex god in big trouble.

Unlike Nancy, Kerry was afraid of pitch dark, so she didn't take the final corner, but turned at the EXIT sign to go back to the front foyer. And there was Pres, flying toward her, running as fast as he could in his eagerness to join her. She was faintly surprised he could even see her — it was so dim and her clothing so dark — but perhaps he'd seen her in the distance walking this way and just knew she was down the hall somewhere.

Pres leaped, ran right up the side of the wall, grunting slightly. His shoes made slick, hard, rubery sounds and left black patches on the wall that she could see even in the dark like ghosts in reverse against the white paint.

"Pres Tilford!" Kerry screamed, absolutely infuriated. "How *could* you! You stupid, dumb idiot. I can't believe it!"

She ran toward him, intending to grab him by the shoulders and shake him until his teeth rattled — no matter that he was six inches taller and heaven knew how many pounds heavier than she. At a time like this! To jeopardize everything

— from the Varsity Squad, to the party, to the victory tomorrow, to his entire school career! Just to show off for her!

It took a lot to annoy Kerry Elliot, and this was a lot.

Shrieking her rage, she rushed up to him. Shadows filled the hall. The face before her was a pale blot in the dark. She had the weirdest sensation of being *afraid* of Pres. Her fingers brushed his sleeve, and the fabric was slicker than anything Pres would wear. "Pres?" she said hesitantly. The arms she had touched came up in her face violently, shoving her, and Kerry cried out in pain and fear, staggering backward and hitting her head against the stone-hard tile walls of the corridor.

"Wonderful game, dear," Mr. Goldstein said. Nancy didn't feel like talking about it.

"Brilliant cheering," her mother said.

Nancy didn't say anything to that either. Her breath was coming shorter and shorter. What if Ben didn't come? What if she had to sit alone in Burger House for hours waiting? What if his game lasted much longer than theirs had? What if he didn't feel like making the drive to Tarenton after all? What if he wasn't very trustworthy to begin with and hadn't really planned on coming anyway?

"Weren't you proud of yourselves?" her mother asked anxiously.

"Oh, yes," Nancy said mechanically.

Her parents exchanged worried looks.

They arrived at the Burger House. Nancy's heart sank even more. A swarm of Tarenton kids — not her crowd, really, but classmates — was pouring into the place, greeting even more Tarenton kids.

I can't handle it, she thought.

It was like the first day of school after she moved here. Sheer, raw panic. *Mommy-take-me-home* type panic.

Nancy peered into the parking lot. The moment she saw Ben, she remembered why she was sacrificing. He was so attractive! He parked, and got slowly out of his car, unfolding his length, and when he had shut the door behind him, he stretched his body, yawned slightly, and looked up at the stars.

Nancy grinned to herself. "Bye, Mom . . . Dad," she said easily, happily. "See you later." She jumped out of her parents' car to go to him. Ben had already seen her. He did not move to greet her but waited, like some carved statue, for her to come to him. The instant she got there he took her arm and escorted her toward the restaurant door.

Panic swept over Nancy again. "I thought we were going to Garrison for a party there."

"We are. I'm thirsty, though. Got to get a Coke before we start driving. You want something?"

I want not to go in there, Nancy thought. She

slowed down, so that Ben was practically dragging her, but he sensed nothing, or else her weight was so minor that there was nothing to sense.

Into the Burger House they walked. Among basketball fans. Groups celebrating the Tarenton win. Kids who hated Garrison. Whose talk was of nothing but tomorrow's smashing of Ben Adamson.

With a soft, muffled thump, the door closed behind them. It was not soft enough that nobody noticed their entry. Ben was too large to go unnoticed, no matter how softly he moved. Nancy, clad in scarlet, decorated him like a shining ball on a Christmas tree.

He loves this, she thought, looking up at him. He can feel the anger we're arousing, and he loves it. She was terribly aware that she was being led in, on his arm, not just walking in with him. Nobody hissed at her.

But they wanted to.

Never had service seemed so slow, or the filling of a paper cup so time-consuming. Nancy thought perhaps an hour had gone by as they stood there. Ben counted out his change with maddening slowness. She refused his offer of a drink for the third time. When he finally turned to leave, he surveyed the restaurant from his extra height in a lordly way, refusing to be hurried or worried.

I would never go into enemy territory, she thought. But he loves doing it. That's what this is all about. I'm his ticket into the fray.

It was a relief to be back in his car! The door slammed behind her, the lock pushed down, the seat belt securing her. It was like a medieval castle — impregnable, entirely safe from the raging eyes of the peasants who hated the lord.

Ben talked about his basketball game. They had won, of course. From Ben's voice this was never in any doubt. He felt totally ready for tomorrow night, he told her. He was in perfect shape, had the perfect attitude. There was no doubt whatsoever about the outcome of the fight against her Tarenton.

She pulled her jacket a little tighter.

It occurred to her that in fact she *was* about to do what Ben had just done. She *was* going into enemy territory. On Ben's arm. Like a piece of Ben's property.

She screamed.

The sound of her own scream was more horrifying to Kerry than the blow on her face. It was a dreadful noise, scraping her nerve, rasping out of her throat like some evil late-night movie.

Her head hurt. It had all happened too fast to be sure of anything. She could not really even tell whether she *was* hurt, or just terrified. The hall echoed with her scream and her head ached in response.

There was a commotion at the other end of the hall: people scrambling, yelling, demanding to know where the light switches were. A second scream stayed in Kerry's throat, choking her.

The vandal, she realized. Not Pres, but the vandal.

She had to notice him. She had to make some intelligent observations so they could catch him, not let Pres be blamed. But she knew nothing. She had seen nothing. A blurred whiteness at the right height for a face. Slippery fabric.

Her face was wet and she realized that she was crying.

The vandal's feet were slamming into the floor as he raced to the dark back of the building. He can't get out, she reassured herself. It's locked.

And then she remembered that the whole purpose of EMERGENCY EXITs was to be able to get out in an emergency. The kid would vanish into the night and nobody would know anything more about him except that it was not a good idea to interrupt him at work.

"Where are the lights?" came a yell.

"It's Kerry!" screamed somebody else.

"She got mugged or something!"

"There he goes! Somebody catch him!"

And then Pres's arms were around her. They closed in comfort, and almost immediately opened with his need to run after her attacker. She could feel his mixed rage and love in that single clasp. "I'm not really hurt," she said, without knowing if this was true or not. "I'm just scared."

The lights came on.

Pres looked her over like a father would his

newborn child. Was she all there? Was she well formed? His hands ran over her face, and then over the back of her head, and light as his touch was, she winced. She had really slammed into that tile wall.

"We got him!" came the chorus of voices from the end of the hall.

The adults arrived by then: the principal, the vice-principal, a few parents, one of the assistant coaches, and the two cops who were always assigned to high school games.

The only other girl still there was Susan Yardley, one of Nancy Goldstein's friends. Even in the horror of the moment, Kerry had time to feel sorry for Nancy, because Susan had all but ended the friendship when she saw Nancy with Ben. Susan's family was Old Tarenton, and people who consorted with Garrison stars might as well be dead.

"But who is he?" Susan said blankly, staring at the culprit the boys were dragging back down the hall.

"Some sophomore," her boyfriend said grimly. "Dill is his last name."

"Jimmy Dill," Pres said, astonished. "He's in my gym class."

They stared at Jimmy Dill.

He was pitiful. Tall, but scrawny. Not good-looking at all — not a hope of ever being good-looking, either. Acne and an ugly nose and fat lips. Now that they had him pinned by the arms, the boys had no idea what to do with him. They felt uncomfortable, as if they were the ones doing something wrong. Jimmy Dill seemed like such an unlikely person to be the source of trouble.

The principal turned to Kerry. "Are you hurt?" she said.

Kerry saw instantly that Jimmy Dill would be in a lot more trouble if she were. He had meant only to ruin the walls — he had not known some girl would attack him in the dark, grabbing his arm. She would have a swelling on the back of her head, but that was it. She said, "No. Just scared. I didn't need to scream."

They accepted this. Kerry thought, *Am I wrong? Is Jimmy Dill a vicious person and I'm going to be partially responsible because I let him go?*

"Let's go," mumbled the other kids. "Come on, Pres. Let's go to your party."

Jimmy Dill seemed so frightened. So pitiable. They could not bear to look at him.

The kids left. The adults could handle Jimmy Dill. They wanted only to walk away and pretend they had nothing to do with the whole thing. How grateful they were to be kids who felt they had something to offer — anything at all — more than Jimmy did, who felt he was nothing. As a group, they shuddered.

How strange it was to come out into a parking lot filled with kids who had not yet left for Pres's house: leaning on their cars, dancing, clowning, yelling, singing and clapping. High spirits filled the entire school grounds. What a contrast to the disaster inside.

"All right, Pres!" they shouted like a cheer, although Pres was the only cheerleader there. "Let's *go!*"

Everybody loves a party, and even more if it's at somebody else's house, and the somebody else is rich and will have terrific food and unlimited space and every single record or cassette anybody ever wanted to dance to.

Some citizens of Tarenton might have thought they felt an earthquake tremor. Mild shocks seemed to travel across the asphalt.

But it was just the basketball team headed toward Fable Point and the Tilford mansion.

Jimmy Dill was forgotten.

CHAPTER

12

Nancy Goldstein was sick with dismay. She could taste it, and she quivered with it as if she had fever from the flu.

She had no idea who might be the host or hostess at this party. Ben had led her into an unknown house in an unknown neighborhood, where he was welcomed with screams of delight, much pounding on the back from the boys, and lots of giggling kisses from pretty girls.

"And who's this?" they all exclaimed. From the way they frowned at her, Nancy knew they half recognized her, but couldn't place her.

"This is Nancy," Ben said simply, giving no details. His arm remained around her so that she was protected from the onslaught of Garrison kids.

"Oh, my *God*!" screamed a Garrison girl, and then burst into half-crazed laughter. "She's a rah-rah from Tarenton. I know her. Look at this, everybody. Benny's brought a rah-rah from Tarenton!"

They gathered around as if Ben had brought a trained chimpanzee.

"I give you credit, Ben," one of his fellow basketball players said. "You not only steal every ball they try to play — you steal their little rah-rah as well."

"She's kind of cute," another boy said, as if Nancy weren't standing within two inches of him.

"Do a cheer for us," said a snickering voice from a girl wearing a fan cap in Garrison colors. "Come on. Do that silly little 'All the Way' cheer for little old Tarenton."

"And does she, Ben?" said the basketball player, digging him in the ribs.

"Does she what?" Ben said innocently.

"Go all the way."

They laughed uproariously. Ben hugged Nancy to his side with such intimacy that anybody would have figured they'd been sleeping together for months. I won't cry, Nancy thought. I won't cry.

Ben led her across that room and several more until they came to a huge buffet. It was a very adult setup: casseroles and fancy finger foods. Nothing like the plain old chips and dip that

Nancy was used to. Gradually she realized, from the number of adults present, that this was a fund raiser. These were alumni, coaches, athletic boosters, parents, and teams.

And I'm part of it! she thought. I'm providing some of the entertainment!

Nancy could not see a single nice person in the crowd. She knew this was ridiculous. Garrison had to have as many nice people per capita as Tarenton. But the room was jammed with staring kids who thought it was the biggest joke in the world that Ben Adamson had snared a Tarenton rah-rah.

And how snide they were about cheerleading.

It was clear that in Garrison, if you were a cheerleader, you were a stupid, sex-crazed airhead. Good for nothing, except maybe going all the way on a Saturday night.

She prayed for support from Ben, but he gave none. For one thing, he was literally unreachable. He was too tall. She had to crook her neck to look into his face, and without fail his eyes were crisscrossing the room, checking out the composition of the party, catching eyes and accepting congratulations and adulation.

For another thing, she really did not know the boy at all. She had no idea how to confess to him that she felt rotten. That she was embarrassed, humiliated even.

He was unaware of her discomfort.

He felt no discomfort, and it apparently did not occur to him that her perspective would be different.

He would not protect her from these gawking, gossiping people. She was on her own. The faces around her blurred, as if she was underwater and they were leering down at her through murky liquid.

She yearned for Tarenton and her friends and her roots and her squad with an intensity that almost made her weep. Here she was on the arm of this splendid boy . . . and she was excruciatingly lonely.

Finally they left the brightly lit buffet and returned to one of the inner rooms, where it was darker, and there was some dancing. Nancy loved to dance. I'll unwind when we dance, she thought. I'll be okay. I won't disintegrate.

But he didn't dance. He took her to a couch in the corner. There was already a couple there wrapped in each other's arms, sprawled out and taking up most of the space. If she had known the kids — or known Ben, for that matter — Nancy would have made wisecracks. But tonight it made her supremely uncomfortable. Ben obviously expected her to cooperate in the same way. *All the way.* Next to a pair of Garrison strangers who were ninety percent there already.

Ben cupped her face in his hands and kissed her.

What do I do? she thought. I don't know Ben

at all. And I don't want to get to know him sexually before we've had a single real conversation!

It was a wonderful kiss.

Nancy burst into tears.

Ben jerked back as if they had burned him. He stared at her, totally thrown, with no idea what to do next. He was not the only one. Nancy Goldstein had no idea what to do next either.

She was at a crossroads. In Tarenton her best friends, her squad, were partying without her. In Garrison she sat in the arms of a tall, dark, mysterious stranger of whom every girl dreams. But how worthwhile was the dream? Parts of it appeared to be nightmare.

Nancy ached for Ben. Momentarily she considered following the example of the other couple. But she ached even more for life as she had known it only a few days before: safe, warm, welcoming, and friendly.

"Ben," she said huskily, "take me home."

"I've heard that line before," he said. "It doesn't worry me."

"I *mean* it, Ben. Please."

"Aw, come on, Nancy. This is fun."

If he weren't so exciting to her, it would be easy, she thought. If our teams weren't competing, it would be easy. If I didn't love Tarenton so much, it would be easy.

But it's not easy. Nothing about this is easy.

"Please take me home."

Ben ignored her.

New panic seized her. What if she *couldn't* get home? What if the decision had already been made for her, by someone who was stronger enough and heavier enough to choose whatever he wanted, *whenever* he wanted it?

"Ben, I made a mistake."

"Not yet. Mistakes are yet to come. You're doing fine." He brushed away the few tears and kissed her cheeks.

"Ben, I'm not kidding. This party is a mistake for me. I don't belong here. I shouldn't have come. Please take me home."

"You expect me to abandon a party in my honor? When you're my date?"

If only she had an ally with her! Some girl, some parent, some friend, who would help her! "Ben," Nancy said, "I know this is rude. You're a wonderful person and I wish things were different, but they're not. I shouldn't be at a Garrison party. It makes me feel sick. I want to go home and cheer for Tarenton. I like you very much. I want you, too. But tomorrow night I want Tarenton winning, not you, and I can't bear to be here another minute."

She had certainly put that strongly enough.

She could not look up at him.

But if the definition of a champion is being a good loser, then Ben Adamson truly was a champion. He did not want Nancy to cry. He did not want to be the reason for any tears, especially in public, on his turf, where he was being watched.

He took Nancy back to his car, amid scores of wisecracks that they all knew what would be going on in the backseat of *that* car, and without argument drove her the several miles to Tarenton.

They talked very little.

Nancy was drained. It seemed a miracle she could even sit there, let alone attempt to be witty and interesting.

As for Ben, it was his policy not to consider failures. He considered, instead, the game coming up, and the strategy he would use to destroy Donny Parrish, the only hope of Tarenton Varsity Basketball.

"Are you sorry you got mixed up with me?" Nancy asked.

Ben had already forgotten her. He was concentrating on driving, which he loved, and the game to come, which he intended to win. "No, I'm not sorry," he said. "You're a lovely girl. And you're making the right decision." No use having an enemy where he might someday want a friend. He smiled at her.

It seemed to please her. She relaxed.

Ben thought briefly of Wendy, the girl he had lined up as his next candidate. His thoughts returned more quickly to Donny. Donny had a tendency to get angry and make judgments without enough thought behind them. A regrettable tendency Ben intended to exploit.

"Turn left here," Nancy said.

Ben thought it must be another route to her

house and obeyed her. They ended up, however, at a road he'd never seen before.

Fable Point. Private, the signs said.

"Where's this?" Ben said, confused.

"The party I should have gone to in the first place. Listen, I'm sorry."

"No hard feelings." Ben leaned toward her.

She yearned to kiss him good-bye, but she knew if she kissed him once — felt that rough cheek, touched that rough hair — she would knuckle under. Tell him, Forget Tarenton. Drive into a deserted lane somewhere and we'll go all the way.

But she got out of the car instead, waved, and began walking, before Ben could swing the car around to go back to Garrison. She knew he had forgotten her already. She only hoped she could forget him as easily. Nobody in Tarenton could compare, except Donny, and that comparison was not in Donny's favor.

She went down the dark lane toward Pres's house.

Every light in the huge place was lit. Even in winter with storm doors and windows tightly caulked she could hear the party raging. Silhouettes of kids appeared in most of the windows. Cold though it was, there was a bunch of them on the lovely front porch that swept around the mansion in circles. The kids were laughing. When Nancy walked in out of the dark, one of the boys exclaimed, "Where did you come from?"

330

"Just passing through," she said, going inside.

The foyer was empty.

The huge, formal front parlor was empty.

She passed the pictures of Tilford ancestors and followed the gallery where a grandfather clock collection ticked mercilessly and an antique harpsichord collected dust.

In front of her was the huge addition Felicia Tilford had designed: the enormous family room with the great glass walls that faced Narrow Brook Lake.

The room was filled with her friends. With noise and laughter and music and the wonderful smell of good hot food.

Oh, please take me back! Nancy thought. *Let me be one of the crowd. Forget Ben. Please, please.*

Only one face looked up.

Mary Ellen.

Her captain, her fellow cheerleader, her friend.

Mary Ellen frowned and turned her back.

CHAPTER

 13

Donny Parrish had no sooner won the game against Grove Hill, than he began to get keyed up about the game against Garrison on Saturday.

He stood in the middle of Pres Tilford's magnificent family room (the Tilfords called it the Lake Room, because its huge glass walls had such a fine view of Narrow Brook Lake) and tried to pay attention to Mary Ellen.

I should go home and get ten hours of sleep, Donny thought. He knew perfectly well he was so wired up he wouldn't be able to fall asleep until dawn anyhow.

He felt he should eat red meat, drink a gallon of orange juice, and swallow a mess of spinach. He reached for a bowl of taco chips and another Pepsi.

There was slow music on the stereo and Mary Ellen wanted to dance. Donny could not possibly dance slowly. His muscles were a jangle. There was nothing slow, calm, or smooth in his entire body or mind. He said to her, "Next fast one, okay?"

She was so lovely! How lucky he was to have Mary Ellen Kirkwood. Donny knew he had her only because he was a basketball star. He was glad he was tall and well coordinated. Mary Ellen wouldn't be caught dead with a short klutz. Mary Ellen chattered away and Donny didn't listen. He could think only of Ben Adamson. Ben's added height was a tremendous asset to Garrison. There was no way for Donny to beat that. And Ben's personality wasn't exactly a liability, either. Donny couldn't make up his mind about Ben. Was all that strutting an act, or was it the real Ben?

"Now it's a fast one," Mary Ellen said, and she jumped up, pulling on his hand. Donny didn't resist. He rather liked fast dances. It took up energy. You would think after an exhausting game he'd be out of energy, but instead he had even more of it. Mary Ellen sang the lyrics under her breath. She didn't have a voice to speak of, but she memorized the lyrics to all the songs she loved and whispered along rhythmically.

They danced vibrantly, bodies swerving and turning, jabbing and thrusting across the floor space. What a house Pres had! Donny's family was well off, too. His parents owned a restaurant and worked long, exhausting hours. But even the restaurant had nothing to compare with the dance floor Pres could offer. It was amazing. Like another world.

As the pulsing rhythm took over his body, Donny relaxed. He could enjoy Mary Ellen again. How he loved that golden hair! And her wonderful smile. Directed at *him*. Mary Ellen was always up when she was with him. It was one reason Donny liked her so much. Oh, sure, there was the usual stuff about her looks, and how sexy she was. But Donny liked a team person. Someone to carry the ball and not complain if she got stepped on. Although Donny could not imagine anyone stepping on Mary Ellen.

A sharp, angry frown creased Mary Ellen's lovely face. She missed a beat in the music and then whirled, her back to Donny now, dancing with a violence in her movements. Donny immediately turned himself, to see if *he*'d been the cause of that anger or if there was something going on behind him.

There was Nancy Goldstein standing in the doorway.

For one blurred, raging moment, Donny thought Nancy had brought Ben. If she had trespassed like that . . . if she had done the unthinkable and brought Ben Adamson *here*. . . .

But when his eyes focused again, he saw that she was entirely alone. She stood in the shrinking posture of the new kid. Nobody spoke to her. Every cheerleader, whether on purpose or by chance, had his or her back to Nancy.

Only Vanessa said anything to Nancy. Her "Gone all the way so fast?" echoed throughout the room.

Mary Ellen took both of Donny's arms and swung him sideways, so that he could not easily see Nancy. The smile on Mary Ellen's face was very strained.

She mad at Nancy or at me? thought Donny nervously.

He had a sense that it would be all too easy to lose Mary Ellen. There were, after all, a lot of boys eager to go out with her. Patrick Henley, for one. It continued to mystify Donny that Mary Ellen didn't date Patrick. He was glad — but confused — especially since it was impossible not to feel the electricity between those two.

Nancy Goldstein stood at the far end of the huge room and nobody said hello. Nobody waved. Nobody said her name. The room seemed too large. Too big and open even to cross. She felt as if she had never known these people, as if they were the same strangers who had terrified her in Garrison.

They hate me, she thought. I hurt them. I was a symbol of loyalty and I dated the captain of the opposite team. I've lost them.

Now she had done it to herself again. She was

stranded at a *second* party she should never have gone to.

Kerry, who would have welcomed Nancy, never saw her. She was too wrapped up in Pres to think of other human beings. As for Pres, he glanced at Nancy, felt anger, and glanced away, because he did not want anything to spoil the evening. Olivia saw Nancy and thought, Why did I ever like her, anyhow? You can't count on Nancy. Olivia went into the kitchen so as to avoid seeing Nancy.

Felicia Tilford, protecting her upholstery, chandeliers, and Oriental rugs, saw her and was shocked. She still found it embarrassing that her son was a cheerleader, but she had to say one thing for his Varsity Squad — they were a tight-knit group. And now they were not only ignoring Nancy, they were making a *point* of not speaking to her.

Felicia Tilford had snubbed many people in her day and she would continue the practice. But in her own home? An invited guest, standing at her door like a waif even the Salvation Army wouldn't want?

"Pres, dear," his mother said, "I believe Nancy needs something cold to drink. Would you like ginger ale, dear, or Coke?" She went to greet Nancy, pressing her soft cheek lightly against the girl's, and escorted her into the room. Nancy seemed pitifully grateful for the attention.

There were moments when Mrs. Tilford wished

she, too, could be sixteen with the world ahead of her, but this was not one. Whatever agony Nancy was enduring, whatever vendetta the kids had against her, Mrs. Tilford didn't want to know about. As Pres brought the soft drink over to Nancy, his mother slipped out of the room.

Nancy took the glass. It was very cold and it slid in her fingers. She had to put both hands around it. Her hands hurt. I'm holding a glass, she thought, instead of Ben. I'm alone in a room full of my friends.

Pres walked back to Kerry.

Nancy was still alone. She was just closer to the people who were not going to welcome her.

Donny saw, and it stabbed at him.

Memory flooded. Years ago, he was a scrawny, unlovable third grader, going to a birthday party, coming in late, all the other little boys laughing at him. The birthday child saying scornfully, "We only invited you because Mom said we had to, anyhow."

Donny danced Mary Ellen backward toward Nancy. "Hi, Nance," he said. "How are ya?"

It was the best he could do. He kept dancing with Mary Ellen, kept smiling at Nancy.

Nancy burst into tears.

Donny Parrish was horrified. He would gladly have faced Ben Adamson in hand-to-hand combat rather than deal with Nancy Goldstein crying. Donny retreated from those tears faster than he had ever left anything in his life.

But Mary Ellen did not.

Breaking away from Donny's grasp, she went to Nancy. Sisterhood overcame envy and anger. "What happened?" she asked. "Tell me. *Don't cry.* Tarenton cheerleaders don't cry in front of a mob of people." Mary Ellen's voice was stern, but her arms around Nancy were soft and comforting.

Nancy cried harder.

The room divided into those kids who would rather have been dead than get involved, and those kids who would rather have been dead than miss any details.

If it had been Mary Ellen, she would have preferred death to exposure in front of her classmates. She took Nancy's arm more possessively than Ben had ever done, and marched her into the pantry. It was the Victorian part of the house: dark wood, long narrow slivers of cabinets enclosing stacks of rarely used china.

"It was awful," Nancy choked out. "I should never have gone with him. I made him take me home. It was awful."

Mary Ellen hugged her. Nancy thought, If Mary Ellen forgives me, then I guess everyone else will. Everyone who counts, anyhow.

Nancy had loved Ben Adamson. It was a love that lasted only days and consisted of only a few moments of contact, but it was no less real for that. Nancy's throat closed and she could not

338

swallow the soda Mary Ellen wanted her to drink.

Angie was there, handing her a Kleenex, and Olivia was there, looking softer than Olivia Evans could in normal circumstances.

"So it's over? You and Ben?" Mary Ellen said. Nancy nodded.

"Well, let's have a cheer for *that!*" said Mary Ellen, and they all giggled, including Nancy. How like Mary Ellen to go right to the heart of the matter. They'd hated this thing with Ben, and if it was over before it began, then let's all have a cheer.

"*Roadway, runway, railway*," Angie chanted very softly.

Nancy shook her head. "It didn't even get on the train, let alone go all the way, Angie. I guess we were both at the wrong station at the wrong time." Weeping overcame her again, but this time she was in a knot of friends: girls who cared, girls who wanted her. The tears ended. The lump dissolved.

"Fix your hair," Mary Ellen commanded, handing over a brush. Nancy wanted to laugh. Mary Ellen could not bear it if anyone in the squad looked messy. If you couldn't look good — even in tears — Mary Ellen had no use for you. For Mary Ellen's sake, Nancy brushed her hair. "So," she said, changing the subject, trying to be breezy, "tomorrow night's the big one, huh?"

"We'll whip Garrison," Angie said confidently. "Marc is coming. With him in the crowd I'll be the best cheerleader in the universe. And with me the best cheerleader in the universe, how can we lose?"

They hugged, a circle of love.

In the dark glass of the butler's pantry cabinets, Mary Ellen watched her own reflection. Oh, to have the life of a Tilford — to live where entire rooms were filled with beautiful, useless china and crystal, to have a sink for nothing but arranging the flowers delivered by the greenhouse!

Someday I will, Mary Ellen thought. I'm not a here-today, gone-tomorrow kind of girl. My life will shine. I'm Number One. I'll always be Number One.

She left the girls and walked out to find Donny again, and kissed him fiercely in front of forty spectators. Donny was embarrassed, but Mary Ellen didn't notice. She was rejoicing in her life.

But none of them *really* knew a thing about their future. Whether they would be winners or losers — whether their lives would sparkle in the sun, or darken in the storm.

Jennifer Sarasin

Splitting

CHAPTER

1

Pres was really out of it. It was a conscious effort, not to listen to his father, but he could do it. He could sit and actually look at him, actually seem as though his gaze were riveted on his father's face, when in reality his mind was on a game or a sexy girl or adjusting the valves on his Porsche. There wasn't much to it, really. Just send your mind out of the dining room, past the maid standing in the doorway with crystal bowls full of chocolate-mint ice cream, and let it go careening into space.

"And we've made a superlative profit, just on this month's statement alone." Preston Tilford II leaned back contentedly in his chair and watched as the dessert dish was placed before him.

"Wonderful, dear." Pres's mother wasn't looking adoringly at her husband's steel-gray eyes or gray hair, though. She was looking at her son, her black-sheep cheerleader son. If only he would

343

respond a little — not even with enthusiasm, but just with mild interest.

Pres's eyes were closed now. He took a mouthful of ice cream and concentrated on separating out the chocolate chips. It was like dividing the Oreos when he was a kid, saving the side with the filling for last. He sure wasn't a kid anymore. He was nearly eighteen, but he felt older, as if he'd been through a lot — except when he was driving the Porsche, or hanging out with Kerry, or cheering with the team. He imagined them standing in a circle around the circumference of his dessert bowl — Mary Ellen the lovely, Nancy the sexy, Angie the dependable, Olivia the silent, and good old slaphappy Walt.

"So, Pres," his father continued. "I'll tell you, even though you haven't asked. Martin's promised that you can start with Investment Services in three weeks. He's going to give you all the training you need. If you won't come to work for me at Tarenton Fabricators, at least we can drill some financial expertise into you. Of course, it will mean giving up all extracurricular activities, including that . . . that team you're on."

Pres's mind slowly returned to the room, then jerked to attention. "What are you talking about?"

"It's about time you took some real responsibility." His father nodded with that little half smile of his that never quite reached his eyes. "And gave up those stupid games you play after school." He hated the notion of his son as a cheerleader so much that he couldn't even bring himself to say the word aloud. "This job will prepare you for the business courses you'll take in college."

Pres put his spoon down on the cherry wood table, his handsome face a frozen mask. For a second, he just sat there, trying not to let his anger show, trying not to let a single emotion out. "It's a joke, right? A funny joke?"

"No joke, Pres. Martin's made you a firm offer."

"Well, why didn't Martin tell me? Isn't that the way jobs are usually handled? When you don't have pull, I mean. When you're not trying to find your idiot son some paper-pushing, boring, stupid way to occupy his time." He gathered steam like a locomotive.

His mother let out a long sigh, then covered her face with her hands.

"I don't like your tone," Mr. Tilford said with deadly calm.

"I don't like the way you treat me, Dad." Pres stood up, his six-foot frame seeming taller in the candlelight. The maid, standing in the doorway holding the silver coffee service, flew back into the kitchen. "I don't have to take this, not anymore. I'm old enough — nearly eighteen. I'm getting out, man. I mean *out*!"

He pushed his knees back against the upholstered chair, feeling power and strength surging through him. The chair hit the floor, but he didn't bother to right it. He kept walking, though he wanted to run. Run and crawl under the covers like a kid, but he couldn't do that anymore. He stalked to the hallway, grabbed his keys from the marble-topped table, and was out the door before his parents could follow. He didn't know where he was going at this hour of night. Just driving, probably. He hardly heard his mother yelling, "Stop him, Preston! Oh, for heaven's sake! Baby, come back!"

No more baby. Not for him.

The crowd was great today. The stands were packed, despite the cold, and the mood was really high. After all, the Tarenton Wolves didn't play the Deep River Killers every day, so it was an event. Now, at halftime, the score was tied, right after Johnny Elliott had tackled the Deep River quarterback, forcing him to fumble the ball, which Bump Daniels recovered and carried over the goal line.

"Boy, did you see that?" Mary Ellen Kirkwood's brilliant cheerleader smile was for real as she raced, arm in arm with Pres, to take her place for the first cheer. Her honey-blonde hair blew attractively across her face, and she didn't bother to brush it away. As involved as Mary Ellen was, she never forgot how she looked. It was one of the most important things in life to her.

"Bump is *on*, man! I mean, the guy's a miracle worker!" Walt Manners didn't usually get this excited about football, but there was something different about him today. He raised Angie Poletti in an impromptu shoulder-sit and she giggled happily.

"Put her down, Walt." Nancy Goldstein tugged at his arm. "Time to get to work."

"Yeah." Olivia Evans, the smallest member

of the cheerleading team, took her place, arching into an effortless backbend in front of the group. "I'm freezing. Let's get this over with."

The crowd's excitement hadn't abated one bit as the Tarenton squad assembled for their opening cheer, a splashy number that Angie and Nancy had choreographed one rainy day. The girls' scarlet skirts swayed in the light wind, revealing their white pleats. Each of the four of them revelled in the outfit, the white V-neck sweater with its scarlet bands and the proud "T" on the front, completing the perfect look that made them one.

The boys hoisted Olivia by all four limbs and spun her as Mary Ellen did a triple cartwheel that ended in a split. Olivia gracefully managed to slip to the ground in time to perform a meticulous series of back flips with the other three girls, while the boys stag-leaped around them.

"We're gonna win it, gonna beat 'em, gonna shine,
We're the team that's putting all the other guys in line.
We can go . . . (stamp, stamp) hot!
We can run . . . (clap, clap) wild!
We can WIN! We can WIN!"

The spectacular close called for super-human energy on everyone's part. Pres was to sweep Nancy up through a pirouette into a flying mount to his shoulders, Angie and Mary Ellen were to form a handstand arch in front of Walt, and Olivia was to do two straddle jumps and end up

347

in a split on the ground, her hands raised in the air in triumph.

But even as they were moving, Mary Ellen sensed something odd. What was it? She prided herself on always getting the big picture on a scene. Even when she was concerned with herself, with her looks, with what other people thought about her, she could still make sense of things.

She knew something was wrong, and looked to Nancy for confirmation even as she bobbed over into a handstand. Then, she heard Nancy gasp and saw her falling, away from Pres. She landed with a hard clunk on the gravel, and there was an almost indiscernible streak of blood along her left thigh. Although Mary Ellen saw pain behind the other girl's eyes, Nancy recovered beautifully. Her tawny complexion was slightly paler, but she was smiling, just the way Ardith Engborg, their coach, always insisted upon.

"What the. . . ?" Walt muttered in annoyance. He didn't like Pres all of the time, mostly because Pres took the easy way out. Walt, who came on like the class clown, was enormously serious underneath. He'd die rather than shirk responsibility. Or drop a girl in full sight of the entire school.

Unfortunately, the team wasn't alone in picking up on the slip. The front bleachers in the stands were practically right over their heads. Susan Yardley and her boyfriend Jimmy stood up in horror as they saw Nancy take the fall, and Vanessa Barlow and her two Deep River boyfriends laughed out loud. Vanessa was the daughter of the superintendent of schools, which made her think that the world of Tarenton High revolved around her needs and wishes. What she seemed to wish, mostly, was for every girl on the cheerleading team to be dropped through a hole in the earth, so that she could take all their glory. But one down would do.

Pres just stood there, his face blank.

"Keep going, for heaven's sake!" Angie hissed at him.

"What's wrong, Pres? C'mon, we just started." Olivia, always thought of as the most retiring one of the team, could speak up when she had to. Her mother had learned this recently, much to her dismay. Because Olivia had suffered from a heart condition as a child, she'd been smothered with care in the name of love until she'd joined this team. Then, and only then, had she found the will and way to strike out on her own.

Olivia bodily swung Pres around into the second cheer, leading the others. Her tiny 90-pound frame seemed to grow larger as she hauled his large one into action.

"Harass them, harass them,
    Make them relinquish the ball!"

Mary Ellen started the "vocabulary cheer," as they called it back in the locker room, and the others joined in loudly. Angie, always the one to try to smooth over a difficult spot, added a pike to her part of the routine, following it with a graceful back walkover. Anything to take the crowd's focus off Pres, Angie thought.

Angie was a peacemaker at heart, the joy of

her big sprawling family. Her mother, Rose, had carried on with her life when her husband died, and worked her way up to owning her own beauty parlor while raising three kids at the same time. Her mother could hoist the weight of the world on her shoulders, but Angie could take the same weight and make it look effortless, smiling, always helpful, extremely popular.

The five of them moved around Pres, pushing him into position, jostling him into doing his part of the routine. But as halftime progressed, it became obvious to the crowd that they were working against an immovable force.

"Poor Pres," Vanessa Barlow said, loud enough for her entire section to hear. "He must have been struck by lightning. He's *sooo* electrifying!" Her peal of nasty laughter coated the air like a thick, cloying syrup.

"Hey, if this is what Tarenton has to offer, they better get the stiffs off the field," one of her Deep River bozos guffawed. "Gimme a team of girl cheerleaders any day — right, Van?" He nudged her in the ribs so hard she nearly fell off her seat.

"I don't know. These girls never impressed me as anything much," she shrugged.

Nancy glared up at Vanessa even as she sprang into a spread-eagle jump, reaching her arms to the heavens and smiling, always smiling. "Don't let her get to you," she hissed through her teeth at Pres. "For heaven's sake, shape up, will you?"

"Leave me alone," Pres demanded. He took her wrist and swung her around so hard, he left burns on her smooth skin.

The last routine was over. The team took a perfunctory bow in their toughest position — a pyramid that fell over into multiple cartwheels — and ran to the sidelines, as much to hide their chagrin as to make way for the football players.

"I don't get you at all, man," Walt said angrily to Pres, as they waited for the first play before they started working the crowd. It was their job to keep the enthusiasm high throughout the game, regardless of what was going on.

"What's to get? I'm just a little bored today." Pres's crooked smile darkened his handsome face.

"We've all got our problems," Olivia reminded him. "But they're not supposed to show when we're performing. How many times has Ardith been over that with us?" After years of struggling back from illness, Olivia was the toughest of them all.

"Don't hound him." Mary Ellen wasn't watching Tarenton's particularly bad skirmish; she was worried about Pres. If there was anything she wanted in life, besides escape from this hick town and her poverty, it was a boy like Pres. Maybe Pres himself, if he'd start asking her out again. It wasn't that she was bored with Donny Parrish, captain of the Tarenton basketball team, but Pres was something different. Donny was a lapdog at her feet; Pres was the dangerous cougar, standing at the top of the mountain, daring her to chase him down.

Angie let out a sigh of frustration and gave the high sign to Kimberley, the leader of the twelve-member Pompon Squad, to start encouraging the crowd. "Let's discuss this later," Mary Ellen said to Pres.

"I don't want to. As a matter of fact," Pres said with grim determination, "I don't want to do anything right now. How about that?" And with no warning at all, he walked off the field. Just kept walking, slowly and steadily, out around the bleachers and back to the parking lot. No one could stop him. No one would dare.

The other five halted only a moment before renewing their efforts to get the audience excited. It was no use, though. Tarenton, for some reason, was losing miserably to Deep River. Nancy couldn't help but think that *they* had done it, that the cheerleaders had let the ball players down and ruined the whole game. Was it possible? Well, Ardith would certainly say it was.

So they tried harder — even when it started to rain, even when the Wolves let Deep River make three field goals in a row, and Bump Daniels completely missed two easy lateral passes. What else could they do but band together, trying to pretend they were still a squad.

The Wolves lost the game, 21 to 18, and the feeling in the locker room afterward was intense. A cold wind swept through them, even inside the steamy hall where they congregated like lost sheep to receive Mrs. Engborg's admonishment.

"Who'd like to explain?" The small ball of fury who was their coach and their inner conscience stood before them, looking about twice her normal height. She was a wiry blonde in her forties, the toughest taskmaster any of them had ever worked for.

There was silence. People stared at the floor or at the door. Walt chewed his gum noisily and Mary Ellen curled the tendrils that crept around her lovely, high cheekbones.

"I saw Pres burn rubber out of the parking lot right after halftime." Ardith bit the words off. "I saw him drop Nancy, too. You know, I don't have a clue as to what you think you're here for, but Varsity means something to me. And if one of you goes off the deep end, that's no excuse. Everyone else is supposed to pick him up and carry on. Ever think of that? No, none of you escape blame for today. Don't look away, Nancy — it's your fault as much as anyone's. And yours, Angie. What about you, Olivia? You're the one with the discipline, aren't you? And why didn't you get Pres back, Walt? Why didn't you cover for him, Mary Ellen? I want answers here." Her hazel eyes took on each of them individually, two lazer beams that pierced their very souls.

"We fell down on the job, I guess," Nancy muttered. She had a terrible fear that, having come so far, she was about to be ditched for this one offense. It wasn't easy, wanting to be part of this group the way she did. Nancy still sometimes felt like an outsider, one of the few Jewish girls in the school, and she needed to be here.

"I'm disgusted with all of you. I'll speak with Pres Monday, but I expect one or all of you to get hold of him this weekend. This is supposed to be teamwork, in case you've forgotten." Ardith marched off down the corridor, shaking her head.

"Who wants to drive over to Pres's house?" Walt asked. "We can all pile into my Jeep."

"No, that's like ganging up on him," Angie argued.

"I'm too tired for a fight now, anyway," Olivia declared, swinging her gym bag over her shoulder.

"Except for a good knock-down drag-out with your mom," Walt countered.

Olivia didn't know how to take that at first, not until she saw the sly smile spreading over his face. Walt liked the fact that she stood up to her mother. She barely returned his smile, but their eyes met and held, a new admiration growing between them.

"I've got to get home," Nancy said. "Anybody need a ride?" She was secretly as thrilled that she was now able to borrow her mother's car and drive alone, as she had been to get on the Varsity Squad. This year's birthday present — private driving lessons — had been her most cherished gift in years.

Mary Ellen hesitated just a minute before accepting the ride. It was the worst embarrassment of her life to have to bum rides from everyone, but Donny had the flu, so she was stuck. The only other alternative was waiting around until her dad finished his bus route and picked her up. That could mean hours of hanging out, letting people know she was so poor she could only afford public transportation when her father was driving it. If she waited too long, Patrick Henley would be sure to appear, eager and willing to escort her home in his garbage truck. Patrick, who loved her, who would probably lay down his life for her. She was terribly attracted to him, and was constantly fighting her feelings for him. How could she fall in love with a guy who was proud of his father's garbage business, and even prouder of the fact that he'd earned enough money to buy his own truck? The trash man — how could he be the heartthrob she was waiting for?

"Sure, I'd love it," she said to Nancy, her brilliant blue eyes grateful. "Why don't we all talk tomorrow? Maybe one of us can go see Pres and hash this out."

As they straggled to the parking lot together, they each had their separate moments of selfish concern. It seemed so unfair, really, to get blamed for something someone else had done. They'd always had trouble being a team, banding together — Ardith was right about that. But this was Pres's craziness, not theirs.

"See you, guys," Walt waved as he climbed into his Jeep.

" 'Bye, see you Monday," Angie called as her older brother, Al, honked his horn and she ran, smiling again, toward his car.

Olivia, bundled up to the hilt, walked to the bike rack where she removed the heavy lock from her Atala five-speed. Until there was snow on the ground, she rode that thing all over Tarenton, just to show everyone she could. She had just stuck her gym bag in her basket and thrust her leg over the seat when she heard the sound of an engine right beside her.

"That bike'll fit right along the back of the Jeep," Walt said. "No hassle."

She squinted up at him. "No thanks."

"The ground is wet. You'll slip."

"I never have before," she assured him.

Walt took a deep breath. Why was he trying so hard? And with Olivia, of all people. "C'mon, will ya? Stop tap-dancing and let me give you a ride. I'll feel like I've done something right today, at least."

Her piercing dark eyes took him in, appraising him. Then she shrugged. "If you want." She watched him jump down from the driver's seat and slide the back door open. Then, without waiting for him to come around to her, she climbed in on the passenger side and let him stow her bike. She felt like a long ride, pedaling slowly through the light rain, but she also felt like talking to someone. It was a weird feeling, and she wondered why she'd given in to it. Olivia rarely let her feelings get the better of her.

Nancy watched Walt and Olivia start out of the parking lot, and she shook her head curiously. She looked over at Mary Ellen, but she apparently hadn't noticed anything, so Nancy didn't comment. She got behind the steering wheel and leaned over to unlock the other door for her passenger. But they'd waited too long. Vanessa Barlow was just climbing into the bucket seat of her latest guy's Camaro.

"Well, you all certainly made a spectacle of yourselves today," she smirked as the big lug beside her started the engine. "If I were a member of the squad, I'd have died of shame."

"Don't hold your breath, Vanessa," Nancy offered. "Since your best doesn't approximate our worst, I don't think there's any danger of your replacing one of us."

Vanessa shook her thick, dark hair over one

356

shoulder with a careless laugh. She swept her
cashmere scarf gracefully around her neck,
wrapping herself in yards of heather as she
snuggled deeper into her warm antique raccoon
coat. "You don't think I'm still pining to be on
your little old team, do you? Mary Ellen, I can't
imagine changing places with you. I mean, I
wouldn't want to ride in the cab of someone's
smelly garbage truck or live in a little turquoise
house." With that, she gave her driver the high
sign and they took off doing forty, screaming with
laughter.

Mary Ellen sat straighter in her seat, pretending she hadn't heard. If only Vanessa's snipes
could roll off her instead of sticking through her
like tiny poison darts.

"She's so ridiculous, she's not even funny,"
Nancy snorted, pressing down on the accelera-
tor. The car grumbled, refusing to turn over.
"It's not even worth thinking up junk to throw
back at her, you know?" She looked at her passenger out of the corner of her eye, knowing
how much it hurt.

"Let's go, okay?" Mary Ellen said in a wan
voice. "I'm really beat."

Nancy turned the key again, and this time, her
efforts were rewarded. She couldn't help thinking as they drove off, though, that Mary Ellen's
reaction was part of what was keeping the team
apart. When you let things get to you, you could
crumble to pieces like a kid's sandcastle. And
then you were finished. She resolved to see Pres
this weekend, and to turn him around.

CHAPTER

The dark-red Porsche careened up Fable Point, taking its own vengeance on the rutted road. Around the last point of the lake, and then, home. Pres laughed at that one. Home? It was ludicrous to even think of *that* place as a safe haven.

He didn't want to put the car in the drive — his father's drive — so he left it by the side of the road. He wouldn't be long, anyway. This was a perfect time to make a clean getaway, since his mother would be at the hairdresser's and his father always did some United Fund Drive charity thing on Saturday afternoons. No one around but the maid.

Even so, he used the back entrance. No need to call attention to himself. He took the back stairs up to his room and, without even thinking, grabbed his duffle bag out of the closet and started packing. As he shoved a pair of sneakers into the deep pocket of the bag, he felt like a man, a guy who could do as he pleased. He even had a place to stay; he'd been planning and thinking about it for weeks. So it was no big sweat — he'd just move out. Plenty of kids did it. Uncle James didn't know he was coming, but he was an okay guy who let things happen.

He threw clothes into the bag at random, trying not to let his mind work.

The other kids on the squad were furious with him, that went without saying. He knew he'd let them down, Nancy worst of all. He liked her, thought she was sexy as hell, even though he'd never asked her out. Maybe he should — maybe that would patch things up. But she didn't have a thing about him the way Mary Ellen did. Probably, of all of them, Mary Ellen would forgive him the quickest. He was kind of fascinated by her — she certainly was beautiful — but she was always trying for a goal she might never reach. Pres knew he was one of those goals, and he wasn't flattered by the idea. Mary Ellen didn't really pay attention to the present because she was so wrapped up in the future, she just couldn't wait to graduate and hightail it to New York and be a model. Well, she'd probably succeed, even if she had to scratch her way up by her long, polished fingernails.

If only Kerry had been at the game. She was visiting relatives this weekend, and had begged off, but at least he'd see her Monday at school. Kerry Elliot was a cool breeze in a dry desert for him: a soft girl, made of different textures and qualities. Only a sophomore, but wiser than most seniors. He'd never known anyone like her before. Of course, his parents weren't wild about her, that also went without saying. You had to have a big bank account to please Preston Tilford II.

He zipped the case and tossed it casually over his shoulder, looking around the room once. There was his stereo and computer equipment. No, better to travel light. Anyhow, he didn't want the old man to say he'd ripped him off. It would be just like him to call the cops on his own son.

He was out the door, skimming down the staircase, out through the kitchen door, past the staircase, out through the kitchen door, past the have to cook for himself! What a laugh. Maybe he could get the team to come over and help. Nancy for meat loaf on Mondays, Olivia for chicken on Tuesdays, and so forth. Then he threw back his head and laughed. They probably didn't know how to cook any better than he did. Only Angie and Mary Ellen, whose parents had to dig for every dime, would know anything about the inside of a kitchen.

No regrets, he thought suddenly as he ran out the door and started up the Porsche again. It would be great, he decided, as he screeched off back around the lake. At least, he hoped it would be.

The Jeep lumbered down the road slowly like an old bear. It could go faster, but Walt didn't want it to. He wanted to savor this moment, this nice, quiet time to mellow out after the game.

"Hello, are you still there?" he asked.

Olivia gave him a look. "Can't you tell?"

"Sure. I can hear the click of the little wheels in your head a mile away."

She laughed, and it was a surprisingly cheery, almost childlike laugh. "Jeeps do it to me. I can't seem to stop thinking that we're about to hit a land mine or something."

"Only the ones the badgers laid. Don't worry, I'm a great driver." This was nice, Walt thought to himself. Cheerleading tired him out, even though he'd never let on. After all, he was The Amazing Rubber Man, the guy who bounced back. He was the happy-go-lucky gymnast who laughed at life and at himself. Why did he think it was nice with Olivia beside him? he wondered, sneaking a glance at her upright, stoic little profile.

He'd never noticed her much. She was great in performance, but sort of a drag at practice. Just like Ardith, always ready to work, always trying for the next hardest level. Tell her to do three scissor kicks, and she'd do six. Tell her to work on her aerial somersaults, and she'd keep going through dinner. A real hog for work. But Walt had been looking at her differently lately. Maybe somebody who worked so hard could play pretty hard, too. Maybe she could listen hard and pay attention to a guy who just didn't seem to draw girls like Pres did.

Olivia wasn't like the others on the squad, he decided. She wasn't concerned with her looks and what other people thought about her. She was just her own person.

"You live pretty deep in there, right?" Olivia

361

asked suddenly, pointing at the thick woods that skirted the lake. The trees were bare now, but you could still hardly see through the branches.

"Right. My folks built themselves this log fortress about ten years ago. Keeps out the elephants, at least."

"A good thing, too," Olivia nodded, playing along. "They do their morning TV show from there, don't they? Their interviews are pretty interesting. I've heard them sometimes, when I'm getting ready for school," she explained.

"Yeah, that's the only time I hear them. I think I've gotten so that I only understand what they're saying when they're talking into a mike. 'Oh, Walt, your mother would like you to empty the dishwasher,' he mimed a microphone in his left hand. 'Would you care to say a few words to the studio audience about that?'"

Olivia actually giggled. He'd never heard her giggle. "What's it like having parents who are celebrities?"

"They're not . . . I mean, just because people know their faces doesn't mean they're the Jackson Two or anything." He shrugged and put the Jeep in first as they struggle up a hill. "One thing, though. They're a team. They work together, eat together, live together. Sometimes I watch them, you know, and I feel kind of —" He stopped midsentence, and she jumped in.

"Superfluous? I feel like that around my mom."

He had to laugh at that. "How could you? She's on your case all the time, following you around school, around practice and games, like you're the only thing in her life."

"Yeah, but it's not *me* she's interested in. It's my pulse, respiration, blood pressure. She doesn't even *know* me," Olivia finished, but there was not a tinge of self-pity in her words.

Walt pulled over to the side of the road and parked. "I find you very interesting," he said quietly. "I bet, if I got to know you better, I'd find you even more interesting." Their hands lay beside each other on the console between the two bucket seats. Walt had an uncontrollable urge to cover her small hand with his huge paw, but he didn't do it. He just stared at their hands, so close.

Olivia was very still, scarcely breathing. She'd been on dates with boys before, of course, but the guys she went out with were always more interested in themselves than her. Michael Barnes thought dating interfered with his goal of becoming a star cross-country runner, and eventually they split up when Olivia started feeling she was coming in a poor second. She never even felt comfortable with Jimmy Hilbert, who'd made such a fuss over her before she discovered he was going out with Nancy, too. With Walt, someone she knew, someone whose voice and hands and body were as familiar to her as the pendulum clock on her bedroom wall, she could almost relax.

"You sure don't say much, do you?" Walt chuckled.

"I was brought up to be super polite," Olivia said with a straight face. "I always let the other guy go first."

"Good. That gives me an opening for another

first." He bent toward her and she felt her own weight shifting, as if she was on the minitramp and about to lose her balance. But she could save herself from falling just by leaning slightly into his large, warm shoulder. He didn't touch her at all, not even a fingertip moved. But his lips were suddenly right next to her cheek, and she felt the cool whistle of his breath before the kiss. Then she turned awkwardly, not knowing what to do, and his mouth was too close to miss. She wished she had some lipstick because her lips were so dry. She didn't even have the chance to lick them before he kissed her, softly and hesitantly.

It was weird. This was Walt, not some strange person, not someone she'd dreamed about and hoped for. But it felt so good, so right. The only problem was, she didn't know what to do next. She didn't want the kiss to end, but she didn't want to seem mushy and emotional by kissing him back. They both hung there in midair, a little astounded at what had just taken place.

A car winging down the road saved them. The loud honk of the driver's horn made Walt and Olivia pull apart at the same time. Then they sat staring at each other, still too dumbfounded to speak.

"So. . . ." Walt cleared his throat. "Oh, boy."

She smiled into her scarf, the corners of her dark eyes crinkling happily as she reviewed the mysteries of the way she felt.

"Well, are you just going to sit there all day grinning like a loon?" he demanded.

"I might. Are you going to drive me home?"

"Sure." Well, that was it, then. He had failed miserably. Walt put the car in gear. Why was he such a dumb cluck? Why couldn't he leave well enough alone? They'd been having a perfectly nice conversation and then, he'd had to jump all over her. Why didn't girls put up signs when they wanted to be kissed? *I'm in the mood* or *Not today, thanks.*

Walt drove steadily around Narrow Brook Lake to the opposite side, near where Nancy lived. Still not a word from the small girl beside him. He plowed on down tree-lined roads to the newer houses, the ones away from the waterfront, which displayed their comfort and wealth in a less conspicuous way. He wasn't exactly sure where Olivia lived and didn't intend to ask. She'd have to speak first, even if it was just to give him directions.

"Next block, it's a right turn — number 33," she nearly whispered. And then she said, "But why don't you stop here so you can kiss me again?"

Angie had just taken the pile of mail off the front table and gone into the living room to sort it, when the phone rang. "Get it, will you, Al? I'm busy," she called, having discovered gold in the mass of bills and catalogs. A letter from Marc Filanno, from college!

"Hey, get the phone, will you, Andrew!" her older brother Al yelled to the next Poletti in line. It was a tradition that the youngest available got stuck with doing things his older siblings scorned.

"Get it yourself, stupid!" came the response from the kitchen.

She held the letter, savoring the neat writing on the envelope, the angle of the stamp, the postmark, the way the paper inside was folded. She was delirious with expectation, almost not daring to slit open the top — not because she worried that the reality would be less than perfect, but just because if she went ahead and read the letter, the ecstasy of waiting would be over.

Marc had graduated from high school last spring, and they'd gone out steadily over the summer. He had a job filling vending machines for some big company, and though the work was boring, it helped his family out with the college tuition. Now he was studying and working simultaneously, so Angie hadn't seen him in over a month. He'd been writing and calling regularly, and she got the impression that he hardly had time for anything.

"Andrew, get me a chicken leg or something would you?" Angie called into the kitchen. "That game gave me the most incredible appetite." Actually, it was the letter that made her hungry. Whenever she was really happy — which was most of the time — she ate. Angie loved to eat. She positively yearned for chocolate cake and double cheeseburgers with bacon. She liked to say that she could eat all day and actually *lose* weight from the exertion, but it wasn't true. She watched her weight like a hawk and was always rationing her treats — a skipped dessert today meant a sinful, gooey one tomorrow.

"Hey, Ange, I'm on the phone with that beautiful girl down the block. You'll have to starve," Andrew chuckled from the hallway, his hand over the receiver.

Angie took a breath and opened the letter, her eyes closed. She inhaled the very being of Marc from the page, thinking of his neat smile, the way his hair flopped over on one side, the way he kind of swayed when he walked. She opened her eyes and read:

Dear Angie,

I've thought long and hard about this, and believe me, I wouldn't write if I weren't absolutely sure that my decision is the best for both of us in the future. It may not look so hot to you now, but in a few months, you'll thank me.

I was talking to Elaine about this the other night, and she agreed that long-distance relationships are practically impossible, particularly when one person's in college and the other still has all those high school activities and concerns to worry about. It's really hard for two people in two such different worlds to make it click.

I'm always going to be fond of you, you know that, Angie, and even now, as I write this, I'm kicking myself for putting the damper on something that was so sweet, so special. But it's only natural that we all grow and change and experience different things and different people. Please, don't sit around and moon over this — go out and cheer on that crowd the way you do so well. I'll always remember your sunny face.

Best,
Marc

"Who the hell's Elaine?" Angie whispered, but of course, she knew. Elaine was some sophisticated college girl who could probably discuss philosophy over a candlelight dinner and knew all the latest foreign films. She probably didn't even have to read the subtitles.

Angie was breathing very hard, all her feelings knotted up in one lump right under her chin. She couldn't cry — that was too dumb. She wanted to throw dishes at the wall, but that would be horribly wasteful. She was going to get control in a minute, in just a second, and as long as none of her brothers came in and started jabbering, she'd be fine.

The doorbell rang and she sat there, pinching the letter hard between two fingers, hoping she was hurting it.

"Ange, get the door, wouldya?" Andrew yelled. "I'm talking."

She didn't move and heard him curse, then put the phone down to see who was there. In less than a second, Nancy was in the room with her, breathless and excited.

"Well, I've located Pres and this is a perfect time for us to talk to him seriously about what happened at the game today. I saw his car parked down by his uncle's house on my way back from Mary Ellen's, see, so if we go corner him there, he'll —" She took a good look at the normally bubbling-over-with-life girl slumped on the couch, gripping a piece of paper. "Oh, Angie, what's wrong?" She felt like a real dolt, to be babbling away when someone right in the same room with her was clearly about to commit suicide.

"If I said *nothing*, you wouldn't believe me, would you?" Angie was as close to tears as she'd been in a long time.

"No, I wouldn't." Nancy sat beside her, feeling the same sort of pain she'd experienced when Vanessa had been so mean to Mary Ellen. Why did she always have to have this awful empathy for everyone else? It was worse than when she went through it herself.

"Marc just sent me a 'Dear John' letter from college," Angie blurted out. "He — and somebody named Elaine — think we don't have anything in common anymore." And then the sobs came, loud and full. She couldn't stop herself; it was like something within her had broken and would never be mended. Even though she knew how useless it was to cry over a split boyfriend, it didn't stop the hurt. Why couldn't he have told her in person, for heaven's sake, or called, or done it gradually instead of all at once, so she could be prepared for it?

Nancy's arms were around her, and she felt an awkward patting on her right shoulder. She wished she could stop this stupid crying — she wasn't really that tight with Nancy, and she felt so exposed.

"I know why he wants to split up, too. I really never thought it was that important to him. I mean, we were as good as married — everyone figured we'd end up together." She knotted her fist and pounded it into her thigh in frustration. "I should have gone to bed with him. Dumb, dumb, *dumb*. That's what guys want, isn't it? No matter how much they truly and sincerely love you, it's no good for them until you've done it. Right?" She turned to Nancy in a blind fury, the tears spilling everywhere.

"I don't think every single one of them is like that, Angie. And if it wasn't right for you —"

"No, it wasn't. He should have known that. We were going to wait, and he *said* that was fine. At least, most of the time, he did. I guess he didn't mean it. And then, this . . . this Elaine came along, and I guess he figured he didn't *have* to wait, so why should he?"

Nancy felt the ache in her own heart. She'd never been that close to a boy, really. Alex Hague had been the deepest relationship of her life, but he'd gone home to England. And then there was her romance with Ben Adamson, captain of Garrison High's basketball team. She'd been crazy about Ben, but that had been a wild, physical attraction more than anything else. He had epitomized sex to her. But dating someone from the enemy ranks was simply more than she could handle. Every time they went out, she'd be looking over her shoulder for Tarenton kids who might disapprove — and everyone did.

For a brief moment, she was jealous of Angie. What she'd had with Marc was really precious. But then, Nancy thought, what's the use if you have to go through all this pain at the end? Keep it light, keep it flirty, and you don't get hurt. You don't get the real highs, but you don't suffer the agonizing lows either. "Angie . . ." she begged.

"I'm all right now," Angie sniffed, holding back a second flow of tears that threatened to ruin all her good intentions. "Or at least I will be in a few decades."

"What a perfect louse," Nancy growled. "I don't know where guys get the idea that they can say, 'Poof, it's over,' and have it be over. It's like they think they're the only ones involved. You really cared about that nerd, too."

"I never felt about anyone the way I did about Marc." Angie sat there for a second, trying to be logical and sensible. Maybe that would stop the crying. "Do you think it could have been more being in love with just the *idea* of having a steady boyfriend? Like being in love with love? My mom always tells me she used to do that before she met my dad."

"Maybe. But what I saw when you were with Marc looked pretty real to me."

Angie's eyes filled again, and spilled over. She didn't want to do it, but she had no control over it. The letter lay, blotched with tears, in her lap.

"I have a box of tissues in my car," Nancy offered. "How about a drive? Just to get you out of the house for a while."

Angie nodded morosely. "If you like, we can

go see Pres. But you'll have to do the talking. I'm a hopeless case."

"You're a great and terrific person who has just been through the wringer," Nancy said fiercely, drawing Angie to her feet. "I want you to tell yourself that there's a lot in store for you, that this isn't the end of the world, not by a long shot."

Angie attempted to smile as she walked toward the door. She thought about being at the end of the world, a bleak place where you had to do trigonometry all day long and there was no rock music and no cheering. Where you'd never have to do your nails and hair before a date, because there were no dates.

Oh Marc, you left your mark on me, she thought glumly as she walked toward Nancy's car. Now how am I going to rub it out?

CHAPTER

I t was five by the time Pres slammed on his brakes in front of James Tilford's house, the small but classy wood-and-glass structure on Beresford Road. The attached studio was hooked onto the back so inconspicuously you couldn't see it from the road. It was mostly skylights and high beams and it faced north — a perfect place for an artist.

"James, you there?" Pres called loudly as he knocked on the door. "It's me."

After a few seconds, the studio door swung open, revealing a small, wiry man with a salt-and-pepper beard, wearing baggy, paint-stained jeans and a T-shirt that was more holes than fabric. He had a pencil stuck behind his left ear, and his gray eyes were only half open, slitted in cynical appraisal of his nephew.

"Well, what little breeze blew you this way, old boy? Your dad want to convey some important message and wouldn't come in person?" James hadn't seen his brother in several years, by mutual agreement, as far as Pres could tell. An artist and a loner, divorced for the past ten years, James was something of a curiosity in Tarenton. He'd renounced his inheritance and decided to make it on his own, something Pres thought was totally commendable, if a little screwy, and something his father thought was grounds for commitment to a mental institution.

"James, I need a place to stay. How about it?" Pres rushed the words out as he stepped through the studio door. The roaring fire in the small wood stove that stood between two easels gave a cheery glow to the room.

"You and your dad have another fight?" James motioned Pres to a sitting cushion in the corner. The place had its own living area, a kitchen, and a bathroom.

"This time it was bad, man. I mean, I don't know how the two of us can even be related. He's totally anti everything I want to do, and I feel like I can't breathe in there anymore. It started with my cheerleading, and now it's —"

"With your *what*?" James guffawed. Then he saw the look on Pres's face. "Sorry, didn't mean to be such a critical boor. But are you pulling my leg? You're not really dancing around out there with the pompons, are you?"

Pres shrugged and decided not to push it. He hadn't talked to his uncle in a while, and maybe James had changed, too. Maybe he'd recently turned into another dictatorial grown-up, just disguised as a funky artist.

"Hey, it doesn't matter. I mean, it's lots of things, you know. The bottom line is that we don't get along. I'm old enough now, and I'm moving out. I just need a place to stay until I can find an apartment, okay? How about it?" This was the acid test. If James didn't ask too many questions, if he just let him be, Pres would know the guy was still okay.

James looked around the studio. "Well, it's humble, and it smells of turpentine, but it's yours if you want it. I'll be in and out of town for a couple of weeks, got a big group show coming up, so I'm not around that much."

"I can really stay?" Pres asked.

"Hey, I don't say what I don't mean." James dug in his pocket for a key, and threw it across the room to Pres. "Just a few house rules. Don't touch the work in progress upon pain of death, and if I catch you in here with drugs or booze or live-in women, you're out on your ear. Understand?"

"Sure, James," Pres's face lit up with gratitude. The guy was on his side! "And thanks, really. My father's going to have a fit when he finds out."

"It'll be good for him," James cackled.

"Say," Pres went on as his uncle started hauling a full crate of canvases toward the door, "is it okay if some of the girls from school come help me get settled? And help me with cooking and stuff?"

"As long as there's no funny business on my property, it's cool. You're young and tender and I don't want to be responsible for your ultimate destruction." He rolled his eyes evilly and tried to twirl his tiny mustache like the villain in a melodrama.

Pres had to laugh at his uncle. The guy was weird, no doubt about it. But at least he could see somebody else's point of view. "You're on. And thanks again," he said as his uncle vanished, hidden behind a large red painting.

Pres looked around, and the thought suddenly dawned on him that he didn't have to be home in time for dinner. With a whoop of delight, he tossed the key in the air. His key to freedom.

Mary Ellen ran toward the gym Monday afternoon, certain that she was going to be late to practice. The halls were practically deserted as she raced along. The only sound was that of her rundown heels on the marble beneath her. If there was one thing Ardith wouldn't tolerate, it was kids who didn't come in on time. To her, it was a sign of not caring enough. That was one thing that couldn't be said about Mary Ellen — she certainly cared. More than anything, probably, except getting out of Tarenton, moving to New York, and making it big.

"You're always in such a hurry. You're going to miss an awful lot if you keep rushing, sweetheart."

Mary Ellen's face flushed, and she didn't have to look up to know that it was Patrick. He had this way of confronting her, of looming over her so large he blotted out everything else in her mind. All she could think about when he was close to her was her body and his, their mouths pressed close in a kiss, his powerful arms drawing her into an embrace from which she never wanted to be released. It was all she could do to keep herself from touching him.

"I'm late for practice." She took just one look up into his deep brown eyes and she was lost, gone, out to lunch for the duration. What was it about him that turned her on this way? He wasn't conventionally handsome, but that wide smile held so much promise, those eyes drew her like a magnet, and that body. . . . It was just sex, she knew that, and she could get over it if she tried, but despite her best intentions, it seemed to get harder and harder.

"You're better than the rest of them — you don't need as much practice. In some other areas, however, you could use a little extra work." And with that, he took her books out of her arms and replaced them with his own massive frame. Bending over her, he smoothed the hair off her forehead, then gently kissed the soft white skin. She closed her eyes, willing herself not to respond. She had the oddest feeling, as if her knees were going to give. She wanted to throw her arms around him, crush him to her, but something inside screamed, *No!* It was too dangerous, practically lethal. Even as his lips moved along the side of her cheek and down to her eager mouth, she started pulling away. This was so wrong!

The more she kissed Patrick, the closer they'd be, and soon the world would acknowledge that they were a couple. *Bus Driver's Daughter To Wed Trash Collector* — she could see the headline now. The only way she'd get to New York would be on their honeymoon. They'd see the sights and take pictures for their scrapbook and then, before she knew it, they'd be back in Tarenton, home sweet home. And then, babies. Her figure and looks would vanish before she was twenty-five.

The scenario scared her so much she literally wrenched herself out of his arms, grabbing her books and mumbling something about seeing him later but she really had to run. She was nearly free and clear, nearly out of his magnetic field, when someone else came around the bend of the hallway. Vanessa.

"Wow, guess I just missed some hot action, huh?" she smirked. "Between you two and Pres and Kerry right down the hall, this school is a regular Love Boat. It's so heartwarming to see two young hearts beating as one." She batted her heavily mascaraed eyelashes so hard they looked as if they were going to break off.

"*Can* it, Vanessa." Patrick stalked away from her as though she had a disease. Mary Ellen had already fled, nearly colliding with Pres and Kerry as she skidded toward the gym door. The two of them weren't looking particularly lovey-dovey, but rather worried and scared, Mary Ellen noticed. Kerry, a sophomore with an open personality and the sweet, soft face of an angel, was looking up at Pres adoringly.

"Oh, great, we can both get some demerits." Pres laughed as he saw Mary Ellen, trying to cover up his real mood. "You sure you don't mind waiting for me, Kerry?" he asked in a different tone, touching her arm.

378

"Of course not. I'll be in the library. You two better hurry." She smiled warmly at Mary Ellen, who couldn't help but marvel at the younger girl's goodness. She was just so *nice* — not Pres's type at all. It was hard for everyone to believe that he'd stopped playing the field for this rather plump, kind of lackluster girl. But when he looked at her, she blossomed.

"Mrs. Engborg's going to kill us, but at least she'll demolish you first, because of Saturday's game," Mary Ellen muttered as they hurried into the gym together.

"That means you get to watch me suffer before your own execution. Could be a gruesome sight." Pres smiled wickedly, ushering her gallantly ahead of him.

"Well, how kind of you two to join us," Ardith Engborg said in a deadly calm voice. "I don't suppose you feel you've missed anything, so if you'll consent to changing into your practice clothes, we'll go right on from where we are. Angie, try that C-jump again. And higher this time. Walt, this is not amateur hour — I expect some real action from all of you."

As Mary Ellen threw off her clothes in the locker room, she was struck by the fact that she felt more energetic than she had in a long time. Usually, when Vanessa got after her and Ardith was on her case, she couldn't help sulking. Today, though, it was different. She was a fireball; she wanted to get out there and lead the others on to glory. She tied her shining blonde hair into a ponytail and fluffed out the little tendrils on the side, strangely impressed with the vision she saw in the mirror. No matter that her practice clothes were old and faded from dozens of washings. She felt good — she actually felt rich!

She practically skipped back into the gym and was smiling until she realized why she felt so good. It was Patrick, his hands on her, his overwhelming presence. His love made her shine. And that was enough to send her spirits reeling back down into the lower depths. Oh, no, she thought as she took her place between Nancy and Olivia for the Tiger cheer. I can't do this to myself — I can't. Starting today, I'll try to stay away from him entirely. No more kisses, no more. It's me and Donny, period. But as she jumped and leapt around the floor, there was Patrick, his wonderful image swimming before her very eyes.

"We got the talent, we got the team,
Watch us now — see what we mean.
There's no limit to our spirit,
We're gonna win 'cause we're really in it!"

Angie tried for a triple roll to coincide with Olivia's, but the two girls collided in space, landing hard on the mat.

"Hey, watch where you're going, will you?" Angie kept trying to concentrate, but it was impossible. There was Marc, of course. One minute she wanted to get him on the phone and scream at him; the next, she was filled with an overwhelming desire to call and beg him to come back to her. And then there was Pres — and what she and Nancy had learned on Saturday afternoon. They'd kept their mouths shut till now, but eventually, the news would be out. She felt funny about knowing it first and not being able to tell.

"You watch it — I was right in place," Olivia huffed, looking to Walt for support. He'd called her on Sunday, just to chat. She'd half expected him to ask her out, but maybe he was just too shy. Anyway, she wasn't going to push — she could wait. In the meantime, this was just fine.

"Stop bickering, you two." Ardith put her hands on her narrow hips and motioned them to the center of the floor. She had on a lavender leotard under a plum-colored jumpsuit, with black leg warmers, and in her current state of mind she seemed very much like an angry, thin bunch of grapes.

"Sit down, everybody. I don't know what's going on here, but it has to stop. I'm going to give you all a chance to speak up, and then we'll get back to work. And I *mean* work! Not this halfhearted attempt at running around like chickens without heads." She did a neat Turk sit and motioned them to join her. "Okay, let's go around in a circle. Pres, you want to talk about Saturday?"

"No," he answered curtly.

Ardith's eyes narrowed. "Anyone else care to shed some light on Pres's problems?"

Nancy and Angie exchanged furtive glances, and shifted uncomfortably. That was pretty lousy, asking them to rat on a team member. Ardith didn't usually do things like this, but she was clearly upset.

"Gee, you're not your usual talkative selves, are you?" she stated sarcastically. "Olivia, why don't you break the ice?"

Olivia, seated next to Walt, just bit her lips and crossed her arms. Walt glanced down at her protectively.

"I think we should get back to work," Mary Ellen offered. "We'll try harder — how about that, Mrs. Engborg?" She bounded up, willing herself to have enough spirit for the whole team. The others straggled to their feet, embarrassed, and eager to get off the hook. There were just some things you didn't tell adults.

"Well, *work*, then," their leader huffed in disgust. "Pres, I want to see you tomorrow in my office, eight-thirty sharp. Is that clear?"

"Very." His tone wasn't sullen or rude, but it wasn't compliant either.

And then they got down to it, pacing through routines until their clothes were soaked with sweat and their limbs ached. They practiced rolls and leaps, carries and lifts; they did enough walkovers and back flips to induce stomach cramps — but nobody complained. Like machines, they worked silently and efficiently, each lost in a quiet physical world where everything else faded into the background. Nothing counted but the grueling, agonizing work.

They were dismissed at six, and Pres raced through his shower, on his way out of the locker room before Walt had even peeled off his soaking sweats. Pres's body was tired, but he was better now than he'd been in a long time. So Ardith would chew him out tomorrow — so what? He could take anything.

"You okay?" Walt stood in front of the shower stall naked, a towel around his muscular neck.

"Hey, I'm cool, man. Don't let it worry you." He was out the door and down the hall without waiting for a response, thinking about the evening to come, about that little studio, and a nice fire, and maybe a frozen TV dinner. There she was. There was Kerry, just where she said she'd be, in front of the library door, her silvery jacket with its thin lavender strip across the yoke slung over her shoulder.

"They closed up a few minutes ago," she explained as he kissed her lightly and led the way down the stairs, toward the front door of Tarenton High. "You look beat."

"Sort of." He smiled down into her clear, brown eyes, so caring and trusting. Having Kerry around was a balm on the wound of all that had happened to him in the past few days. "Grocery shopping first, okay? You have to tell me what to buy."

She grinned, her round face lighting up. "I made a list after I finished my French vocabulary. Real healthy stuff — I hope you can take it."

"Baby, I can take it if you can." They started laughing and didn't stop until they were outside in the parking lot. The cars of the people on the team and those of a few faculty members were the only ones left. It was starting to get dark.

As Pres opened the door of his Porsche for her,

Kerry turned to him, a look of deep concern furrowing her brow. "Hey, what about this? How about if you just stop off at home and let them know where you're living? That wouldn't be so hard, would it?"

He sighed and was about to answer, when a husky voice spoke up, startling them both. "You mean you haven't told *them*? Oh, Pres, how cruel of you." Vanessa had been sitting on top of a Toyota right beside them, and they hadn't even seen her. She was like the wicked witch in a fairy tale, popping up when you least expected her.

"What do you know about it?" He peered at her suspiciously. Pres had dated Vanessa off and on for the past year. He had to admit she turned him on. She was always so willing. But he could anticipate most of her fast moves by now. He was one of the only people she couldn't con — possibly because he had a lot of the same instincts about dealing with life that she did. What saved him was that he generally used his better judgment and most of the time, he didn't stoop to being a louse.

"I just couldn't help overhearing you two chatting in the hall before practice," she shrugged casually. The wind blew her thick ebony hair out, fanlike, and picked up the collar on her loden green coat. She drew it closer around her as she smiled at Pres, running her tongue over her lips, relishing the sound of her own words. "So you moved out. You're cutting the apron strings. Bully for you. Actually, I have my eye on a place of my own for this summer. It's simply perfect. You'd love it, darling." She put a kid-gloved hand on his arm. He shook it off, but her words brought definite pictures to his mind.

"Let's get going, Kerry." He determinedly opened the door for her and, without even a backward glance at Vanessa, Kerry climbed inside. She still had trouble believing that she was dating Pres Tilford, that he liked her as much as she did him, that he wanted to hold her and kiss her and be with her. So when something like this happened, when a verbal duel was going on right in front of her, she figured the smartest thing to do was shut up and act as if she wasn't there.

"How about a lift, Pres? My dad's late tonight," Vanessa flirted. "The three of us would probably fit, if Kerry squeezed those nice round thighs in a little. You don't mind, do you, dear?"

"I. . . ." The younger girl, huddled in her silver jacket, thought it was unkind and unfair of Vanessa to discuss her weight. But she was simply not in Vanessa's league and couldn't begin to think of a suitable comeback.

"Forget it, Vannie. Not tonight." Pres walked around to the driver's side.

But Vanessa wasn't phased in the least, even though Pres had used her most-hated nickname. She stood calmly, hiding the fact that her brain was working overtime. "Kerry, do you know we all used to call your boyfriend Presto Chango? That's because he was out with a different girl practically every night. Isn't it true, Presto?"

"We better get going, Pres," Kerry said uneasily, "if we're going to make all those stops and do all those errands."

"Vanessa, you ever hear the one about sticks and stones? Names will never hurt me."

"No, of course not, Presto. But moving out of your parents' house could do some irreparable damage, couldn't it? I was just thinking — it might get you kicked off the team."

"What are you talking about?" He slammed his door and came back around to her, grabbing her by the arm.

"I'm sure my daddy knows some rule about high school kids living in proper settings." She bent down casually, giving a tug to her polished boots.

"What do you want, anyway? What's in it for you?" Pres demanded in a hushed whisper, so low that Kerry couldn't hear.

Vanessa smiled, her hot-pink lips inviting and threatening at the same time. "Well, for one thing, Presto, I want *you*. And for another, I just never believed that boys really belonged on the field or the court, unless they were in the game. They look weird jumping around, doing all those acrobatics. I mean, imagine telling somebody your boyfriend is a cheerleader. It's tacky."

"Well, I'm sorry to make things tough for you, but *I'm* going to tell everyone, so you don't have to. I'm living with my uncle, and that's got to be a perfectly all right arrangement. So don't get your hopes up, Vannie." He stalked around the car, threw himself into the driver's seat, and turned the key hard in the ignition. The Porsche pulled out like a beast that had just been released from its cage.

"Take it easy," Kerry pleaded. "I don't care

386

what that girl says. It's dumb. All I care about is you."

Pres let up his pressure on the gas pedal slightly and glanced over at her. "You're a sweetheart. Hey, you know she was lying, don't you?"

"I know what I see and feel." Kerry settled back in her seat, running her hands through her flyaway hair. "Now tell me, how do you feel about fish for dinner?"

"Fish?! Are you kidding! Fish is one of the things I left home to get away from."

Kerry giggled, and her laugh lifted his mood. "But it's brain food, Pres. You'll think better."

"Tell me about it." And yet, as they drove along, it occurred to him that he was going to have to do a lot of fast thinking tomorrow when Ardith confronted him. And once he'd told the truth, once she knew what was bugging him, what was he going to do then?

CHAPTER

Pres didn't sleep very well. After Kerry had cooked the fish for an an hour, they'd discovered that it was more inedible than it normally would have been, so they scrapped it and ate chips with their Cokes instead. Then, because she had to be home by nine on weeknights, they'd driven back to her place, and after that, he'd been alone — by himself in a strange, unfriendly place.

He mooned around the studio, wondering why James didn't have a TV, wondering what Ardith was going to do to him, wondering (only once or twice) what his parents were thinking. Then he'd opened up the sleeper-sofa and plopped down on it, willing sleep to come. He was drowsy one minute and wide awake the next. Finally, the fire went out and he huddled in the thermal blanket for the rest of the night.

There were only a few cars in the parking lot when he pulled the Porsche into his favorite spot under a large spreading maple, now bare and majestic in the morning sun. He noticed Vanessa's father's car — that guy was always up at the crack of dawn to do his laps around the track. He tried to get his daughter to join him, but she hated any kind of exercise where you couldn't show off in front of other people. Jogging was much too solitary an activity for somebody as flashy as Vanessa.

But Pres was surprised to see Vanessa standing in front of the principal's office, as he walked into the front hall of Tarenton High. She looked very pleased with herself, not like she was about to be chewed out. He was immediately suspicious. Vanessa just oozed trouble — and if it wasn't around, she'd make it. He shouldered his way down the corridor just as the principal's door opened and Mrs. Oetjen ushered Vanessa inside.

"That girl deserves twenty to life for making people miserable," he muttered to himself on his way up to Ardith's office. Down the hall, silhouetted against the glass, he could see his coach's diminutive form pacing back and forth in the tiny room. He took a deep breath and approached her inner sanctum. Then he knocked once and opened the door.

"You didn't have to pick me up." Olivia grinned happily, settling back in the seat of Walt's Jeep with a look of total satisfaction on her face.

"You're absolutely right. Want to get out and walk?" He kept his eyes on the road, but he might as well have been staring deep into Olivia's for all the attention he was paying to the other drivers around him.

"Hmm. Well, since you went to all the trouble of getting to my house so early, and since you had to get the third degree from my mother, I guess I'll stick around. Hey, watch that pothole!"

The two of them bounced in the air as the Jeep veered to the right just a bit too fast.

"That was not a third degree," Walt protested as he got back in line with the other drivers. "That was a fourth, fifth, and tenth degree rolled into one. Boy, I try to think nice thoughts about most people's parents most of the time, but Livvy, it's hard with her. What did she mean about my intellectual potential, anyway?"

"Oh, if you don't have an IQ of 947, there's clearly something wrong with you," Olivia giggled. "Not to mention your health, your looks, your moral character, and all your ancestors back to year one — and their health."

"Well, I do have a sense of humor," he said. "Is that on her list?"

"Nope. Unimportant."

"How about my charming personality?"

"No good."

"How about my phenomenal gymnastic ability?"

"Absolutely no points." Olivia gave him the thumbs-down sign.

"How about a date?" Walt said softly. "Like a movie and a burger after? Or a burger and a movie? Or two burgers and two movies?" He pulled into the school parking lot and looked at her eagerly. It was really difficult for him to just blurt things out like that.

"I'd love to." Olivia looked at him with shining eyes. "Anytime," she added, deciding that she would make it easier for him.

"Tomorrow night," he said, helping her down from the high seat. Her hand was warm and it fit perfectly in his. "So you'll have time to go through the shopping list with your mom."

They were both laughing as they walked into the hall and passed Nancy on her way to first-period math. She looked at them, then did a double take. They could tell she was trying to put some pieces together.

"Good morning, guys," she said cheerfully.

"Hi, yourself," Walt practically sang. He would have given a cheer right there in the crowded first-floor corridor if Vanessa hadn't at that moment walked out of Mrs. Oetjen's office, with the principal's arm around her shoulder. The very sight made him itch all over.

"Look who's just polished up an apple for the teacher," he said to the girls under his breath. "Now what's she up to?"

He didn't have to ask because Vanessa was only too delighted to tell. As soon as Mrs. Oetjen had turned around, the girl was rushing over to them, eager to spread her bad news as fast as possible.

"Well, it's finally happened," she began by way of greeting. "You kids are in for a real surprise. Nancy, where *did* you get that darling hat? It makes you look so . . . sweet," she growled.

"What's happened, Vanessa?" Walt demanded. "Don't tell me you're going to fulfill our wildest dreams and move to Outer Mongolia?"

She didn't smile, didn't even bother to acknowledge his remark. "Pres is off the cheerleading squad. He's on probation," she announced, "which puts all of you in a rather big pickle, doesn't it?" And with that she flounced away.

"*What* did she mean by that?" Olivia screwed up her face in annoyance. Walt just shrugged, but Nancy had one hand pressed over her eyes.

"What do you know about this?" Olivia asked when Nancy made a strange little noise way back in her throat.

"I can guess what Vanessa was discussing with Mrs. Oetjen," she said slowly. "I suppose you guys may as well know. Angie and I have been busting to tell someone since Saturday. And if everybody already knows. . . ." She thought about it for a second, then took a deep breath and spilled the beans.

"Mrs. Engborg, listen, I'm under perfectly good supervision. My Uncle James is just as much a parental authority as my parents. More — he actually cares what happens to me." Pres laughed disparagingly.

"I'm very sorry, Pres, but this is out of my control." The coach looked very businesslike and solemn. "There happens to be a school rule. Unless a student's parents have split up or there's a death in a family or there's some extenuating circumstance that would make regular family life impossible, you have to be living at home.

You cannot pick up and leave just because it suits you."

"But I've got a home. My uncle's practically a live-in chaperone," he lied. Technically, he'd only seen James once since Saturday.

"I'm not going to argue," Ardith said firmly. "Not living at home means probation. Probation means no extracurriculars. And that means you're off the team."

His face was stricken. Of course, somewhere, deep down, he'd expected this. When Vanessa had brought it up, he'd had some wacko hope that he could wangle his way around any rule. But now he'd have to face the responsibilities of moving out, and getting bumped from cheerleading was just one of them. Fleetingly, it occurred to him that he'd only tried out for the team to spite his father, so now it didn't really matter. But the point was, *now* cheering was a big part of his life.

"Ardith," he began, just as her office door opened. Mrs. Oetjen was standing there.

"You've told him." She stated this — didn't ask it.

"Yes, he knows," Ardith said. But she turned back to Pres with a softer expression on her face. "How about you solving this problem for everybody, Pres?" she asked rather kindly. "You've made your point, so now you can get on with life. All you have to do is move back home and the restriction will be withdrawn. Isn't that true, Mrs. Oetjen?"

The principal hesitated a moment, then nodded. "I suppose that would be acceptable."

393

Pres's mouth curved upward in a half smile that was vaguely reminiscent of his father's. "Not on a bet," he murmured. "I didn't do it just to prove something. I did it because I had to, don't you see? I was going nuts in that house."

"We could all see that your work has been suffering," Ardith acknowledged. "But this doesn't help matters. Pres, you know as well as I do — and the rest of the kids on the team know, too — that you're preoccupied and lacking in concentration. Nothing you do has the same energy or enthusiasm as before. And then there was the incident at Saturday's game. If you're capable of dropping a girl during a cheer, you're jeopardizing the whole squad, don't you see? As long as you persist in this self-centered behavior, you can't be a team member."

The principal walked inside and sat down in Ardith's second chair, facing Pres with a look of desperation on her face. "Your parents are extremely concerned, as you may well imagine. They'd do anything to have you come back."

For a second, Pres's cockiness faded. "You mean, they called you?"

"Well, naturally. They wanted to know if you'd turned up in school yesterday. When I assured them you were here, they seemed rather surprised, but pleased. At that point, they begged me not to tell anyone, which is why Mrs. Engborg didn't know at your practice in the afternoon. I take it they've been talking to your uncle every day, without satisfaction."

Pres started to laugh. It began as a snort and amplified to a roar. The tiny office shook with his sound. The two women glared at him, incredulous. "Don't you see?" he gasped when he finally caught his breath. "This is exactly what's so screwy! They never talk to *me* — *never*. They go to everybody else and talk *about* me! Geez." He thought about the phone in Uncle James's studio, how he'd sat next to it for an hour the previous night, hoping it would ring.

"They are clearly having some difficulties expressing themselves, Pres, but perhaps, you would, too, if you were the stricken parent instead of the rebellious child."

He stood up, his shoulders squared off as if for battle. "Well, I'm not giving in or giving up. You can do whatever you want to me. I have a place to stay and it suits me fine. And as for cheerleading," he spat the word at Ardith, "you can get yourself another guy. Because I don't need it — or you." With that, he stomped out, feeling a lot less sure of himself than he wanted to. He'd be late to math on top of everything — what a bummer. His only satisfaction right now was in imagining how burned his father must be. What he wouldn't give to see the look on Preston Tilford II's face!

Donny Parrish followed Mary Ellen down the cafeteria line, picking dishes at random. He was too busy staring at the luscious long legs in front of him, admiring the way they neatly curved upward to the thighs and small of her back. Mary Ellen sure was something! And that hair — long silk he could run his fingers through endlessly, perfect strands that curled around his giant

hands whenever he wanted them to. Yeah, come
to think of it, he was a lucky guy. Dating a girl
who wasn't only gorgeous, but who really had it
together. Sometimes she was a little hard to
handle, because she always expected more than
she got, but he was used to her moods by now.
They were kind of cute, in a way.

"Say, you must be starving." Mary Ellen
laughed, her brilliant smile gleaming at him.

"Huh?" Donny snapped out of his trance and
looked directly at her. "What do you mean?"

"I know being the captain of Tarenton's basketball team is a huge job and you work up a
terrible appetite and everything, but *four* ham
and cheese sandwiches for lunch on top of chili
seems like overkill to me."

"Oh, yeah. I forgot. Must be a little fever left
from my flu or something." He quickly put three
of the sandwiches back, feeling dumb and embarrassed. He hated being shown up — it just
wasn't right for someone to point out his mistakes — even if it was Mary Ellen, the most
desirable girl in school doing it.

Mary Ellen had only picked a salad herself.
Dieting had nothing to do with her choice — the
problem was financial. Of course she brown-
bagged it every day, to save money, but when
Donny asked her to eat lunch with him, she
simply couldn't drag out a homemade peanut
butter and jelly and eat it with any kind of grace.
So she'd scrimp on something else that week.

As they walked to the cashier's station and
paid, Mary Ellen caught a glimpse of a dark head
at the other end of the line. Her face turned red

as he spotted her. Patrick! *Oh please*, she prayed silently, *let him just leave us alone. I can't deal with him and Donny at the same time.*

But of course, as soon as they had found their seats and Donny had gallantly pulled out a chair for her, nuzzling her neck and shoulders as he sat beside her, Patrick went into action. Leaving his tray with the cashier, he took a high-flying leap in the air and hurdled the counter, landing on both knees only inches from Mary Ellen. As the kids around them cheered at his acrobatic antics, he steadied himself with a hand on her leg. She reacted immediately when he touched her.

"This seat taken?" he asked Donny casually with a wink up at Mary Ellen.

Donny weighed the alternatives before speaking. "Well, actually, some of the guys from the team said they'd join us. . . ."

"They're not here yet, though. Guess it'll be okay. I'll eat fast. I'm not that hungry today — for *food*, that is," he added meaningfully to Mary Ellen.

Donny shrugged angrily and turned to his chili, as Patrick went to retrieve his tray.

"Donny," Mary Ellen said quickly, "he doesn't have to eat with us, you know. Just tell him to get lost."

"Well, why don't *you* tell him?" Donny asked brusquely, his wholesome, all-American face suddenly turning mean. "You're the one who knows him so well."

"Donny, you sound like you're jealous," Mary Ellen forced a casual laugh. "And that's perfectly ridiculous." She was lying, of course. Donny's jealousy was perfectly justified. All Patrick had to do was sit down next to her and her stomach would whirl around like a top. She dug into her salad, hoping to be finished by the time Patrick got back.

But it was Walt and Angie who made it to their table first, with Olivia bringing up the rear. The three of them looked like survivors of a shipwreck.

"Can we sit down?" Angie asked hopelessly, taking the chair Patrick had reserved without waiting for a response.

Walt nodded a perfunctory hello to Donny, then took two chairs for Olivia and himself. "Nancy's coming over later. She had a hot and heavy session with a frog in bio lab. Right before lunch, too. Yuk." He wrinkled his nose.

"Cut the jokes, Walt." Angie just kept looking at Mary Ellen as if she was about to burst into tears.

"What *is* it with all of you?" Mary Ellen put down her fork, suddenly forgetting about Donny and Patrick and her elaborate juggling act with the two of them.

"I knew she hadn't heard yet," Olivia sighed.

"It's bad, Melon," Angie shook her head, forgetting how much Mary Ellen hated that nickname. "But I better just blurt it out. Pres has been kicked off the cheerleading squad, as of this morning. It's official."

"You're crazy!" Mary Ellen looked at each one of them, but their eyes all said the same thing.

"What's going on?" Donny asked eagerly, but

no one paid the slightest attention to him.

"Yeah, what *is* going on?" Patrick asked as he strode back toward them with his tray, and squeezed a chair in between Olivia and Mary Ellen. He was so close, their knees bumped under the table. "All of you look like death warmed over."

"You remember how awful Pres was at the game Saturday," Olivia went on to Mary Ellen, completely ignoring Patrick as well as Donny. "Turns out he was going through some real hard times at home, so he just moved out. His uncle has some studio he's staying in, but he's not supposed to, according to school rules. So Mrs. Oetjen put him on probation until he moves back home."

"Which, rumor has it, he's not about to do," Walt continued. "He was pretty hard on Ardith — told her to look for some other cheerleader. He never was awfully gung ho about getting on the team. Remember how I had to pressure him into it?"

Mary Ellen sat there stunned, hardly moving, as the information sank in. She was ashamed to realize that her first reaction was annoyance that she hadn't found out first. After all, she was the captain of the squad. And on top of that, she'd dated Pres. Why couldn't he have told her? That little Kerry must know, she thought suddenly, recalling the scene outside the gym the previous night. That's what they were talking about! That's why they looked so worried.

"Well, what are we going to do?" she asked at last. "It's absurd to think that some other guy could take over for Pres at this stage. I mean, we've got one game this weekend, and from then on till the end of the season we're booked solid. How can somebody come in cold and learn all our routines?"

Donny, feeling totally left out, decided to contribute something to the conversation. "Aw, it's not like putting in a new shooter on the basketball team. Anyone can learn a few high kicks and cheers."

The other four just glared at him. Patrick laughed aloud. "Oh, boy, you've done it now!" he guffawed at the basketball star. He turned to Mary Ellen. "I think you should lodge a protest with Mrs. Oetjen and get Pres back."

"Olivia and I already tried that, Patrick," Walt sighed. "Talking to that woman is like talking to a rock."

"Oh, how could Pres *do* this to us!" Angie wailed as Nancy walked over, looking as grim as the rest of them. She was holding her food tray at arm's length from her body.

"Well, at last! There you are," Walt nodded, pulling over a chair for her. "Why are you holding your tray like that?"

"Because I stink of embalmed frog, that's why. I don't want to get too close. I've washed my hands three times, and I still feel that slime. One of you is going to have to feed me so I don't get my hands near my mouth. What have we decided about Pres?" she asked in the same breath.

Donny made a big show of pushing back his chair and clearing his throat. "I'm done with lunch, Mary Ellen, and since you're so busy over here, I think I'll take a walk. See you later, okay?" He stood there for a minute, hoping she'd tell him to stay, hoping Patrick would take the hint and leave, but all he got was a shrug.

"Sure. Later, Donny." She couldn't be bothered keeping up a front, couldn't even bother to smile.

As soon as Donny'd walked over to the tray return, Mary Ellen felt Patrick's arm slip around her. "Hey, it's not so bad," he whispered soothingly in her ear. "You kids are wonderful at improvising things. Just cut out all Pres's parts and work around the holes. It'll look great — you'll see."

"It'll look dumb!" Angie proclaimed. "He does all the big lifts! It's all coordinated, don't you see? And we're going to look really awful, going up against Muskeagtown's Twinkling Twelve on Saturday, staggering around like we don't know what's what."

Muskeagtown's twelve Varsity cheerleaders were something to see. They had a graceful, ballet style that caught the eye and flowed like honey over a crowd. Mary Ellen had to admit Angie was right. Five of them improvising against the Muskeagtown squad doing their finely honed steps would spell disaster.

"All right, listen, here's the plan. We'll find a new guy. The school is full of guys who want to fool around with four girls." Mary Ellen said firmly. "A couple of us will work with him every minute, day and night. We'll drill him till he's perfect. But Ardith's going to have to make it clear to him that he's only a temp. In the meantime, the rest of us will work on Pres. He's got to come back," she said despairingly, not really knowing whether she wanted him back because he was good for the team or because someday, somehow, he might be good for her.

She hadn't given up hope that one day their relationship would really click and together, they'd waltz off out of this podunk town forever. Pres had it all: looks, brains, wealth, and the proper attitude about taking what was his from life. Moving out on his folks proved that beyond a doubt.

"Well, we'll try it." Walt nodded, getting up as the next bell rang and everyone started for the tray return. "But we're going to need an awful lot of luck to get by this Saturday."

"I'm willing to work hard if you can find another guy who is, too," Olivia said staunchly.

"Me, too," Nancy agreed.

"Hey," Angie said softly. They all stopped where they were and looked at her. "What about Pres? He must be feeling absolutely awful." She couldn't help but relate to this. She was still seeing Marc everywhere, hearing his voice, smelling his clean, starched shirts, no matter how hard she tried to concentrate on forgetting him. She knew all too well how personal problems could blot out everything else in life.

"Pres is tough," Patrick assured her, his hand reaching for Mary Ellen's as they started out the cafeteria door. "He'll get by."

"We'll all get by," Angie agreed. "The question is, what'll it cost us?"

No one had an answer for that.

CHAPTER

Five rather disgruntled cheerleaders lay sprawled on the gym mats, waiting. Ardith usually beat them to it, and was generally warming up as they arrived, but today she was closeted in her office, and there was someone in there with her. The new guy, whom she had found.

"Did you see Pres today?" Angie stretched her long, lean legs out on the floor in front of her, pulling down the bottoms of her forest green sweat pants. "He hardly even nodded at me when I passed him in the hall this afternoon. He looks just awful."

"Mr. Sanders called on him in history and he drew a blank," Nancy offered. "Either that, or he was thinking of something else."

"How could he not be?" Mary Ellen demanded. Her hair was done in intricate braids, overlapping and crisscrossing on top of her head. That generally made her feel queenlike, but today, her head felt heavy and overloaded. Whether it was the braids or her thoughts, she didn't feel up to a strenuous practice. "I don't know — this whole thing is a terrible mess."

"The only thing worse is if Ardith decides to replace Pres with Vanessa," Nancy muttered. "Seeing as how she knows all the cheers already, I mean."

"But . . . oh, come *on!*" Walt practically yelled. "It's gonna be a guy. She couldn't do that to us — she wouldn't!"

"She wouldn't do it to herself," Angie giggled. "I think Ardith hates Vanessa almost as much as we do."

But there was no more time for gossip, because the coach's door opened and she marched out briskly, her maroon, velour sweat suit a beacon in the tan and gray gym. Behind her was a kid about her size with a mop of curly black hair and prominent high cheekbones, above which black eyes looked wary and cautious.

"Oh, no!" Nancy shut her eyes tight and hugged her knees to her chest. "Not him. Why did it have to be him?"

"Who is he?" Walt whispered.

"Guys, this is Josh Breitman," Ardith volunteered. "I guess you all know each other, at least by sight. Josh is a senior, a very fine gymnast, and a really quick study," Ardith rushed on. "He understands that we've got an emergency here, and he's willing to give his all to work with us. He feels sure he'll be ready by Saturday's game, and I have complete confidence in him." She glared at them all. "That means I have confidence

404

in you five to make things easier for him."

"Hi, everyone." Josh's voice was extremely deep, a rumble that came from down in his chest. "Hi, Nancy. How're you doing?"

Nancy just nodded. She looked as if someone had just stepped on her toes during a routine. Angie gave her a nudge in the ribs, but she didn't respond.

"So, let's get going," Ardith suggested. "Mary Ellen, would you please start the warm-up. And talk as you go — I want Josh to get everything the first time, if possible." She took a seat facing them on the mat that lay in front of the mirror. The others straggled to their feet and took their places in front of her. She reached over and turned on the tape recorder. A Stones number blasted off the gym walls.

"Okay," Mary Ellen willed herself to seem enthusiastic and energetic, but she couldn't stop thinking about Pres. He should have been there with them. He should have at least sought them out earlier in the day to talk about things. But that was Pres all over — he had to be himself, and insist he was right about it at the same time.

"Arms overhead, and swing your torso, right and left and keep it going!" she shouted, her mind a zillion miles away. Luckily, she knew the warm-up so well she didn't have to think about it. Her hips and torso swung and swiveled, her toes arched and flexed on command. While her body worked, the rest of her was free to consider what she really wanted to do about this lousy situation. As captain of the squad, she felt it was her duty to get things back in shape. Of course, she had to admit to herself as she caught a glimpse of Josh working behind her in the mirror, he was pretty good. Nice relaxed movements, good tempo, and a smile on his face. But what was Nancy all bummed out about? She looked as if she'd rather be doing calculus.

"Walt, you take over," Ardith said after about twenty minutes, when all the kids were sweating profusely. "Let's work on the minitramp for a while, get in some jumps and leaps. From there, we'll go to ground work and do cartwheels and walkovers. Josh, you shouldn't have any trouble with this part — it's just like gymnastics class."

"Sure, Mrs. Engborg. No problem," he said confidently.

Walt led the group in a series of increasingly complex maneuvers on the minitramp, stuff that was easy for him and Olivia, the most athletic of the team. Mary Ellen and Angie, although not naturally adapted to difficult moves, performed them flawlessly because of their years of practice. Only Nancy still had trouble with this part of the workout, and today her faults seemed magnified ten times over. When she missed her third doubleback somersault on the tramp, it was Josh who stopped the next person in line from going on.

"Ah, do you mind if I just give you a couple of pointers, Nance? If you spot on that wall over there, and be sure to tuck your knees as you're in the air, you can't help but go over. It's a cinch! Watch me." And with that, he leapt high and flew through the air, his body becoming a tight ball of energy as it curled into itself and spun backwards not two, but three times. The others gasped. Nancy grimaced.

"Now you try it," he offered, a cocky smile on his broad face.

"No thanks. I couldn't begin to duplicate that." She was so curt with him, even Ardith looked up in surprise. Nancy was usually happy to get help from anyone who'd offer it.

"Enough of that for today. Let's work on the cheers. Josh has to know the most basic by Saturday. Mary Ellen, let's go over the 'Tiger,' 'Victory,' and 'Beat 'Em' cheers this afternoon. We don't want to overwhelm you, Josh, but there's a lot to learn."

"Hey, that's fine with me," Josh said with a shrug. "I'm having a ball. This is fun."

Angie distinctly heard Nancy mutter, "I'm glad *you* think so," and, while Mary Ellen was showing Josh where to stand, gave Nancy a sideways kick in the ankle.

"Straighten up, will you?" Angie hissed. "Whatever's bothering you about him will have to wait."

Nancy took her place, which happened to be between Walt and Josh, and stood facing the mirror as if it was her executioner.

"Now," Ardith instructed, "the cheer begins with you two guys holding Nancy under the arms. On the second line, we all start high kicks, and you lift her while she's kicking and help her to flip over backwards. Got it? Let's try it."

The six of them just couldn't get it together. Whether it was the mood of despair, the awkwardness of having a newcomer, or Nancy's terrible attitude, the thing would not gel, no matter how many times they tried it. They went from one cheer to the next, and although Josh seemed to be picking up the steps easily, the overall effect was one of chaos. When the clock on the far wall hit six, Ardith stopped them with a sigh.

"All right, let's quit, shall we? Look, kids, we really don't have a lot of time. Tomorrow, I want to see you warmed up and ready to go by three-thirty, and then we'll work on the cheers themselves all afternoon. But you have to concentrate — *you* have to make it happen. If any of you have any thoughts about this not working, then it won't." She was looking directly at Nancy. "So leave your little concerns and big problems home tomorrow, will you?" She turned on her heel and swiftly left the room, and the kids breathed a sigh of relief. One by one, they started toward the showers. Josh looked at Nancy as she passed him at the door, but she didn't look back. She marched stolidly down the hall and followed Mary Ellen into the locker room.

"Now," Angie asked Nancy when the four girls were alone, stripping out of their clothes, "would you care to explain?"

Mary Ellen and Olivia were both staring at Nancy. There was no way she could avoid their annoyed and curious eyes.

"Josh Breitman is the son of my parents' best friends," she moaned.

"So?" Olivia was unyielding. "What does that have to do with anything?"

"Ever since we moved to Tarenton, they've been after me to date him. At family events, the

408

Breitmans always show up, and there's Josh. At summer barbecues, there's Josh. I mean, it should be clear to everyone by now that we're not interested in each other and never will be. But they keep pushing it!"

"Why?" Mary Ellen stuck a shower cap over her gleaming hair and threw a towel over her elegant white shoulder. "I mean, if it's not love at first sight — or second, or tenth — why bother?"

"Because, don't you see?" Nancy ran her hands through her thick, dark hair. "He's a nice Jewish boy. He's smart. He's probably going to get into Harvard. He's everything they ever wanted for me. Ugh!"

Angie couldn't help but laugh, although she felt for her friend. "But what's he like as a person?" she demanded.

"Oh, you know, conceited, stuck on himself."

"I didn't see that in him today." Olivia shrugged. "I suppose he could have been nervous and all, it being his first day, but —"

"Josh Breitman is never nervous. He's the cockiest kid I ever met," Nancy said decisively. "You saw that demonstration on the minitramp when I botched it. You don't call that nerve?"

"He was just trying to help," Angie offered. Then she shook her head and sat next to Nancy on the wooden bench. "Look, no matter how you felt about him in the past, you have to ditch it for now. What's important is getting us all to work like a team, and we'll never manage that if you're set on keeping up this feud, right?"

"Promise you'll try," Olivia begged her. "And who knows, you might get to like him after all."

Nancy wrinkled her face. "You've got to be kidding."

"Just *try*!" Mary Ellen insisted. "Pretend it's. . . ." She nearly said Ben Adamson and caught herself just in time. "Pretend it's your knight in shining armor."

"Pretend it's Pres," Angie said quietly. The others were suddenly silent, each of them realizing that, for all their complaining and being annoyed, they missed him. They knew he must be suffering, too. He'd just been given notice that he no longer belonged, and that had to be devastating to anyone's ego, let alone his. And just when he'd taken on all his own personal demons, he had to assume responsibility for splitting up the team, too.

"I'll try," Nancy agreed. "But it's not going to be easy." She thrust her face into her hands and shook her head in misery. "I've been so nice to people lately — I even helped some little kids cross a street last night. I don't deserve this! And the worst part is, my parents will find out and then they'll start a total campaign. 'Elect Josh Breitman Boyfriend of the Year.' Yuk!"

The other girls laughed, but tenderly. None of them could really make fun of Nancy's plight. Aside from the fact that they liked her a lot, every one of them knew that it could have been them. When it came to matters of the heart, nobody escaped.

As Mary Ellen showered and changed, she kept relating Nancy's problem to her own. She'd never stand for it if someone came along and designated the one boy for her. If her father put his foot down and said, all right, it's Pres Tilford and that's it, or it's Donny Parrish and I don't want to hear any guff about it, she'd undoubtedly rebel and lose interest in both of them. In India, she remembered, they still had arranged marriages. Sometimes, the poor bride didn't even see the groom until their wedding day! It was positively weird!

She threw on her blackwatch-plaid skirt and high-necked white blouse, tucked up the few wheat-colored tendrils that had fallen out of place, and raced out of the locker room. Donny hated it when she kept him waiting, and his practice was generally over before hers. Naturally, he showered and was ready in no time.

She was halfway down the corridor when she felt a tug on her arm. Suddenly she was being whirled around, and she felt giddy even before she saw the tall shape clearly before her.

"Let me take you home tonight," Patrick breathed. He was wearing his white coveralls, the uniform he always wore when he was working. His wide mouth was smiling gently, and she could feel the heat behind his offer.

"I . . . someone's waiting for me. In the parking lot," she answered needlessly, her voice cracking. No, she couldn't walk out there with him! He'd probably even parked his garbage truck somewhere near Donny's Chevy — on purpose, to embarrass her!

"Let him wait. I know you want to." Patrick didn't need to say more. He pulled her close against him. His mouth hovered over hers, threatening and tantalizing, both at once. Nobody was around. Mary Ellen could hear only the distant sound of the floor waxer, as the janitor hummed away down the corridor, going in the opposite direction. No one would see them, and how she wanted to kiss those full, warm lips!

"Listen, Patrick, this is just impossible." She squirmed slightly in his grasp, but not enough to sever their delicious contact. "When are you going to get the message?"

"I've got the message. Sweetie, what you say and what you mean are two different things entirely. You know it as well as I do." And then he kissed her, deliberately and thoroughly, leaving no room for doubt as to how he felt and what he wanted. She clung to him hopelessly, realizing she was lost and hating herself for it.

She *did* care about Patrick, and that was the awful part. Her heart was his, and had been for a long time. It was just her stupid sense of propriety, of what she pictured for herself further along the road, that stopped her from giving in entirely. He was never going to change, never going to want more than his lucrative garbage route and a nice house in Tarenton and a comfortable suburban life. She couldn't settle for that! She just wouldn't!

"I've got to go," she muttered, wrenching away. Once she broke out of his embrace, she could breathe again, but it was still hard to think.

"Run if you want to." He shrugged, looking very pleased with himself. "I have all the time in the world, and believe me, babe, I've got longer legs. This race is an open and shut case." And then, to her amazement, *he* walked away from her, whistling a silly little tune as he swaggered toward the stairwell. *Guys*, honestly!

As she ran to the parking lot, she still tingled everywhere Pat had touched her. And when Donny blew the horn at her, she hardly heard it. She walked toward his car dreamily, the evening breeze taking her neat hairdo and adding its own finishing touches. Like her feelings, she thought as she let the wind carry the blonde strands wherever it would, she just couldn't stop them.

"Your lipstick's smeared," Donny said when he saw her.

"And I'm late, don't tell me." She gave him a peck on the cheek, self-consciously dabbing at the pink stain she left there. Patrick had most of it, of course, and he probably hadn't bothered to wipe it off. Was there something wrong with her that she could behave this way with two different boys within minutes of each other? Not that she'd done anything really reprehensible, but still. . . .

"There's that guy with the garbage again," Donny muttered, as he turned on his headlights and pulled out of the parking lot. "He sure gets around," he laughed. "Well, forget about that creep. How was your day?" He reached for her hand, and she let him take it, but there was very little enthusiasm in her response. She wanted Donny to be *it*, to be the one she not only was proud to be seen with, but also the one who made her stop in her tracks, made her breathless with excitement. Unfortunately, it wasn't like that with them. They dated, they had stuff to talk about, they were both pretty big socially at school, and that was all.

Mary Ellen sat beside him in silence on the way home. Would her choices be any easier if she weren't involved with any boys at all, if she only had herself to depend on for emotional support? No, things would be miserable without guys. But why did they have to make everything so messy? She was beginning to think that an arranged marriage might not be so stupid after all. At least it would take the confusion out of her life!

Pres left school early. There was nothing to be gained by hanging around, and Kerry had a drama society meeting till late, so he might as well split. If he went to the library and waited for her, he'd probably run into the guys from the team coming down from practice, and that was the last thing he wanted. Boy, what a lousy deal — to toss him out on his ear without a day's warning, without so much as an afternoon's detention! And they'd even gone behind his back and gotten a replacement already — some kid, some senior who measured about five-foot-zero, according to Vanessa, who'd wasted no time in telling him. What a bummer!

He got in the car and drove, covering the few miles of the town a couple of times before heading out toward Narrow Brook Lake. He found himself winding around back into town, and suddenly, he was terribly hungry. There was nothing that would taste as good right now as a burger and fries, washed down with a chocolate milkshake. The problem was where to go. If he stopped at Pete's, the whole crowd would be there. Too early for the team, but the whole rest of his class'd be there, practically. And they'd all be talking about him. How could he show his face there? With Kerry, he might have considered it. But alone, forget it.

Nowhere to go. Nothing to do. The idea of a warmed-up TV dinner at James's studio was more than he could take. He drove back to school and sat in the parking lot again, hoping something would happen. Anything.

"Isn't that Pres?" Olivia peered out of the Jeep's windshield in the gathering dark. "What's he doing back here?"

"Waiting for us, maybe?" Walt offered. He had his arm around her, and was feeling pretty mellow. His limbs were tired and all stretched out from the difficult practice, and had been burnished to a fine glow in the hot shower. And he was even warmer because of the presence of the small, delicate girl beside him.

"You want to go talk to him?" Olivia had her hand on the door handle, but Walt leaned over and snapped the lock.

"Not really. I'd rather kiss you."

She smiled into the dark, but shook her head slightly. "I want to talk first. What do you think of the new guy?"

"He's okay. I guess he could even work out." Walt shrugged. "But he'll never be part of the team." He was disappointed, longing for a kiss, but figured it could wait if it had to. Immediate gratification was nice, but not always practical.

"You mean he's a hog for his own glory, right?" she grinned. "A John McEnroe type?"

"Like some people are part of the chorus, but others just have to sing the solo." Walt laughed and thumped the steering wheel. "Listen to me! Making like Pres is some kind of self-sacrificing, lovable pushover."

"Like you?" Olivia teased, unsnapping the lock behind her.

"Exactly." Walt snapped the lock again. "Okay, we've talked. Come here, you beautiful, smart, wonderful girl."

"I want to see Pres," Olivia said decisively. "That doesn't mean I don't want to see you." She kissed him lightly, then thought better of it and kissed him again, this time lingeringly and happily. "I hate making out in cars," she grumbled as she dodged his hands and undid the lock, slipping out of the Jeep like a shadow. "Come on!"

Walt lumbered behind her, savoring his good fortune. She was a girl who said what she meant, at least. And she meant she wanted to be with him, which was the best part of all.

"Pres!" Olivia yelled. "Hey, it's us!"

Pres rolled down the window of the Porsche, half delighted and half embarrassed to have been spotted. "How's it goin'?" he asked casually, as if today had been a day like any other and he was just sitting there, waiting for the light to change.

"We missed you," Walt answered. "We want you back, man."

"Sure. Tell it to the judge."

"But you could move back with your folks and solve the whole thing," Olivia begged. "Believe me, I'm an expert when it comes to running-away-from-home schemes. I've got so many plots to escape my mother's clutches, I could write a Gothic novel. But I don't act on them because there are things I want more — like cheering. Can we come inside? It's getting cold."

"Be my guest," Pres shrugged, opening the door on the passenger side, and watched his two ex-teammates climb in. And then he noticed that Walt had his arm around Olivia and he felt even more miserable than he had a few minutes ago.

"What's the deal?" Walt asked him. "Just tell us why."

"I want to be free, man," Pres said in a muffled tone. "That's the bottom line. I'm sorry to mess you guys up, but you've got somebody else, right? Hey, I was just another gorgeous body. You'll get over me."

"Not true." Olivia's stern, heart-shaped face was shaded with a variety of emotions. "You were one of us."

Pres's flippant words died in his throat. He sat there, his hands gripping the steering wheel, until finally Walt and Olivia got out of the car and walked away.

CHAPTER

6

The Tarenton games were always well attended, but this one was packed. There were no seats at all left in the gym bleachers, and the fans who were determined to get in had jammed themselves along the rear doors of the gym.

"It would have to be a full house our first time out," Angie mumbled, adjusting the pleats of her cheering skirt. There had been a last-minute panic about Josh's uniform, because, of course, he was too short to fit into Pres's. But Rose Poletti came to the rescue when her daughter begged her, quickly altering an extra pair of scarlet pants with the white stripe down the seams as well as the white sweater with the scarlet "T" for Josh. He looked great, Angie thought.

Nancy was jumping rope in the corner of the practice room, her white pleats unfolding and overlapping against the scarlet skirt every time she went up and down. It had been a grueling week, and her spirits were no better than they had been on Tuesday, when this whole thing started.

On Wednesday, during practice, Josh had held her in the air just a minute too long and later, had hung around so that he could meet her at her car. On Thursday, he'd stuffed a silly panda bear in her locker with a note attached that read, "I'm really not so hard to bear." On Friday, he'd come up to her at lunchtime and demanded to be allowed to sit with her. What could she do? She just couldn't figure out why he was going to such lengths to spend time with a girl he'd purposely shunned for the past year and a half.

Olivia and Walt sat together at Nancy's feet, doing two-person stretches. They looked kind of funny holding hands with their feet spread wide, rocking back and forth like one big seesaw, Olivia's short legs coming only to Walt's muscular calves, but they seemed to be having a wonderful time. Mary Ellen glanced over at them from her backbend and considered them. They were going home together every night now, and they seemed to appear and disappear at exactly the same moment. Was it possible? Little Olivia and big clown Walt?

"Well, what are you all standing around for?" Ardith bustled into the room like a whirlwind, her hair tousled, as though she'd been running her fingers through it for the past hour. "It's late, kids. I know you can do it. Just concentrate on your moves and remember what game you're cheering for. Whatever you do, don't yell for any touchdowns."

She laughed at her feeble attempt at a joke.

Tarenton was the only school in the district whose football and basketball seasons overlapped. This caused occasional upsets among the players who were on both teams, and perennial confusion among the fans. "Josh, how are you feeling? You think you can do it?" Ardith ran her sentences together to save time.

"Great. Never been better." Stealthily, he maneuvered himself over to Nancy and jumped into her next turn of the rope. She stopped moving abruptly and they bumped heads.

"I'll line us up, then," Mary Ellen suggested. She patted her golden hair and, catching a glimpse of her perfect profile in the glass panel of the door, she decided she was ready. With determined steps, she led the way toward the rear gym door. The others, bouncing on their toes, were right behind her.

"And one, and two. . . ." She began the cheer before opening the door. This was one the whole crowd knew, so it didn't matter if they heard every word clearly.

"We're here for you!
And three and four,
Let's mop up the floor!
And five and six,
Just watch our tricks!
Seven, eight, nine,
Stayin' right on line!
Tarenton — you're a ten!
Yay!"

Mary Ellen kept a close eye on Josh as he

cartwheeled his way to the center of the floor and the others flipped or somersaulted around him, but she really didn't have to. The guy knew what he was doing. He was working into the routine as though he had done it a thousand times, and had even made it his own. Pres, the great cartwheeler of all times, had a smooth, even pattern to his turns, but Josh seemed to bounce all the time. It was kind of cute.

As Mary Ellen looked up from her place, a wide smile on her lovely face, the cheer springing from her throat fully and happily, she knew the crowd loved her. It was times like this that fulfilled her and made her dissatisfied all at once. Cheering gave her a tantalizing taste of what it might be like when she was a model, coming down that runway to the applause of every top designer in New York. It made her feel as if she was riding a swing, being pushed higher and faster. It was like delirium, like a fever.

She came out of a fast spin into Walt's waiting arms and held a second, her eyes taking in the second row of the bleachers. For an instant, the smile faded from her face. There were Pres and Kerry, holding hands, looking on in grim anticipation. She knew that scowl of his all too well. It must be eating him alive to be here and not be with them, to have to sit on the sidelines.

She spun again and now she was facing Patrick, who was grinning directly at her with a really ridiculous expression on his face. He did look terrific today. When he stood up to cheer the cheerleaders, she couldn't help but notice his sharp Fair Isle vest over the starched white

shirt and those neat gray cords. The guy really
had it all together, she sighed to herself as she
took a turn away from Walt and Angie and led
the way, clapping and yelling, toward the door
where the Tarenton basketball team was strain-
ing to burst through.

> "Tarenton,
> In the sun!
> Tarenton,
> You're the one!
> Son of a gun!
> Ready to run!
> Beat 'em! Beat 'em! Yay!"

The "Beat 'Em" cheer was nearly drowned
out by the sound of the crowd, welcoming each
player to the floor. As Donny passed Mary
Ellen, he grabbed her hand for a second, but let
go so quickly that no one noticed. The rest of
his team followed him, ready for a victory, tast-
ing the win they knew was nearly theirs.

The Muskeagtown Maulers ran out next, their
own cheering team trying to outdo Tarenton's —
in volume if nothing else. They had some good
players, but the Tarenton Wolves were generally
considered to be the best team in the district,
running neck and neck with Garrison High. With
Donny Parrish, their power forward, and Hank
Vreewright, the star center, they couldn't miss
tonight.

The two teams lined up as the cheerleaders
took their places on the sidelines, stepping over
the fans who crowded the aisles. The referee

threw the ball up between the two centers and Hank tapped it first. The game was on.

The first half was wild, the score hovering at a tie the entire time. One of the Muskeagtown shooters was really hot tonight, which put Donny on his toes. Nearly every time he captured the ball and dribbled it down the floor, he eluded the defense and lined himself up for the best shot. If he couldn't shoot, he'd pass, but you could tell it was costing him something to give the ball away.

"These guys are terrific," Josh whispered to Nancy as they stood working the crowd, giving the "Growl, Wolves, Growl!" cheer.

"Haven't you ever seen a basketball game before?" she asked sarcastically.

"Not with you. My eyes have been opened to all sorts of new things," he grinned. Nancy looked at the ceiling and took Mary Ellen's cue for the "Victory" cheer.

But at that moment, something seemed to distract Donny, just as he was about to shoot. The six-foot-seven Muskeagtown center easily knocked the ball from his hand and passed it downcourt to one of his open teammates. The Muskeagtown guard made a long shot, a three-pointer, and that wrapped up the first half of the game. The visiting team's cheerleaders went wild. They were winning.

Mary Ellen started the halftime routines with less than the gung-ho spirit the squad needed. Josh was the only one who was still bouncing, and even Angie's straddle jumps lacked oomph. They were all super-aware of Pres, now sitting glumly, now getting up to shake a fist, or make a face, or both. It was like having Big Brother watching.

"C'mon, Donny," Mary Ellen whispered, as they retreated for the second half of the game. "Show 'em what's what."

But Donny wasn't concentrating. It was evident from the beginning, when he simply stopped guarding his Muskeagtown opposite and started watching something — or someone — in the bleachers.

"What is he *doing*?" Olivia asked in a panic, even though it was strictly forbidden to talk at games. Nothing was supposed to distract them from what was happening on the court. "Donny never lets anything get in the way of a win."

Mary Ellen had known all along; actually, she'd seen the problem coming before Donny did. Every time she moved, every cheer she led, Patrick got up and started blowing kisses at her.

"Donny, don't look at him," she pleaded under her breath. It was too late, though. As the clock ran down to almost nothing, he fouled, and then, unbelievably, fouled again. When the ball finally was back in play, he let Muskeagtown make three baskets in a row. His teammates were looking at him as though they wanted to kill. Ahead 64-59, Muskeagtown simply ran out the clock, practically rubbing Tarenton's nose in it, to win the game.

The Muskeagtown cheerleaders filed onto the court in triumph several seconds later, doing a splashy windup routine that had at least half the crowd on their feet. The Tarenton kids and their parents looked angry and disappointed as they made their way out of the gym, and the cheerleaders could scarcely wait to disappear. Mary Ellen didn't want to see Donny, didn't want to get anywhere near him. It was so embarrassing — she knew the whole awful thing was her fault.

She passed Vanessa, just climbing down from the bleachers, and looked the other way. But Donny was coming right toward her, and suddently she felt trapped — nowhere to run.

"Well, that was *quite* a performance, Mr. Parrish," Vanessa cooed at Donny, who was dripping with sweat, his shoulders hunched under the thin towel his coach had thrown at him. "Congratulations! You just about lost that game single-handedly." She positively oozed venom.

"Shut up, Vanessa," Mary Ellen said, for some reason jumping to Donny's defense.

"Now why do you think we lost, Melon?" Vanessa sounded really interested. "Do you have any idea?" With that, she walked away, head held high. Mary Ellen would have liked nothing better than to wipe that smirk off her face, but Donny stopped her.

"Look," he said softly. "I know I didn't do my best, and I feel rotten about it, but how could I concentrate with what was going on out there? This has to stop. Did you see that guy, making a fool of himself over you? It was disgusting."

"Donny, get dressed. We'll talk about this some other time." She wanted to be furious with him for losing, but some part of her felt oddly flattered. She meant more to him than the game! His feelings for her were that strong!

"No, I want to talk about it *now*. That bozo thinks he owns you, and you've got to set him straight."

"That's not true. Patrick and I —"

"Used to have something going."

"That's a lie!" she fumed. "We never did. I never let him hope that —"

"Hey, he wouldn't behave that way if you didn't!" Donny was yelling now, but they were alone in the gym, so it didn't matter. Donny's usually placid features were distorted with rage, and he had that fierce, powerful look he sometimes got when an opponent on the court handed him a real challenge. "Mary Ellen, I can't take this being played off against another guy. You better make up your mind. One or the other — not both of us. That's all I have to say." He stalked away from her, his long legs striding swiftly to the gym door and out into the corridor.

Slowly, Mary Ellen sank down on the nearest bleacher and put her head in her hands. He was right, of course. If she wasn't leading Patrick on, she certainly wasn't turning him off. And it was Donny she wanted to be with. Wasn't it? Of course, it had to be. He was captain of the basketball team, tall, handsome, lived in a lovely home near the lake, really popular at school. At least, she thought ruefully as she got up and made her way to the locker room, he was popular until tonight. After what he'd done, there probably wasn't a kid in school who still thought of him as a hero. What she still couldn't figure out was whether he ever had been.

* * *

Josh was dressed before Walt, so, after saying good-night to his new teammate, he slung his sheepskin jacket over his shoulder and walked down to the girls' locker room. He slid down the wall and sat cross-legged, barring the way. She's be out in a minute or so.

He felt pretty good about the game, actually. Of course he wasn't thrilled that Tarenton had lost, and probably nobody would remember his performance because of that, but at least he'd shown the squad that he could do it. Not that he'd ever doubted it, really, but it was vital to have other people know his worth. If there was one thing his dad drummed into him over the years, it was the importance of getting along, and of making a good impression. He carried that a little too far sometimes, but in this case, it was working.

But was it working with Nancy? He knew she was pretty mixed up about him, and that was only natural. After all, they'd avoided each other like the bubonic plague for a year and a half. He'd always thought she was a real bubble-brain, just another dumb girl, but when he'd seen her Tuesday, working out with the squad, he'd seen an entirely different person. He admired people who committed themselves to something, who worked hard to get what they wanted. Not to mention the fact that she was a damn sexy, good-looking girl.

The door opened and Olivia walked out, followed by Angie. They both looked devastated, and his infectious grin did nothing to revive their spirits.

"Hey, you win some, you lose some," he said with false cheer, standing up to greet them.

"Josh, we shouldn't have lost this one," Olivia pointed out.

"By the way, Josh," Angie said, smiling kindly. "You were awfully good. I don't know how you did it, but you have all the routines down without a hitch. You're doing a brilliant job."

"Really," Olivia chimed in.

He was just about to thank them for the compliment when Nancy walked out the locker room door. He thought she looked fantastic, her complexion ruddy from the shower, her dark eyes vibrant and oh, so deep. When she saw him, she hesitated a second, then her hand flew nervously to her hair.

"How about a Coke?" he asked her in front of the other two. He really would have preferred waiting until they were alone, but he was worried she might run off if he didn't pounce immediately.

"I don't think so. Not tonight. My parents are waiting out in the parking lot."

"They wouldn't mind," he grinned knowingly.

They'd be tickled pink, Nancy thought. The kid was maddening. He still annoyed her, but there was something kind of appealing about him, if you liked that type.

"Well, Walt is probably wondering where I am," Olivia cut in, taking Angie by the arm.

"And I'm going out with some of the guys," Angie said mysteriously. Since her breakup with Marc, she'd dated sporadically, but everyone seemed to know she was still tender from her wounds, so there was nothing serious going on.

"See you Monday. 'Bye!" Josh waved at them deliriously as they beat a hasty retreat down the corridor. He faced Nancy, his hands on his hips. "Well?"

"Josh, I really don't —"

"You don't hate me, do you?" he asked frankly, softly.

"Of course not." She smiled indulgently.

"I'm not really that terrible. If our parents hadn't introduced us, you'd probably jump at the opportunity."

That did it. Why, of all the conceited, arrogant. . . ! "Josh, why don't you go cool off your swelled head in the night air. It'll do you good." She stormed past him, her boot heels clicking on the marble floors.

"Wait! Hey, give me a chance, would you, Nancy?" He was pleading now, all his self-assurance slowly waning away. "I didn't mean anything by that. I just think we're at an unfair disadvantage. You know, when your parents tell you to do something, you naturally run in the opposite direction. So, taking that into consideration, I would like — really I would — to start all over again, as if we didn't know each other. Hello, I'm Josh Breitman."

She stared at him for a second, then gave a funny, exasperated laugh. "Why are you trying so hard?" she asked quietly.

"Because I get a kick out of all this *trouble* you're giving me, is why," he joked.

She shut her eyes tight, wondering why she was so compelled to go out with him at the very same time that she wanted him to leave her alone. "Well, maybe just a Coke," she sighed.

"Super! Great! Well. . . ." He made a wide flourish toward the stairs. "Shall we?"

"Just let me . . . I have to go tell my folks. I'll meet you by your car," she explained, suddenly anxious all over again.

"If you don't want to say it's me you're going out with, you don't have to." Josh smiled lightly. "If that would make it easier for now."

She looked at him curiously, amazed that he knew her worst fears and that he was so easy about letting her off the hook. He *knew* her parents would jump all over her with how thrilled they were that she'd finally seen the light about their friends' son, and he *knew* that would be awful for her. Suddenly, she liked him. He understood her. Was that partly, she wondered, because they came from the same kind of background?

"I'll see you at your car in ten," she promised, already speeding down the stairs.

Josh stood in the empty corridor, threw his sheepskin coat in the air, and gave the "Victory" cheer to the still air.

"Pres, let's go. It's stupid to hang around here," Kerry said, pulling on his arm. The parking lot was deserted, but Pres hadn't moved from his position behind the old maple tree since the game started letting out forty minutes ago.

Pres didn't move. He had rarely felt lower, even when he was fighting with his father.

"Look, they lost the game. But they would

430

have anyway, you cheering or not. It has nothing to do with you," Kerry said.

"Of course it does!" he exploded at her. When she jumped back, he took her by both shoulders and pulled her to him. "Sorry, I shouldn't take it out on you. Kerry, it's not only losing, don't you see? It's that shrimpy kid doing my stuff. It's the rest of the squad. They'll probably never speak to me again. Just like my folks," he added with a sardonic grin.

"Why don't you call your mom?" Kerry asked quietly. "You could say hi and then hang up." When he was silent, she added, "It wouldn't kill you."

He put his arm around her and started to walk her toward the car. "Maybe I should call the kids. Talk to them . . . I don't know."

"Maybe you shouldn't worry so much." Kerry leaned up and stood on her toes to plant a kiss on his lips. He responded immediately, crushing her to him as he pressed his mouth over hers. They stayed like that for a long time, held together by a feeling that rocked them both. When at last Kerry pulled away, Pres was staring down at her, a trembling smile covering up for his childish fears. He needed her — he really did — and it took a lot out of him to admit that.

"Don't go anywhere, will you, Kerry?" he asked softly when they started back to the car. "Stick by me."

"Like glue," she promised solemnly, and she meant it.

CHAPTER

It was a beautiful Sunday morning. Even the birds had forgotten how cold it was and were ducking merrily in and out of tree branches, doing all the silly aeronautical maneuvers birds do when the weather suits them. Pres had rolled up the sleeves of his flannel shirt and was splitting logs for the wood stove. Uncle James was parked on a nearby tree stump, drinking pitch-black coffee, and contentedly watching his nephew work.

"You have a real aptitude for that, you know?" he commented. "Look at those splits now, just as clean as lightning. I think you should go into the lumbering business."

"Oh yeah?" Pres lifted an eyebrow at him. "You're only saying that to get me to cut extra for you."

"Not true. I know an artist when I see one, and you're one."

432

"Hey, if you call this art, you better hang up your easel," Pres teased. He stopped a moment, spit on his chilled hands and rubbed them, then grabbed the ax handle again.

"Well, how do you like living alone?" his uncle asked, more serious now. "Is it all you thought it was cracked up to be?"

"Sure," Pres lied. "It's great. Do what I want when I want, come and go without anyone looking over my shoulder. It's the life, man."

"And I was thinking you were looking kinda peaked lately," James said, getting up and starting toward the main house. "Shows how observant I am." He could tell that Pres just wasn't ready to tell him the truth. "Want some fresh-brewed coffee?" he offered.

"It that what you call that stuff?" Pres glanced quizzically at James's stained cup. "I thought it was diesel fuel."

Laughing, James started back to the house, but he stopped and turned at the sound of a car coming up the road. Pres saw it at the same time and cursed, then planted the ax firmly in the wood before him.

"I'll bring two cups," James said. "Looks like you're going to need it strong," he grimaced, and quickly vanished into the house. This was no time to stick around.

Mrs. Preston Tilford II parked the black Mercedes beside the studio and slowly, she got out of the car.

Pres stared at his mother as though she were someone else. He'd seen that gray skirt hundreds of times, and that camel's hair jacket with its

433

matching beret. He'd seen her fine-boned, aristocratic face a lot lately, when he was lying in front of the fire just about to fall asleep, and he'd known every expression on it for eighteen years now. And yet, she didn't *seem* like his mother. She was different somehow.

"Hello, Pres," she said, standing about five feet away. The breeze tugged at her hat, and she pulled it down firmly over her dark, graying hair.

"Hi." What was he going to say? What should he do? "You . . . ah, want to come in?" he asked politely.

"Thank you. That would be fine," she nodded.

They were being so careful with each other! He couldn't stand it. And where was James with the coffee? He shouldn't be expected to go through this by himself.

Together, they walked into the small studio, where the fire was crackling.

"Have a seat," he offered graciously.

She sat, neatly arranging her skirt around her. He sat opposite on the unmade bed, then jumped up when he noticed the carton of milk sitting on the counter. She always hated it when he left the milk out to sour at home.

"Pres. . . ."

"Mom. . . ." They began at the same time, and both laughed nervously. "Ah, you first."

"Listen, Pres. I would have called this week, but your father convinced me that I should wait. And then I decided to come on over, just in case."

"In case of what?"

"Well, it did occur to us that you might hang up if we called." She wasn't the least bit nervous

434

about saying this, he noticed. She assumed he hated them!

"I wouldn't have," he told her quickly. "Anyhow, it's good you came. This way you get to see I'm in a nice place, doing great on my own, right?"

"Dear," she said, sitting forward in her seat, "I want you back. Very badly." Her face didn't betray much. She hardly ever cried, although Pres liked to think that maybe she'd shed a few tears over him in the past few days. Now, however, she was totally dry-eyed.

"*You* want me back — what about him?"

"Well, your father, naturally . . . he does, too."

"So why didn't he come with you?" Pres demanded, covering the small room in three strides. "If he cares so much, why didn't *he* ask me to come home?"

"He's got his pride." She shrugged. "He doesn't like to beg. And he didn't want to put himself in the position of losing his temper with you. That never solves anything."

"He's mad, huh?" Pres asked.

"What do you expect? Pres, he was trying to do something helpful for you. He never dreamed you'd take offense, let alone run off like you did. For heaven's sake, he got you a job! He didn't like to see you wasting your time with —"

Pres cut her off quickly. "With stuff like cheerleading. With normal stuff like hanging out with my friends."

His mother gave him a disparaging look. "Oh, dear, you really don't understand him at all."

"Yeah, well, he doesn't get me either. So it's

435

just as well we're not living together anymore."

Felicia Tilford shook her head, then stood up, wondering whether it would do any good at all to try another tactic. "I've been talking to Mrs. Oetjen," she told him. "And I know you're on probation. You're off the squad anyway, Pres, so what does it gain you to persist in this . . . this silly game?"

"Mom," he said between clenched teeth, "if you think it's a game, you have a lot to learn about me. This is a decision I made, for good or bad. I'm happy here, which is more than I could ever say about being home."

She turned away suddenly, but he caught a glimpse of tears glistening in her eyes. He'd hurt her, and he was glad of it.

"I'm sorry to hear you say this, but I don't think you really mean it, so I won't argue." She marched briskly to the door, stopping with her hand on the knob. "You can always come back — I want you to know that," she said in a much softer tone. And then, to his amazement, she walked over and roughly kissed him on the cheek. He couldn't remember the last time she'd kissed him.

After she left, he stood by the door, listening to the sound of the car's engine starting up and moving away. He wanted to forget the whole incident, but hard as he tried, it stayed with him. *She* stayed with him, and he hated her for it.

It was about four when he heard the sound of another car on the road, and then a second coming right after it. He peered out the window into the afternoon sun.

Could that be Walt's Jeep? And it looked like Nancy's mother's car following it. He grinned, then leapt out the door like a crazy person, waving his arms and dancing around the yard.

Walt blared the Jeep's horn and pulled alongside the studio, spraying gravel. Olivia had jumped down before the car had come to a complete stop and she waved back at Pres, mimicking his ridiculous dance in the middle of the road.

"So, how's everything?" Angie called, stepping out of Nancy's car. Mary Ellen joined her, shading her eyes to get a better look at James's house. Nancy and Walt brought up the rear, their arms full of packages and bags.

"Everything's *great*." Pres nodded, still grinning. "C'mon in and see my place. What's all this?" he asked, gesturing at the paraphernalia they'd brought.

"Well, everyone knows a young bachelor has no idea how to keep house for himself." Angie laughed, as Pres opened the door for them and ushered them inside. "So we've come to help you make this house a home. Well, will you look at that!" She stared, wide-eyed, at the painting in progress on the easel. It was pretty abstract, but no one could miss the subject matter. A green-limbed man with pink toes was passionately embracing a blue and yellow woman with a very large belly.

"My uncle's latest," Pres said apologetically.

"Must be kind of weird having that facing you when you get up in the morning, huh?" Walt wandered around the small space, taking in the roughhewn wooden beams and smooth soapstone

437

mantel over the wood stove. "Other than that, it's cool. I like it," he pronounced decisively. "What do you guys think?"

"Terrific," Mary Ellen sighed. She could just imagine herself here in a little hideaway when she'd tired of the nightlife of the big city and needed an escape. She and some devastatingly handsome movie producer would come up here, light a fire, and never answer the telephone.

"It's a little stark," Nancy said, running her hand along the kitchen counter. "How about some curtains, Pres? I made one once."

"You made *one* curtain?" Mary Ellen asked skeptically, sitting on the floor in front of the fire next to Olivia. "What happened to the other?"

"It died a horrible death in my mother's sewing machine. Don't ask me to describe it," Nancy shuddered in mock horror.

Angie gave her a playful push on the shoulder as she went to one of the shopping bags and withdrew a jar of popcorn kernels. "I don't know about anyone else, but I'm starved. Can we do this over the fire?"

"Why not?" Pres agreed, going to the refrigerator to get a six-pack of soda for everyone. He felt like a genial host, about a thousand percent better than he had twenty minutes ago. His pals had come to see him! They didn't hate him! With everyone pitching in to pour soda or heat the oil for the popcorn, it was like old times before he'd split the squad apart. And suddenly, he felt less guilty about it, like he could even talk about it.

"Kerry and I caught the game yesterday," he said casually, wandering over to the counter to turn on the small portable radio to a good rock station. "Pretty foul, if you ask me."

"Yeah, look who's talking," Walt said, grabbing an uncooked kernel from the pan and throwing it at Pres.

"Well, it was bad, man. That doofus Ardith got to replace me looked like he was trying out for the Olympic klutz award."

Everyone looked at Nancy, who turned three consecutive shades of crimson. "Oh, I don't think he's that awful," she said noncommittally. "After all, it was his first time out, and he'd only had four days to learn about a dozen routines. He'll get better."

"If you let him." Angie turned to Pres, then got up and moved closer to him. "It's all in your hands, you know."

"Don't start with me, Ange," Pres warned her. "I got a lecture from my mother this morning — I don't need five other parents."

"Hey, have you lost it completely?" Walt demanded. "You saddled us with a klutz from the word go *and* the hassle of teaching the kid everything from scratch. You know, that's a lot for the rest of us to handle."

"He's not a klutz," Mary Ellen said, looking at Nancy. "As a matter of fact, I think he's really good. He's got a special flair. Don't you think so, Olivia?"

They all caught her drift at once: Shame Pres into coming back. "I think he's dynamite," Olivia agreed. "Gives a breath of fresh air to the squad."

"Hey, you're stuck with him now." Pres shrugged, trying not to let them get to him. "You better like him."

The room was stilled by an awkward pause, the kind everybody wants to break but no one knows how to. Finally, Angie grabbed the pan off the fire and made a big deal of offering the popcorn around.

"Don't you have any clean bowls in here?" she asked, rummaging through his cupboards. "Honestly."

"What are we cooking tonight, anyhow?" Mary Ellen asked the others, ignoring Pres. "I think pot roast — how about it?" She fished in one of the bags and brought out a large slab of pinkish-red meat.

"What are you going to do with that?" Pres asked, wrinkling up his nose.

"Cook it, stupid." Angie put her hands on her hips in exasperation. "Don't tell me you never saw a pot roast before."

"Not before it was dead," Pres grimaced.

"Boy, this guy has a lot to learn." Nancy took the meat from Mary Ellen and went to the stove with it, where she began rummaging around for a pan.

"You're not going to start cooking that without sandblasting the stove, are you?" Mary Ellen asked in disgust as Nancy lit the gas. She reached up to run her finger over the stove top. "Ugh, how can you live like this, Pres? It's criminal."

"You take care of the stove, Melon, and you start seasoning the meat, Nancy. I'll do something about the bathroom, okay?" Olivia told

440

them, her mouth full of popcorn. "Did you bring the cleanser?"

"In the bag," Mary Ellen nodded, already busy with a sponge.

"And I'll do the laundry," Walt grinned. "I'm wonderful at laundry," he confided to Pres. "Where do you hide the stuff? No, wait," he said, a finger to the side of his nose. "I just got a whiff. I can find it myself."

"Don't forget to sort the colors," Mary Ellen yelled in to him.

Pres watched in amazement as the five cheerleaders whipped around the studio, dusting, polishing, and scrubbing. They were so enthusiastic about their tasks that he actually got interested. Like Tom Sawyer's fence before it was whitewashed, the dirty studio became a challenge too good to pass up. Pres Tilford, who had never done a lick of housework in his life, whose mother would have fallen over in a dead faint at the sight of him with a bucket and mop, started washing the floor.

At one point, Angie stopped peeling potatoes and looked at him curiously. "Oh, what I wouldn't give for a camera. A perfect blackmail shot," she giggled.

"What do you mean?" Pres growled.

"Big bad Pres with his hot car and his own digs and his sexy ladies — cleaning! No one would believe it!" Walt chuckled.

And then they all started laughing at him. He laughed, too, pelting them with popcorn, trying to stuff it down the girls' shirt fronts, getting it right back again in direct hits to the face and

441

neck. They were so busy fighting, they didn't hear the door open, and for a minute didn't even see Uncle James standing there in amazement, staring at all of them.

"What in the name of. . . ?" he boomed.

The battle ended as quickly as it had begun.

"We're making this house into a home," Pres explained. "James, these are the guys on the squad. Guys, my uncle, who has so kindly provided me with a place to live."

Everyone murmured hellos and started cleaning up the popcorn.

"Well, I thought I smelled something funny." James shook his head, going over to the stove and peering inside.

"Stay for dinner, James? There's plenty," Pres offered.

"Hey, no thanks. Home cooking is a little more domesticity than I can possibly stand," James laughed. He was still looking around, noting the shining counters and dusted surfaces. "I thought kids were supposed to raise hell and mess things up."

"Right, Mr. Tilford," Mary Ellen said with her most appealing cheerleader smile. "But we do that *all* the time. It gets boring."

James gave her a lopsided grin and swiped some popcorn from the overflowing bowl before starting back toward the front door. Pres followed him. "How's your mom?" he asked Pres under his breath so the others couldn't hear.

Pres shrugged. "Old story: She wants me back, my dad doesn't. I'm staying right where I am — if it's okay with you," he added.

"I don't mind, kid, not in the slightest. But watch it with the cleaning. I don't want you to turn into a wimp under my roof, understand." With an unbelieving shake of his head, James left the six of them to their craziness.

"When do we eat?" Pres demanded, coming back to the group, relishing the wonderful smells and the comfort of being surrounded by friends — such extraordinary friends who would even forgive a louse like him.

"When you set the table, wise guy." Walt slapped some paper napkins into his hand.

Pres did as he was told, realizing as he did so that family wasn't always the people you were related to. Sometimes, he thought as he put a fork at each place, family was closer than blood.

CHAPTER

"Okay, kids, that's it for tonight," Ardith sighed, stretching from one side to the other. "Everything's looking basically all right except for the new tumbling cheer. Work on it, would you. I don't want *you* working harder, though, Olivia. One jump higher and you'll go through the roof."

Everyone except the leaping gazelle in question looked gratefully at Ardith. They did worry about Olivia every once in a while. She had an almost obsessive need to do better — regardless of how perfect her routines looked — and she was always trying for something more difficult, more daring. It was very nerve-racking for the rest of them, when they watched her propel herself into the air like a person shot out of a cannon. They were certain she was about to land on her spinal column and end it all.

"And Walt," Ardith continued, "try not to

land on top of everyone when you take that spread eagle. Looking good, Josh," she added quietly to the newest member of the team.

"Thanks," he nodded, following Nancy out the door of the gym. He was feeling okay about himself these days. After all, Tarenton had won the last three games they'd cheered for, and everyone now freely acknowledged that the cheerleaders were back in shape again. Naturally, a bunch of kids doing their splits and backbends didn't make the touchdowns or baskets, but the morale-building factor they provided was important — everybody said so.

The girls were almost at their locker room, and Josh hurried to catch up. "Hey, wait a sec," he called to Nancy, who didn't turn around.

"I think someone wants you," Angie whispered to her.

Nancy gave her a look. "You don't have to remind me," she muttered as Angie swept inside the locker room with Mary Ellen and Olivia giggling meaningfully behind her. "Yes?" she asked, turning to Josh.

"I was just wondering about the dance a week from Saturday."

"Yes?" Nancy repeated. She liked him, she actually enjoyed being with him, but he was so persistent! Every day after practice, he'd been waiting to take her home. And after she'd finally agreed to their first date, he simply assumed they were a couple, and was there every time she turned around. She tried being frosty, being flip, being almost rude. Then she demanded her privacy, saying that it was every American citizen's right. But he wore her down with flowers, with sticks of gum, with double-chocolate malteds. She hated to admit it, but he was growing on her, sort of like a vine you have to cut off a building after a number of years.

"Well, you do dance, don't you?" Josh asked, his black eyes devouring her.

"I could dance circles around you," Nancy proclaimed.

"Sure you could. I guess we'll have to see. I'll pick you up at eight," he nodded cockily, starting down the hall toward the guys' lockers.

"Just a second," she fumed. "I haven't said anything about going with you."

"But you are. You have to!" He rushed back, looking terribly upset. "It's destiny. Kismet. You and I were matched in heaven. That means we're stuck, boogying together till the earth turns cold."

"Josh, honestly!" She threw her hands up, and he grabbed them.

He kissed her lightly, but underneath the playfulness was a deeper feeling that Nancy responded to.

"Say it — tell me you love me. Tell me you *like* me for now. I'll settle." He looked so earnest and anxious, she had to laugh.

"I do. I like you despite my best intentions."

"Then the dance is on?"

"I guess." She shrugged, wresting her hands away and walking through the door of the girls' room. There was something she couldn't put her finger on, something new about him that made her feel silly and giddy. It wasn't like with other guys she'd gone out with. With Ben, for instance, everything had been intense and passionate. Every moment seemed to weigh heavily; every word had meaning. She had never wanted to keep her hands off Ben. Or wanted his off of her.

With Josh, it was easy, almost carefree. And it was weird, since she'd fought her parents so long and so hard on this very subject. For over a year, she'd protested that Josh was too short for her, too overbearing, too aggressive.

When the Goldsteins had first moved to Tarenton, her father had begged Nancy to join the temple youth group, and consequently, she had stayed as far away from the temple as possible. It wasn't that she was ashamed of being Jewish — the tradition meant a lot to her. It was just that she wanted another, more exciting destiny than her mother's. And when she'd first met Josh, he reminded her of everything she was familiar with.

Now, though, she saw something more in him. Oh, he still tried too hard to please, and he was still kind of stuck on himself, but he was stuck on her, too, and the attention was pretty nice. She couldn't tell her parents, though. They didn't know she was going out with him, and if *she* had anything to do with it, they weren't ever going to find out.

"You look gooney," Olivia said, sticking her head out of the shower and glancing at Nancy, who was waiting with a towel wrapped around her middle. The girls' volleyball team had just finished practice, and showers were at a premium.

"You're no one to talk," Nancy huffed at her,

sighing as one of the Eismar twins beat her to the next available stall. "I've never seen you dancing around like an idiot before, but now you do it every time Walt trips over you."

"Just to get out of his way." Olivia smiled coyly.

"Oh, admit it, Livvy." Angie came up behind them, her long hair twisted under the shower cap. "We know you two are an item."

"I think it's wonderful," Mary Ellen chimed in. She was already in her underwear, putting cream on her long, slender legs. "The two of you go so perfectly together. Like cars and gasoline."

"Like rock 'n' roll," Nancy agreed.

"Like ice cream and hot fudge sauce." Angie sighed, her mind never off its favorite subject for long.

Olivia grinned sheepishly at them. "All right, I confess. He's just about the ideal boyfriend. He even tolerates my mother. The other night when he took me home she kept flashing the porch lights at the Jeep. And when I didn't pay any attention, she marched right over and demanded I come in the house. I was out of my mind, naturally, but Walt just smiled at her and said good evening. He's amazing. Never loses his temper, even though I lose mine all the time."

Mary Ellen wandered away from the group, the smile still fixed on her face. She was pleased for Olivia, although she'd never been one to revel in another person's happiness. What was theirs was theirs, and it didn't touch her too much. It was difficult for her to be as enthusiastic as the others, given her present situation. There was Donny, and then there was Patrick. It was a royal pain.

She glanced over at Angie as she drew up her navy blue tights, making sure that every wrinkle was pulled out and that the mended run didn't show. Now why should Angie be so thrilled for Olivia? — she didn't have anyone at all. Since Marc had ditched her, she'd made a point of playing the field, but Mary Ellen knew she didn't have a date for the dance. I could give her one of mine, she thought glumly, zipping her corduroy jumpsuit to the top with a neat flourish. But which one?

"Good-night, gang. Get some rest. That practice tomorrow is going to be a killer, I can tell." She stuffed her wet clothes into the old gym bag she carried, picked up her books, and started out of the locker room.

"See you tomorrow," Nancy sang, her thoughts on Josh.

"Have a good one," Olivia called out, rubbing herself thoroughly with her towel. Walt was probably doing the same thing right now. She blushed slightly thinking about it, and was surprised. She was aware Walt had a body but she always managed to keep her physical feelings under control. It was part of her determination to run her own life.

"Good-night, Melon," Angie said, giving a cheerful wave.

They were all so good-natured. Mary Ellen scowled into the darkened corridor. Even when they had nothing in particular to celebrate, they were generally on top of the world. Whereas she

449

had deep-rooted fears that wouldn't stay in their proper places; anxieties that she wasn't doing enough, looking good enough, going far enough. All those worries kept her from really enjoying life — like Angie, for example. Now there was a saint if she ever saw one. Able to make light of a less than luxurious background, able to smile at disaster, able to go to a dance without even the promise of a date.

"I'm just different, I guess," she muttered to herself, throwing her parka over her shoulders and tugging at the front door of Tarenton High. "I'm really more like Pres — a loner." And then, for a brief second, she wished for him back again, too. "You malcontent," she grumbled into her scarf. "He's got Kerry now — leave him alone."

When she saw Donny's car, she walked toward it as though it were dangerous. And when she slipped into the passenger seat and snapped her seatbelt into place, she distinctly heard the clang of a prison door shutting in her mind. But a number one guy was what she wanted. Wasn't it?

Pres and Kerry looked at the curtains Nancy had dropped off. After that Sunday afternoon, she'd gone into a sewing frenzy, finding fabric at a flea market sale and rushing home to "create," as she called it. The curtains were bright orange with yellow flowers, and they almost reached to the bottom of the studio windows. There was only about a five-inch gap.

"What do you think?" Pres asked, examining

them as though they were some exotic species of animal.

"They sort of remind me of my grandmother's kitchen — I don't know," Kerry sighed. "They don't do much for me."

"Me, either." Gratefully, Pres started to put them back in the box.

"But she's here so often. She'd be hurt if you didn't hang them up."

"So, she'll be hurt. Kerry, they're disgusting," Pres moaned.

"I say they go up." Kerry, for all her sweetness, had opinions. Though most people saw her as kind of vague, drifting through life, that was really just a cover for her shyness. She didn't speak her mind with just anybody, but now that she felt more comfortable with Pres, she wasn't afraid to be up front with him.

"You hang them, then," he muttered, thrusting them at her. "I want nothing to do with it."

She had just begun to string them on the curtain rods when they heard the sound of a car coming up the road. Pres tensed at once.

"What's the matter?" Kerry had become an expert at sensing his mood changes.

"Nothing. It's just . . . I wasn't expecting company." He *knew* that sooner or later his father was going to come and have it out with him. There was no way that he was going to leave the situation as it was, when it was well known all over town that Preston Tilford II couldn't even keep a tight rein on his own son. If there was anything his father hated more than losing money in business, it was being thought of as a chump.

451

"Whose car is that?" Kerry peered out into the gathering dark.

Pres joined her at the window, noting with relief that the car parked beside the studio was a beat-up Volkswagen Beetle. His father wouldn't be caught dead in a Beetle.

There was a quick rap at the door, followed by a raucous war whoop. As Pres put his hand on the knob, the door flew open, and in crashed a tall, muscular guy with a curly red beard that scrawled all over his thin face like graffiti.

"Well, who are you?" the stranger asked.

"I'm Pres; this is Kerry."

"Pres? Not little Pres! You're kidding!" The bearded wonder extended his hand and pumped Pres's up and down for a long minute. "The last time I saw you, you didn't even know how to put your socks on straight."

Pres scowled. "A.J.?" he asked. It couldn't be anyone else.

"The one and only." The guy started giving Kerry the eye. "And what's your name, cute stuff?" He reached out for Kerry.

"This is my cousin, A.J.," Pres told Kerry quickly, stepping between them. "Just passing through, I would think." A.J. was James's only son, but they hardly knew each other. He'd lived with James's ex-wife after the divorce, but he was apparently quite a handful, and she got fed up, sending him off to boarding school somewhere in New Hampshire. Pres's mother had mentioned a few months ago that A.J. had just started at Columbia University and wasn't doing awfully well.

"Hey, you living here now?" A.J. dropped his leather carryall and plunked himself down on the couch.

"Yeah, I am," Pres said a little defensively.

"You don't mind if I crash here for a while, do you? I'm kind of on leave from college, if you know what I mean." He winked at Kerry.

"James is out of town for a couple of days at a show, but I'm sure it would be okay if you stayed in the main house," Pres told him. "He left me a key." He dug down deep in his pocket and produced it, then tossed it to his cousin who let it fall on the floor in front of him.

"Oh, hey, that's cool. Really. But, honey, I still don't know your name."

"It's Kerry. Pres, I think I better be getting home," she said, clearly uncomfortable with this boy whose thoughts were obvious.

"Want a ride?" A.J. asked. "I've been driving for eight hours straight — might as well keep going."

"That's okay," Kerry smiled as nicely as she could. "Pres, let's move it, shall we?" She tossed her jacket over her shoulder and was out the door without even saying good-bye.

"So, I guess I'll see you whenever," Pres told A.J. firmly.

"I'll be out by the time you get back. Just have to shut my eyes a sec, okay?" A.J. yawned widely, then put his boots up on the couch and lay back.

Pres drove Kerry home slowly. He was not looking forward to finding his cousin right where he'd left him — and knowing A.J., he probably

453

hadn't made an attempt to move and wasn't going to for the rest of the night.

"You two don't have much in common, do you?" Kerry asked when Pres had been silent for ten minutes or so.

"Not a whole lot. He always goes home to his mother in Virginia. I don't remember when James last saw him. They never got along."

"I can see why."

"Well, I'll get him out of the studio tomorrow. Wonder how long he intends to stick around Tarenton." He didn't think James would evict him from the studio, but if he really couldn't stand having A.J. under the same roof with him, that would mean it was share or move out. And *then* what was Pres going to do? He couldn't go home. But he doubted that he could stay in the same space as his cousin for very long without starting a fist fight.

"See you in school, okay? Sleep well," Kerry told him as he pulled up in front of her house. He leaned over and kissed her gently, feeling her warmth creeping over him and into him. Their kisses were gentle to begin with, soft and whispery. He hugged her rounded shoulders, enjoying her curves against his leanness. Then he kissed her harder and pulled her closer.

With a sigh, before Pres's hands could move from her shoulders, she reached back and opened the door. Then she was gone, and he was alone.

"Why won't you let me come with you? Hey, I'm not gonna bother anyone," A.J. assured Pres early the next morning. Pres had made himself a cup of instant coffee, and his cousin was looking at it covetously.

"Look, I gotta go," Pres said, grabbing his books and starting for the door. He purposely poured the dregs down the drain so A.J. couldn't drink them.

"I can't believe you're still going to school," A.J. shook his head in disbelief. "You have your own place, your own sexy little girl, everything copacetic, but you trudge off to Tarenton High like a good little doobie — don't even want to be late." He laughed scornfully.

Pres kept his temper, but just barely. "A.J., I'd really appreciate it if you were out by the time I get back this afternoon. We'll probably get along much better if you're in the house and I stay here. And keep away from Kerry, too."

"Hey, man, don't give it a thought. Don't you worry your little head." And with that, he turned over on the couch and went right back to sleep.

Pres wasn't concentrating awfully hard that morning. There was a spot quiz in first-period math that he totally blanked out on, and history was nearly as bad. Five of the kids were asked to sit in a circle and discuss the coming of the Industrial Revolution for the whole class — and Pres was one of the lucky ones who got picked. He said something off the wall about winning the revolution with guns instead of bows and arrows, and everyone in the room cracked up.

By lunchtime, he was ready to give it up and go home. He wandered into the cafeteria, looking for Kerry, but couldn't find her. Swarms of kids

were hitting the steam table at the same time, so
he grabbed a sandwich and a container of milk
and took a seat with some of the football jocks
and their girls at a table near the window. What
was he going to do, anyway? He didn't really like
living alone, yet he couldn't own up to that. But
A.J. could ruin everything by *forcing* him to
move out. And he hated being off the squad. He
itched to move again, his body doing mental
gymnastics at every game he watched. He could
see himself in a stag leap, or carrying Olivia on
his shoulders, or swirling Mary Ellen and Angie
each on an arm. He could *feel* it.

There was another problem, too, and it was
getting a lot worse. Pres was out of cash. He had
barely enough for groceries now, even though
Kerry had been chipping in. He hated taking
money from her. How ironic that the richest kid
in school didn't have two cents to rub together —
his father had seen to that. But then, Preston Tilford II had always been tight with a buck. He'd
made it clear, when he apportioned his son's allowance, that if he wanted more, he could earn
it by working at Tarenton Fabricators. Pres
didn't want it that badly.

He'd been out of the house for three weeks
now, and he had just about polished off the cash
he'd had. He hated the idea, but soon he was
going to have to dip into his savings account.
He knew that as soon as he did that, his father
would put a stop on it — on the whole deal.
Because it was a joint account, old dad knew
when things were moving over at the bank. He
made it his business to know.

"Well, a free seat — exactly my size!" Vanessa's throaty sounds were so close to Pres's ear, he could hear them over the cafeteria din. "And then Goldilocks sat down in the baby bear's chair to cozy up to the big bad wolf. How're you doin', Wolf?" Her tone was blatantly suggestive — there was no doubt in Pres's mind what she was after.

"What's going on, Vannie?" he asked, as casually as he could under the circumstances.

She pulled the chair up and sat so that they were touching. He could feel her leg under her tight skirt right through his jeans.

"Just wondering how long you're going to stay out of the action. I've missed you. Where is that girl you usually hang around with, anyhow? What's her name — Kelly something?"

"I've got as much action as I want, Van," Pres said decisively, balling up the sandwich wrapper in a tight fist. "But thanks for asking."

"You keep me in mind if things get dull, all right?" she told him.

He was on his feet and moving away from the table when he spotted the one person who could rattle him faster than Vanessa. With a grunt, he waited as A.J. approached their table.

"Hey, little cousin, I found you! How's the school trip today?" A.J. asked, his eyes all over Vanessa. She was asking for the attention, and she got it.

"Hello," she sparkled at him. "I'm Vanessa Barlow, your welcoming committee at Tarenton High. And whom do I have the pleasure of welcoming?"

"A.J. Tilford, Pres's cousin, just in from New York for a visit." His deep-set gray eyes narrowed a little, sizing her up. "I didn't think I was going to stay long, but now I might."

Vanessa gave him one of her slow, lingering smiles, and flung her dark hair invitingly over one shoulder. "You live in New York?"

"Temporarily. Officially, I'm at Columbia, but my real reason for being there is to attend the New York City University of Life. The street action's really wild, if you know what I mean."

"Of course," she said. A.J. had just risen several notches in her estimation. Not only was he a college man, but he was above and beyond organized education. The pirate king, the highwayman robber amidst all these dumb high school boys.

"You free for lunch?" A.J. asked her. "And I don't mean this garbage," he scoffed, indicating the unappealing food strewn over every table.

"I sure am." Vanessa was on her feet and moving toward the door instantly. She looked back once to make certain that A.J. was following her, and caught Pres's eye. "You don't mind, do you?" she asked him.

"Hey, Van, I think you two deserve each other. Have a great time," he added sarcastically.

As Pres watched them go out of the cafeteria, it struck him that despite his various and multifaceted problems, he wasn't that bad off. He might be lonely, he might be off the cheerleading team, he might have money troubles, but at least he wasn't a creep. And that was more than could be said for a lot of people.

CHAPTER

9

"Oh, no, he's early," Olivia moaned, looking out the window at the Jeep parked at an angle in the drive. "Now he'll get stuck with my mother!"

Hurriedly, she splashed on some cologne, then started on her makeup. Olivia generally didn't put much on her face at all, except for moisturizer, but tonight was special. And besides, she needed something to bring out the luscious lavender color of her new angora sweater with the pink pearl buttons along the side of the neck. She dabbed on some gleaming brown shadow, then outlined the crease of her eye with a soft lavender pencil. A little blusher, a little pink lip gloss, and she was ready. She just prayed her new shoes wouldn't cause too many blisters. After all, she had practice on Monday, and self-imposed blisters from wearing the wrong footgear were definitely frowned upon by Ardith. She whizzed down the stairs, jumping the last three. There he was, cornered.

"Hi, Walt. 'Bye, Mom. We won't be too late." If she could just whisk them out of there without a scene!

"I was just telling Walter, dear, that smoke-filled rooms make it difficult for you to breathe. No one smokes at that school of yours, do they?"

Olivia gave Walt a look. "Oh, no, Mom, they wouldn't dream of it. Shall we go?"

Mrs. Evans rose to her full height, glaring at the two of them. She wasn't tall, but her broad shoulders and hips gave her a massive presence. She wasn't the kind of person you'd feel comfortable meeting in a dark alley.

"I want you to know, Walter, that my daughter is still very frail. This strange break dancing and disco junk is strictly inadvisable. Do you understand?"

"I certainly do, Mrs. Evans," Walt said seriously, before Olivia could jump in with a sarcastic comment. "We will confine ourselves to very slow moonwalking." And with that, he swept up his jacket and Olivia's coat from the hall rack and steered his date outside. She was nearly convulsed with giggles as they got to the car.

"You're a riot, you know that?" She laughed as he took the time to kiss her forehead, then her nose, and finally, her inviting lips.

"Oh, is that it? And your mother led me to believe that I *cause* riots. Let's hit the road, kid!"

They were off, driving through the still, chilly night. Tarenton dances were generally big events, and tonight's was no exception. The kids on the entertainment committee always provided the best decorations, the hottest DJ, and some really good refreshments. They were only able to manage the finances by asking all comers to donate at the door, of course, and though some kids objected to this, they all gave. It was a tradition.

"There's Angie's car," Walt commented, as they pulled into the already crowded school parking lot and he turned off the ignition. "Did she come alone?"

"She said her brother Andrew was taking her. Didn't seem very broken up about it, though," Olivia said. "I think she has her eye on somebody who promised to be here," she added mysteriously.

"Who?"

"Wouldn't you like to know? Buy me a Coke and maybe I'll tell."

Laughing, they ran into the building. All the lights on the upper floors were blazing, and the chaperones were standing around the front hallway, waiting for enough kids to show so that the dance could start.

"Door prizes? No, thanks. Hey, I never win anything." Josh was standing with his arm around Nancy at the entrance to the gym, as Walt and Olivia approached. A senior with thick glasses and a very serious expression was trying to convince everyone who entered to sign up for a prize. That meant extra admission, of course.

"What's the prize?" Nancy wanted to know. Her cheeks were flushed, nearly matching the deep red of her silk vest. Under it, she wore a

461

white silk blouse with billowing sleeves.

"I don't know," the senior told her.

"Well, if you don't know, who does?"

"I have an inkling." It was Pres. As he strolled up to the gym door with Kerry on his arm, he looked happier than he had in weeks. He leaned over and whispered in Nancy's ear, then did the same to Kerry, who gave him a dubious look, then shook her head. "Old exam books with answers in them, huh? Doesn't sound too exciting to me. Not tonight, anyhow." She looked so proud, so sophisticated, as Pres escorted her inside the noisy gym.

"In that case, fella," Josh said to the disgruntled senior, "I'll just take two regular tickets. And two for my friend, Walt."

The gym looked magical tonight — nothing like the sweaty arena they worked out in every day, although the smell still hung on. There were Mylar balloons everywhere, and Japanese paper lanterns over the old hanging light fixtures to dim the glare a little. The walls had been plastered with rock album covers, and a miniature stage had been set up under one of the baskets for the disc jockey. He was a college kid, dressed all in black leather, with unbelievable hair. Nancy didn't know whether to watch his yellow-and-green-streaked concoction bobbing in time to the music or Pres dancing with Kerry.

"Place looks terrific!" Josh said, sweeping Nancy into a fast twirling pattern on the floor. He certainly had style, Nancy thought. She didn't always feel that she was the lightest person on her feet, but Josh made her feel positively ethereal.

Mary Ellen and Donny walked in next, saying rather subdued hellos to the other two couples. Olivia caught Mary Ellen's eye, but she looked away. One thing was certain — she wasn't delirious about being here. Or was it being with Donny that was upsetting her? Although she looked lovely in a soft blue-gray velveteen top and tight-fitting jeans, her mind was clearly elsewhere. And her eyes scanned the floor hungrily. Olivia was certain she was looking for Patrick. The thing was, if Patrick was here, *he* would find *her*, Donny or no Donny.

"Hello, everybody! Party time!" Vanessa's deep voice made everyone turn suddenly, their light moods darkened somewhat by the appearance of one of their least favorite people. "Do you know my date? A.J. Tilford, this is the rah-rah crew — you know, those cheerleaders your little cousin Pres used to associate with. And this is A.J., guys, direct from New York City." She spoke quickly, looking around the floor instead of at them. She wanted to make sure everyone was suitably impressed with the big fish she'd snagged.

"Oh, is that Angie?" Vanessa continued, peering out into the corridor. "Poor little Angie had to come all by herself. I really feel for her," she sighed in exaggerated concern.

"And we really feel for you, Vanessa," Walt said quietly, starting toward Angie before she could hear any of this.

"So that makes it even," Olivia called over her

shoulder. She caught up to Walt and whispered, "Ask Angie to dance. Go on. I'll go grab some food so I can tell you what's good."

He beamed at her, loving her for her generosity, her open spirit. And then, before Angie could even say hello, she felt herself whisked through the door of the gym, onto the crowded floor. The senior at the door waved at them, but there was nothing he could do. Walt and Angie were moving too fast for him, doing double pirouettes and fancy lifts to the wild music.

Olivia watched them for a second, then wandered to the refreshment table. A.J. Tilford had fixed himself a large plate of pizza, chips, and dip, and was leaning back, blocking the table from Olivia's view. She walked around him, then grabbed a glass of Coke.

"Vanessa went to the little girls' room," he said without further preliminaries. "You want to. . . ?" He moved his finger in a circle, indicating dancing.

"Ah, not really. Thanks. I'll sit this one out," Olivia nodded.

"Not much to get excited about, right? Hey, this place is a drag already. But in a podunk town, with a podunk high school, what can you expect?"

He was so smug, she wanted to smack him. "Oh, and I suppose it's just *fantastic* in New York City." Her small body fairly bristled with rage.

"Are you kidding? Babe, school dances are really out. I mean, we're talking *tired blood*, you know what I mean? You want to split?" He looked at her through dull gray eyes. The odd thing was, he didn't seem to care whether she said yes or no.

So she said neither. She put down her glass and simply walked away toward the ladies' room. If Vanessa wasn't out of there by now, she'd just ignore her. All she knew was that it was important to put as much distance as possible between herself and this big hairy ape.

There was someone in the ladies' room, but it wasn't Vanessa. Mary Ellen was standing in front of one of the sinks, splashing water on her face and gulping air. It was evident that she had been crying.

"Hey, it's too early to fall apart. The dance has hardly begun," Oilvia said. "What's going on?" When Mary Ellen just shook her head, Olivia crossed her arms and looked at her through the mirror. "It's Vanessa, right? She was in here and said something horrible."

"Sort of. Not really. It's not important." Mary Ellen sniffed, her breath coming in shuddery jerks as she tried to calm herself down. It was all coming to a head, and for some reason, she just wasn't coping very well anymore. She knew it was dumb to believe anything Vanessa said, but somehow, with things going bad with Donny and her own mixed-up emotions, anything seemed possible. There was something so logical about what Vanessa had told her — that Angie had come to the dance specifically to see Patrick. "Isn't that sweet?" she'd gushed on her way out the door. She loved to drop megaton bombs, then waltz away just before everything crashed around her.

But Mary Ellen wasn't going to let this news spoil her evening. She had to be happy and cheerful — everyone expected it of her. "Hey, we better get back." She tried a laugh, but it sounded hollow to Olivia. "How do I look?"

"You always look beautiful," said the ever-practical Olivia. She didn't believe in getting overly emotional about anything, so she didn't press Mary Ellen for an answer. All she said was, "Watch out for Vanessa's date, by the way. He's perfectly awful, and seems to want to go home with the first girl who looked bored or unhappy. You, Melon, are a prime target."

"I'll be careful," Mary Ellen promised, taking a deep breath. The music swirled over them as they walked back onto the floor. It was loud enough to vibrate in their stomachs, and the dancing was crazy enough to get lost in. They stood to one side, scouting the territory, and then Olivia spotted Walt looking for her and edged her way toward him. That left Mary Ellen standing alone.

She'd never been a wallflower in her life. It felt weird. And yet, she wasn't surprised that Donny didn't want to dance with her. She'd been making things pretty tough for him lately, and as soon as they'd entered the gym, he'd gravitated right to his basketball buddies, some of whom hadn't come with dates. She could see him now, going over a tough pass he wanted to use at the game next week. His pal Hank took the imaginary ball from him and feinted to his right, nearly knocking over a couple who were swaying together on the dance floor.

"Why so glum, lady?" Pres saw her moping there and dragged Kerry and Angie over to her corner.

"I'm not!" Mary Ellen protested much too cheerily. "How are you guys doing? Great music, isn't it?" She was wound too tight, talking too fast. No one believed her for a minute.

"How about a dance?" Pres asked her, half turning to Kerry for permission. She smiled and motioned them both toward the floor.

"If you don't mind, I think I'll pass. I didn't sleep very well last night and I'm kinda beat." Her eyes were focused straight ahead of her, on Patrick's strong, broad back. He was hopping around with two girls, a couple of juniors Mary Ellen didn't know very well. She told herself to stay where she was — if he wanted her, he'd find her.

"Okay, but you're missing the chance of a lifetime," Pres cautioned her. "Kerry?"

"Nope. I've had it — for a while, anyway. Angie, it's up to you. I'll be over there with my shoes off. Have fun!"

Pres shrugged, then pushed Angie onto the floor before she could bow out. The DJ switched turntables, and a slow number boomed from the huge speakers. Angie moved closer, and Pres put his arms around her protectively, steering her in a tight circle. She was the one girl he could hug without any mixed feelings. She was a friend, and touching her was just nice — not a sexual invitation. He had never, for one minute, been turned on by Angie.

"How are you and your cousin working out together?" she asked solicitously, lifting her blonde head from his shoulder.

"We avoid each other, period," Pres laughed. "He moved into the main house after I told him for the tenth time, but he threatens to come back to the studio when Uncle James gets home tomorrow. And the worst part is, I don't know how long A.J. intends to stay. Looks like he's getting very comfortable."

"So what'll you do if he crowds you out?" Angie looked deep into his eyes, demanding honesty from him. She liked Pres a lot — always had — and she hated to see him do dumb things. "Have you considered moving back home?"

Pres rolled his eyes up to the ceiling, then spun her under his arm. "No lectures or I drop you right here. Just dance, will you, please?"

"Don't you avoid me, Pres." Angie stopped in the middle of the floor and took him by the hand. "Don't you dare. I want you back on our squad, and this is the only way I'm going to get you."

"What's wrong with Mr. Wonderful?" He jerked his head over at Josh and Nancy, who were locked in a close embrace, swaying slowly on a dime-sized spot on the floor.

"Nothing. He's good, perfect sometimes. But he isn't part of our team and never will be. He doesn't mesh the way you do. We all feel it, even though no one's talking about it — partly not to hurt Nancy's feelings. She's pretty gone on the guy."

"I can see. Hey, could we talk about this some other time? I have to *move*, Ange." He did a few snazzy dance steps in place, feeling itchy all over. Other people could talk to him about this subject, and he'd just laugh it off. But Angie was different. She looked deeper inside him than anyone, except maybe Kerry, who was always on his side. But Angie didn't pull any punches. She said what she thought.

"You want to move; I want to stand still for a second. Who wins? I can't talk and dance at the same time."

He sighed, then nodded reluctantly. They fought their way off the dance floor and walked past the refreshment table, over to the big windows that faced the back of the school. It was about a hundred decibels quieter here, which was not saying a great deal.

"Why won't you move back home, Pres?" Angie demanded, her clear blue eyes like a beacon in the huge room. "You've been away for weeks now. Wouldn't this be a perfect time to make peace with your folks, particularly since you have that unwelcomed visitor hanging around?"

"No time is a perfect time, Ange. Yeah, I know, sooner or later I'm going to have to bite the bullet. If only. . . ." He let the thought trail off.

"It's your dad, isn't it? Have you talked to him?"

"No, just to my mother. She wasn't a lot of help. I don't think Preston Tilford II really *wants* me back. I mean, talk about a laissez-faire policy! The man's oblivious to me. I might as well not

469

even be there." He balled up his fists. Just the thought of his father made him want to hit something.

"Pres, I don't know your parents. But even if you aren't crazy about the guy, he's the only father you've got. I may sound like a sap, but that's my opinion, for what it's worth."

He looked at the floor, then out at the dancers, slick now with sweat and the excitement of the pulsing beat. They were all so *normal*, with their normal families and normal school activities and normal boyfriends and girl friends. And he was such a misfit. Except that Angie didn't think so. She was a rock, no doubt about it. He put his arms around her and squeezed hard, taking her completely by surprise.

"You really want me back, huh?"

"Do I!"

"Well, I'll think about it." He let her go, a little nervous about hugging somebody who wasn't Kerry right in sight of everybody. Kerry wouldn't blink, because it was Angie — but a lot of other people might start some nasty rumors. They had before.

"Look, I've got to go rescue Kerry from the chorus line over there. See you later." He was smiling as he walked her over to her brother and ducked away, over to the line of chairs against the wall. Angie gave the V for victory sign behind his back.

"Are you ready to dance yet?" Pres demanded as he swept Kerry up off her feet. "Because it's either that or I do a loony number by myself. I've got to blow off some steam, lady!"

"You're on," she murmured, stepping away from Mary Ellen, who'd been standing beside Kerry's chair for the past ten minutes.

"We'll be back when we fall down, Melon," Pres called to her, but she didn't hear him. Patrick was walking directly toward her, tall and determined and giving her that wide, lopsided grin that never failed to turn her insides to the consistency of hot oatmeal.

He didn't ask her to dance; he simply took both her hands and drew her toward him. They weren't on the dance floor, but suddenly, they were swaying together, their fingers interlaced, their bodies brushing with tantalizing eagerness.

And for the first time in a long time, Mary Ellen didn't give him a fight. She let herself be drawn forward, let her head drop heavily onto the front of his chest; let her eyes close dreamily as he led her in a small, slow circle. They might have been the only people in the room. As for Donny, she had no idea where he was, nor did she care.

"You smell so good," Patrick said at last, whispering below the sonic boom of the record. "I'm going to remember this smell when I go to sleep tonight."

She turned her head to him, looking into his dark eyes, feeling the wall of his muscles surrounding and encasing her.

"Kiss me, would you, Patrick?" she asked softly. It didn't matter that they were in the middle of the Tarenton High gym; it didn't even matter that the guy she'd come in with was somewhere nearby. Nor did it matter that she'd promised herself not to let Patrick get any closer than a room's length away. Tonight, she needed some security, some place of her own. And he wanted her — despite what Vanessa had said, she could sense it. He'd always wanted her.

His wavy forelock dipped over his right eyebrow as he stooped and placed his lips on hers. They were warm and wonderfully slow and easy on her anxious mouth. He simply let them both enjoy the moment, touching her gently. Their movement stopped completely, and for a moment, they were suspended in time.

"Just what the hell do you think you're doing?!" In the next instant, their contact was rudely broken. Mary Ellen felt Patrick wrenched out of her arms, and then she saw Donny. His face was red. There was no emotion in his eyes at all.

"We were dancing," Patrick said quietly. "Since you haven't danced with her all night, I figured she might be bored. Might be bored even if you *had* been paying attention to her," he chuckled.

Donny's arm was a steel piston, ready to pump. As Mary Ellen screamed, Walt, Hank Vreewright, and three other guys from the basketball team jumped on top of Donny, holding him off, but just barely.

"I'll fight for her, if you want to," Patrick told him brusquely. "But wouldn't it be more sensible just to ask her whether that's necessary?"

"Aw, who cares?" Donny spat at Mary Ellen, as he shook the guys off him angrily. "This thing's been over for weeks now. I'm glad to get her off my back. But you, mister," he growled at Patrick, "you just better stay out of my way." And with that, he stalked off, the muscles in the back of his neck bunched like a mass of granite.

The chaperones, too late to stop the fight, were busy trying to restore order on the floor and get the dance going again. The other kids were buzzing about the commotion, which made Mary Ellen feel exposed and bruised. Patrick's arm circled her protectively, and he tried to walk her away from the main action, but it was difficult. She was still the center of attention. Yes, it was true she'd wanted to end the relationship with Donny, but why did it have to be like this, in front of everyone? She could *feel* Vanessa smirking at her all the way across the room.

"Are you okay?" Pres was at her side in a second.

"Sure." She smiled weakly at him, then turned to Patrick. "You better take me home."

"Your wish is my command." Patrick, through the whole thing, had been cool as ice. He'd come to the dance with one purpose — to take Mary Ellen home — and now that she'd asked him to, he didn't need to preen or make a fuss.

"We're leaving, too," said Angie, who'd dragged her brother Andrew over as soon as she'd seen Donny march out of the gym. She took Mary Ellen aside for a moment. "I never could stand that overblown beanpole. He shoots a mean basket, but the rest of him is all over the court, if you know what I mean."

473

Mary Ellen nodded glumly, grateful for the support but still furious with herself for causing all this ruckus.

"I think I've had it, too, Pres," Kerry sighed. "Do you mind?"

"No, it's fine." He scanned the floor for Vanessa and A.J., but couldn't see them. Luckily, he'd managed to avoid them all night, and that was certainly okay with him.

Josh and Nancy, and Walt and Olivia were still dancing, still so wrapped up in one another that it would have been a shame to stop them to say good-night. Mary Ellen let Patrick help her into her jacket, and together, they walked steadily out of the gym, past the small crowd of gawkers, and down to the parking lot. Only the feeling of his hand holding hers kept her going. She didn't know whether this was going to be a turning point in her life or a night she'd regret as long as she lived.

She let Patrick help her up into the cab of his garbage truck and waved down at Pres, who was helping Kerry climb into the Porsche. The contrast might have amused her at some other time, but now, nothing seemed awfully funny.

"I love you, Mary Ellen. I hope you know that," Patrick said solemnly as he put his key in the ignition.

"I do. I've known for a long time." It wasn't much of an answer — she knew that — but it was all she could manage now. She didn't know how to deal with Patrick's love — how to accept it, enjoy it, and not let it take over her life.

CHAPTER

"You can't tell me you didn't have a wonderful time." Josh softly stroked the hair out of Nancy's face and let his hand rest for a moment on her cool cheek. They stood together on the porch of her house, listening to the wind and to each other.

"No, I can't tell you that," she admitted.

"And you can't deny that you and I really hit it off together," he persisted.

"All right, I give. We're a match. Good-night, Josh," she laughed gently, her hand on the doorknob.

"Nancy, you forgot something." He turned her around again, taking her by the shoulders. He was still smiling, but there was an intensity behind the grin that cancelled out any thought of laughter.

She could see herself reflected in his dark eyes, and feel herself melting. They drew closer, and then their bodies touched. She wrapped her arms around his neck and inhaled the sharp soap smell of him. He hugged her to him, his small, muscular form insisting on the kiss, holding her, demanding her response.

Just as their lips separated, the front door was pulled open. Nancy jumped so far away from him, she might have been executing a particularly difficult cheering maneuver. Her heart was going as if she'd run a mile.

"Oh, dear, I'm so sorry!" Her mother stood there in the dark, her robe wrapped around her. She ran her fingers nervously around the base of her neck. "I heard voices but no one was coming in and I just thought . . . oh, I'm really sorry!"

"What's going on?" Nancy's father, looking rumpled from sleep, stood behind her in his pajamas. "Is everything all right?"

"Yes, certainly, dear. Let's just get back to bed and let these two young people say good-night." Mrs. Goldstein, to her credit, remembered what it was like to come home from a dance and have your parents hovering in the background like hungry wolves about to pounce.

"I'll be right in, Mother," Nancy said softly. Had they seen Josh? He was hanging back, out of the dim glow of the porch light.

"You know, sweetie," her father said as he turned his back on them, "it's not against the house rules to invite the gentleman in for some hot cocoa. Except I guess you kids don't drink cocoa nowadays. Oh well, good-night."

There was a muffled chortle from the dark side of the porch. Josh had started to laugh and couldn't stop himself. Nancy looked despairingly in his direction, but it was too late. Her parents had already noticed his bush of dark hair and heard his distinctive laugh.

"Josh? Josh Breitman? Is that you?" Mrs. Goldstein took a step toward him. "Why Nancy, you never. . . ." She looked from one to the other, incredulous.

"Hi, Mrs. Goldstein, Mr. Goldstein." Josh walked into the light, coming over to shake each of their hands. "Nice to see you again."

"But Nancy, you always told us that. . . ." Her father rubbed his chin, then his thinning hair. "I will never in a million years understand teen-agers," he muttered as he rubbed his eyes. "Say, it's awfully cold out here. Could everyone please come inside?"

"Josh, it's so wonderful to see you," Mrs. Goldstein said. Nancy wanted to crawl under the porch.

"Uh, Nancy, I don't know if I should really come in right now. I kind of said I'd be home at a respectable hour — and it's been past 'respect-able' for hours."

Mrs. Goldstein sighed happily, relishing the very idea of a seventeen-year-old boy who did what his parents asked. "Of course. Well, we'll see you soon, I hope. Good-night, dear." She pushed her husband back inside and closed the door. Josh and Nancy could hear them on the other side, laughing.

"You're sunk now," Josh said to her quietly. "Cat out of bag; boyfriend's cover blown."

Nancy tried to look mad, but she couldn't. The

477

whole thing was too funny. "Did you see the expressions on their faces? I love it when I completely blow their minds." She giggled, then roared.

"Now you'll never get rid of me," Josh said happily, leaning over to kiss her nose. "They won't let you."

"That'll be my decision, mister. Now, get out of here."

He kissed her again, a soft brush of the lips that grew deeper as they stood there. She pulled away after a long time, breathless, craving more. Still, she couldn't help thinking of her parents somewhere on the other side of the door. It sort of put a damper on her ardor. "Call me tomorrow," she whispered as she ducked inside.

Josh Breitman could have flown home. But since he had the car with him, he decided he might as well drive.

"You're sure you want to go home alone?" Andrew Poletti looked at Angie through the open car window.

"Don't worry about me. You guys go get your ice cream sundaes and have a great time," Angie told him cheerily.

"But I've never known you to pass up ice cream before," her brother persisted. "You sure you're not sick?"

"I'm not sick — just feeling slightly flabby around the middle these days. You know, I have to at least try to stay normal-sized for cheering. Honest, that's the real reason. Now will you get out of here? They're waiting for you."

And indeed, as Andrew looked over toward the Ford pickup his pal Sonny was driving, the horn honked and eight kids yelled at him to get a move on. He shrugged and looked at her again. "Okay, tell Mom I'll be home in an hour." He started to walk away, then came back to her.

"What is it now?" She waggled a finger at him.

"Did you have a good time tonight?"

"I had a wonderful time," Angie asserted, "and a wonderful date. But now, I wish he'd get lost." Without further ado, she turned the key in the ignition and started off briskly, so he wouldn't have the chance to come back and bug her again.

She didn't really want to go home, and yet, there was nowhere else she really wanted to go, either, so she figured she might as well call it a night. The odd thing was, she'd been boyfriend-less before, and it had never gotten to her at all. She could go to a school dance by herself and have a ball and never think twice about the fact that she was going to end the evening without a good-night kiss, without so much as a friendly handshake. So why was tonight different?

Maybe it was seeing everyone she cared about matched up, even Walt and Olivia, for heaven's sake — and Walt had never been attached with anyone before. Maybe it was realizing, after her talk with Pres, how precious the fundamentals were. Of course, of all her friends, and certainly of all the guys on the team, she had the best family, hands down. Her mom and brothers kept her on target — they really cared deeply about what happened to her — and that was about as fundamental as you could get.

She missed Marc. She couldn't deny that. But she couldn't be expected to get over him within one month. She tried not to look back, not to feel sorry for herself. But something else was bothering her, and she would just have to forget it. That something was Patrick Henley.

What difference did it make if she'd recently been having lunch at his table, or going over her lab notes with him, or even walking from fifth to sixth period with him? None whatsoever. Because he was so stuck on Mary Ellen that other girls were merely background noise as far as he was concerned. And it was true that Angie and Patrick had never been more than good friends, whereas he and Melon had had this love-hate thing going for over a year now.

There were other guys she could date, and some of them really liked her. If Angie set her mind to it (except that she hated the idea of purposely going out to snag a boyfriend), she could probably go out with any one of half a dozen guys on a regular basis. Did she just develop this thing for Patrick because she knew he was unavailable? Was she that crazy?

She sighed as she pulled the car into the driveway and parked. Nothing was so bad, really. Nothing that was going to hurt so terribly in the long run. But tonight, she felt wistful. The thing of it was, she was happy that Melon had finally gotten rid of Donny. Could you be happy for someone else, and also a little mad at her because she had something you wanted, all at the same time?

"Home so early?" Rose Poletti was sitting in

front of the TV, knitting, when her daughter came in. "Turn that thing off, will you? I'm not even watching it. How was the dance? Did you have a good time? And where's your brother?"

"Don't be a worrywart," Angie cautioned her, kissing her on the top of her head. "Dance was fine; Andrew's out with the gang. I'm going to bed. See you in the A.M."

She was on her way up the stairs when she heard her mother say, "Dancing must be harder than cheerleading. You look pooped."

"Just a bit. I'll sleep well tonight."

And she would, too, if she could just resign herself to the fact that Patrick and Mary Ellen were now a unit. That was that.

Pres and Kerry sat in the Porsche for a good half hour and talked. He didn't tell her what Angie had said, nor what he'd vaguely promised her. He had to chew on that for a while, had to see how it fit in his scheme of things.

So instead, they covered all the likely topics: how crazy they were about each other (capped by a kiss), Mary Ellen's problem with guys, Walt and Olivia, Josh and Nancy, A.J. and how awful he was, and how crazy they were about each other (capped by another, longer kiss). It was after midnight when they said good-night and Pres reluctantly put the car in gear. He would have loved to have driven Kerry right back to the studio, made a fire, and curled up with her in front of it. He thought about going further than that. He thought about it a lot, but she was too young and anyhow, sex might mess up the great

481

thing they had going. What Kerry gave him was more than just physical thrills. She gave him part of her soul.

He drove slowly, savoring the quiet. Tarenton couldn't have been called busy at any time of day, (technically, there *was* a rush hour, except that it was only ten minutes long), but at night the town was like an empty shell, waiting to be filled. Pres loved the feeling of having it all to himself. The road was his, and he could drive as fast or as slow as he wanted. The big maples and sycamores were his, the bare branches arching over the narrow highways. And the night sounds were his, too — the scurry of a startled rabbit, the brisk wind, the creak of a cracked tree limb. Driving at night in Tarenton made Pres peaceful, as he never could be during the day.

He was cruising along, about fifty yards from his destination, when he noticed the smoke coming out of the studio's chimney. He *always* let the fire die down before he left the place — that was one thing he'd promised James. The answer was plain and neat: A.J. was ensconced again. And the lights were out, which meant that the louse had plopped down on the couch and gone to sleep, damn him.

With a set jaw, Pres parked and stalked up to the studio door. He stuck his key in the lock and turned it, but nothing happened. What was going on? He never double-locked this place — there wasn't any reason to. He turned the key around again and the door moved under his hand. But he didn't move. He didn't like what he heard inside.

"A.J.," he stated firmly in a loud voice.

Silence. He took a step into the room. Then he heard a covered whisper, and throaty, muffled laughter.

"Look, whatever you're doing in here, you better can it." He felt like a jerk, talking to the dark room.

Then he heard two feet hit the floor and the shuffling sound of someone coming toward him. The red beard looked lopsided in the pitch dark.

"What's going on, A.J.?" Pres asked indignantly. "I thought you said you'd stay in the main house."

"Sure, little cousin. I am. It's just a lot cozier in here, with the fire and all. Here, why don't you take the key back and *you* stay in the house tonight?"

Pres took the proffered key and peered at A.J. suspiciously. He was bare-chested and bare-footed, and even in the backlight of the wood-stove, he could tell that the guy was looking pretty smug.

"What'd you double-lock the door for?" Pres asked. He knew there was something going on, and he intended to find out. Then he intended to get his studio back and throw the guy out.

"Can't a man have any privacy?" A.J. asked. "Listen, good buddy, I'd really like to continue this conversation some other time if that's okay with you. I've, uh, kind of got something going here, get it? So how about you get lost for a few hours?"

Pres took a step into the room. He could now make out another form on the couch, and it was female. "Sorry," Pres said staunchly. "Hate to break up the party, but she'll have to go. House rules. I told Uncle James there wouldn't be any overnight dates on the premises." He couldn't believe himself, acting so responsible. And it wasn't even his problem, strictly speaking.

"Boy, are you a party pooper," said a familiar husky voice from the vicinity of the couch. "Pres, we were just making out, nothing more serious than that — so far." Vanessa lifted herself up on one arm, and Pres could see in the firelight that she still had all her clothes on, although they'd been sort of rearranged.

"I said out." Pres felt perfectly wonderful about destroying Vanessa's good time.

A.J. sighed and padded back to the couch, where he helped himself to the cigarettes lying on the end table. He lit two at once and handed one to Vanessa, which she held out before her like the Statue of Liberty brandishing her torch.

"I've put up with a lot from you, A.J.," Pres continued. "But I told your father I'd see to it that nothing got out of hand here."

"Nothing's out of hand, little cousin. Vanessa and I just have this date, see?"

"Not in the studio you don't. And not in the main house either. Why don't you take her home to the Barlow residence and see what the superintendent of the Tarenton schools has to say about it?"

A.J. frowned, then looked over at Vanessa, who suddenly seemed very bored. "C'mon, honey," he said to her, throwing a couple of shoes in her direction. "Somebody has just rained on our parade. Let's adjourn to the car."

"It's too cold in the car," Vanessa whined. Then she shrugged and stood up, rearranging her clothing precisely, making Pres watch. "You might as well take me home — now that he's spoiled everything."

Taking their time, the two of them gathered their things and sauntered to the door of the studio. Pres didn't move; he didn't say another word. He'd gotten his message across and he was oddly proud of himself. It was weird — when he was living with his parents, and before he met Kerry, he would have done just what A.J. was doing. A strange girl in a strange place. Tonight, though, he felt older and in control of the situation.

"Good-night," Vanessa growled at him as A.J. ushered her out the door.

"Hey, little buddy, I'll need that key to the main house back, now that you've evicted me." A.J. held out his hand, and Pres just let it hang there in mid-air.

"Key? That's funny, I thought I had it here somewhere." He pretended to search his pockets. "Must have lost it. I guess that means you sleep in the car tonight, *good buddy*." He closed the door on them, double-locked it, then leaned against it for good measure. There was nothing wrong with being a mean son-of-a-gun every once in a while, he thought. As he got ready for bed, he whistled a little tune, then threw another log on the fire.

CHAPTER

The six cheerleaders ran in a line, then physically threw themselves forward, cartwheeling their way across the floor. When they reached the other end of the gym, they repeated the move, but this time, they each added a back flip and a straddle jump before turning into the amazing whirling dervishes. Back again at home base, Walt and Josh hoisted Mary Ellen and Olivia into two spectacular flying mounts as Nancy and Angie did handstands in front of them.

The music stopped as they assumed the ending pose. No one breathed. And then, suddenly, the room went wild, with even a few Garrison High spectators unable to keep themselves from jumping to their feet and cheering as if for their own team. A perfect end to a perfect basketball halftime. Tarenton was beating Garrison, 31 to 22.

"Pretty good if I do say so myself," Josh whispered to Nancy, as they made room for the Pompon Squad and scuttled back to the sidelines.

"If only Donny didn't look like he was going to smash the ball into someone's face," Nancy said.

Mary Ellen looked slightly chagrined, but not a whole lot. If Donny wanted to sulk and pout, that was his business. As for her, she felt she was well rid of that relationship. She'd dated him for his looks, his status, his self-assurance — and now, a week after their breakup, it was clear to her how shallow Donny really was. And how shallow she must be to have wanted someone like that so badly.

She watched him, trying not to let the others see she was watching him. As the second half wound down, he seemed to be working even harder, the sweat spraying off him every time he hurled himself into the air for a shot. Yes, he was very good at what he did. But so what? Patrick was kind and sexy and nuts about her. She had decided that this time, she'd be able to keep her relationship with him on an even keel. It wouldn't get too hot and heavy; it would just be nice and very romantic. Certainly, she hadn't changed her mind about what Patrick Henley had to offer her, but that didn't mean she had to eliminate the possibility that he might change, in time. That he might actually learn to want the same things from life that she did.

When the final basket hit home, she raced the other cheerleaders up to the front for the closing cheer. She was sparkling, exhilarated, and Tarenton's win of 59 to 42 had very little to do with it.

> "Let's get the ball, now,
> Move it down the court!
> Never let 'em run away,
> With Tarenton's sport!
> Pass it, shoot it, dunk it, loot it!
> Win it is our aim!
> C'mon team! This is our game!
> Yay!"

Mary Ellen's blonde hair flew around her head as she led the cheer. Angie looked over at her, sensing something different about her, something that hadn't been there just an hour ago. She admired Mary Ellen for so many reasons, and one of them was her ability to turn on that crowd-pleasing dazzle any time she set her mind to it. She had seen Patrick in the stands, blowing kisses and making the most ridiculous lovesick faces at Mary Ellen throughout the game. It didn't really hurt Angie that much to see it, because he did look pretty silly. But then, she remembered from her own experience with Marc months ago, love sure does make you silly — among other things.

"Boy, could I use a swim about now," Olivia sighed as they filed out the back door of the gym, avoiding the worst of the cheering crowd's crush.

"You're on," Walt agreed, putting an arm around her. "Of course," he added, feeling her soaked cotton turtleneck, "you're wet already."

"Yeah, and *you're* all wet all the time," Nancy

smirked. "C'mon, girls, let's race these guys to the pool."

Technically, no one was supposed to be in the Tarenton pool after school hours, but Ardith had lobbied the head of the health ed department on behalf of her kids. She liked them to work out the kinks after a game, and swimming was certainly better for them than going on a soda-and-pizza binge. Since all of them had passed the junior lifesaving course, she wasn't worried about leaving them alone at the pool.

Walt and Josh were already doing laps when the four girls staggered out into the chlorine-filled atmosphere. The Olympic-sized pool had six lanes, five for serious swimmers and one larger one for the kids who just wanted to fool around. There was a net for water volleyball strung across it, and Angie executed a neat leap over it, nearly landing on top of Josh, who was doing a slow breaststroke in the second lane. "Yow! Watch it!" he yelped.

"Sorry, Josh." Angie splashed him lightly, then ducked under the rope, back into the first lane.

"You don't have to apologize to him," Nancy laughed. She was doing her leg lifts at the shallow end, pressing against the force of the water. "He's impervious to injury." And with that, she dove underwater, swimming toward him like a shark, aiming for his legs.

"Hey, what is this? How come everybody's ganging up on me?" Josh complained, fighting off his attacker with a low feint at her waist. "Sure glad it's almost track season and I won't have to hang around with you nuts anymore."

Nancy emerged from underwater, her hair dripping, to see the four faces on the other side of the ropes frozen with apprehension. "What's that? What'd you say?" she asked. "What'd he say?" she asked Mary Ellen, who had just swum to Walt's side at the deep end and was standing with only her head sticking out of the water.

"Josh, what did you mean by that?" Olivia demanded.

He laughed nervously, then looked at all the panicked faces. "Hey, I'm not leaving tomorrow, guys. I wouldn't strand you without a sixth cheerleader. I just meant, the season's changing, and once basketball and football are over. . . ."

The group continued to stare at him, and he grew increasingly more uncomfortable with the attention. "But you don't cheer in the spring-time — do you?"

"There are lots of group meets, and the state-wide championships, not to mention working up new routines for next season," Mary Ellen explained as calmly as she could. "We have plenty to do in the spring."

"Josh, you couldn't. You wouldn't." Nancy shook her head. She had grown to like him so much in the past few weeks, and now, all the things she used to hate about him were rising to the surface: selfishness, arrogance.

"Look, guys, hey, you're putting me in an awful spot," Josh said, feeling really stupid just standing around in the water. He hoisted himself up on one side and sat, his legs dangling in the water. "You knew I was on the track team last year, and Ardith told you I was just temporary. I mean, I've loved every minute of the cheering — well, after you all stopped being convinced that I was a klutz, I mean — and it's been terrific being part of your team. But what can I say? It's not my goal in life or anything like that."

"That means we'll have to find another guy," Angie said quietly.

"I don't think Ardith wants to do that again," Olivia cut in. "I overheard a couple of the kids on the Pompon Squad saying that if we lost another Varsity member, they might just scrap the old team and start fresh with six new people."

"They couldn't do that!" Mary Ellen was horrified by the news.

"They might," Nancy said solemnly. She looked at Josh again. "Please say you won't cut out now."

Josh wiped a few drops off his face, then looked around at their anxious faces. "I can't promise that, Nance. Sorry."

When nobody said anything, he shrugged, then grabbed his towel and walked down the side of the pool toward the exit door. He didn't look back.

"I never even dreamed he might quit," Olivia moaned.

"Me, either." Angie climbed up the steps on the shallow side and made a turban of her towel around her wet blonde hair. "Well, back to the drawing board, huh, guys? I'm going to take a long, hot shower and ponder this one." She walked to the girls' exit and disappeared quickly from the humid room.

Nancy felt awful, almost as if she were to blame for this. After all, she should have known — she could have warned them. But why hadn't Josh mentioned it to her? Because he just assumed that she knew? Shaking her head, she got out of the pool, too, and then Olivia followed suit. Nobody felt like splashing around in the water anymore.

"See you outside, Walt," Olivia said quietly as she walked past Nancy. "Give me a while to get my hair dry."

That left Mary Ellen and Walt, standing in the deep end with only their heads above water. And this was a precise mirror image of the way they both felt — up to their necks in trouble.

"Walt," Mary Ellen grimaced, "we're in the midst of a crisis."

"And I thought the whole thing was fixed. I mean, losing Pres was awful, and breaking in a new guy was tough, but this is *really* bad news."

"We've all been much too pie-in-the-sky about our future as a team," Mary Ellen said, leaning back against the soft water. She floated for a while without speaking, gazing at the ceiling of the pool room as though it might give her the answer she wanted. "The six of us — and I'm including Ardith," she continued at last, "we've all been beating ourselves to a pulp, working harder, doing more spectacular routines, hoping everything would get better. Instead, it's getting messier and messier. Sure, we've been doing great at our last few games, but nobody's going to remember that if we lose one more member. It'll mean splitting for good."

"You know what?" Walt said, running a hand over his water-slicked hair. "We need Pres back. And he *needs* to come back."

"Sure," Mary Ellen agreed, coming out of her float and swimming to the side of the pool, where she climbed up the ladder and sat on the edge. "So what else is new?"

"I personally don't think Pres is all that happy with his new arrangement, particularly since that wacko cousin of his moved in. His grades have been going steadily downhill — Kerry let that slip — and he seems pretty torn up about not seeing his parents. Maybe I'm imagining that part, but I don't think so. I tried to put myself in his shoes the other day, and I decided it would be damn hard to swallow my pride and go back home. But if I was miserable enough, I just might."

"Are you saying we should remind him how miserable he is?" Mary Ellen suggested, a hint of a smile on her lips.

"Not exactly. I don't think he needs any reminders. What I'm suggesting is an alternative." Walt swung up beside her by one lift of his powerful arms.

"What do you mean?"

"Well, suppose, just for argument's sake, he moved in with me? Right now, he's breaking school rules because there's no one really supervising him. As I understand it, that uncle of his is hardly ever home, so he's on his own. But if he were staying with parents of another Tarenton High kid, it should be perfectly acceptable. My folks' house is plenty big enough, and they're

493

there all the time, except when they're around the community scouting out stories for their show. If Pres were under their wing, nobody could squawk about his breaking school rules. Even Vanessa couldn't make anything out of his living with the illustrious Manners family. What do you think?"

"Eureka!" Mary Ellen yelled, throwing her arms around his neck and toppling them both over into the water again with her enthusiasm. "That might do it. And it would only be a step away from a reconciliation with his own folks, I bet. Oh Walt, do you think your mom would agree?"

"Hey, sure. She and Dad love an audience, you know. They'll probably insist Pres go on their show some morning and talk about teenage rebellion and crime in the streets."

"You're great, Walt," Mary Ellen tossed over her shoulder, climbing up the ladder again and sprinting toward the locker room. "I can't wait to tell the others. And be sure you tell Josh everything's okay if he wants to go out for track. We're getting *Pres* back!"

Walt swam around in a slow circle, mulling over his plan. It would probably work, and Pres would probably be pretty grateful. It was even likely that Mrs. Oetjen would let him back on the squad. Only one thing bothered him, and that was such close proximity to Preston Tilford III. Walt liked being Mr. Hospitality, but he wondered if he could put a time limit on his invitation. Too much Pres around the house, as well as at school, might give him a slight inferiority complex.

He got out of the pool and dried himself off, then went to find Josh. But the locker room was empty, so he showered and dressed quickly, then grabbed his things and started for the parking lot. Olivia was waiting for him at the front door of the school building.

"You're pretty smart, you know," she said, wrapping her arms around his neck. "Mary Ellen just let the rest of us in on your brainstorm."

"Good idea, huh?"

"I think it's the best idea anyone's had yet."

He looked at her seriously, wondering about her reservations. "But. . . ?" he prodded.

She tucked her arm in his and together they walked out to the parking lot. "*But*," she admitted, "there may be a few loopholes, like Pres agreeing and your folks agreeing and Ardith and Mrs. Oetjen agreeing."

"You think it could work anyway?" he asked.

She didn't say anything. They walked to the Jeep in silence.

Angie took a deep breath and walked into the office. She waited quietly, smoothing her hair and rubbing her tongue around her teeth, just in case she'd gotten lipstick on them. She hadn't, of course, but it never hurt to check.

A young woman with dyed red hair done up in a fashionable sweep stood there staring at her. "May I help you?" she asked.

"I'd like to see Mr. Tilford, please," Angie

said in a solid voice. She didn't want to appear nervous or flustered in any way.

The secretary looked at her dubiously. "Do you have an appointment?"

"I'm afraid not," Angie stated bluntly. "But I know he'll see me. Just tell him it's about his son."

The woman paused a second, then opened the door so that Angie could step into another reception area, a wood-paneled room with huge oil paintings of clipper ships on every wall. She stood there, wishing she had something to do with her hands.

"Wait here, please. I'll see if he's free. Who shall I say wants to see him?"

"Angie . . . Angela Poletti. Uh, he doesn't know me, but I go to school with his son," she told the woman, sinking down into one of the nearest low plush leather chairs.

The secretary nodded, then left the room. Angie was too busy rehearsing her speech to look at any of the magazines that were piled neatly on the end table beside her.

So *this* was Tarenton Fabricators! The office spoke of money and hard work and power — all those things that Pres claimed to detest. And certainly she could understand his not wanting to work for his father. As crazy as she was about her mother, she knew it would be disaster if she ever started helping out at Rose Poletti's beauty parlor, in whatever capacity. Parents and children had to know where to draw the line — and working for a parent was simply out of the question as far as she was concerned. *Living* with a parent, on the other hand, was more than a necessity. It was a fact of life.

The secretary returned. "You may go in," she said briskly, showing Angie the way down the corridor. "I wouldn't take up too much of his time if I were you, though. He's a busy man," the secretary added.

Angie kept her eyes forward and walked to the door of Preston Tilford's office. A worried-looking man with steely gray hair and eyes sat before an enormous desk. There were exactly three pieces of paper cluttering it.

"Come in, please, have a seat." He rose, as he saw her stop in front of the open door.

"Thank you, Mr. Tilford. It's very kind of you to see me," Angie said in her politest tones. "It's about Pres," she went on.

"Yes, well. . . ?" He looked impatient even as he ushered her to a high-backed leather arm-chair and began to pace in front of the large picture window on the opposite wall.

"Mr. Tilford, Pres doesn't know I'm here, and he'd probably kill me if he did." She laughed, trying to break the tension, but got no response. "I'm one of the kids on the cheerleading squad, see. . . ."

"Oh, that group that Preston had belonged to," Mr. Tilford said with a touch — just a touch — of disdain.

"But he still does belong, you see. Oh, we got a replacement when the principal docked Pres, but it wasn't the same. You know, it's like in business," she said, fishing for a comparison Mr. Tilford would readily understand. "When you have an item that's selling, you don't try to sell something else in its place. Right?"

"I suppose so." He stopped pacing and leaned back against the windowsill, his long legs in their neatly pressed gray pin-striped pants stretching out before him. "But there's nothing I·can do about that, young lady. Pres has made his choice."

Angie sighed. Now came the hard part. "Well, he did make a choice, that's true. But we all have a right to reconsider the decisions we've made. Sometimes, it just takes one push in a different direction." She looked into his face, but got nothing back. "You see, Mr. Tilford, he's not that happy living by himself, and even though he won't admit it to any of us guys on the squad, or even to Kerry, his girl friend, it's my gut feeling that he's ready to come home. The thing is, he doesn't think anyone *wants* him to come home."

"Why . . . why that's ridiculous. His mother and I have been waiting patiently all this time, and —"

"Maybe you *shouldn't* wait patiently. Maybe you should just rush in there and tell him what you feel. Not that it's my business to tell you what to do, sir," she continued hastily, "but it really would help if you'd go over to his uncle's studio and ask him back. He needs that."

Mr. Tilford looked exceedingly confused and not very pleased. "Young lady," he said, shaking his head, "in effect, you're telling me to go and beg my son to come back to the home that *he* decided wasn't good enough for him. That doesn't make much sense to me."

Angie was getting very exasperated. The man really was impossible. Everything had to be perfectly logical for him to get it. But if you loved your kid, you wouldn't give a flying hoot about logic. "Naturally, it's up to you. But I wish you'd go see him. Even if it's just to say hi and see how he's doing."

She got up because she had played all her cards and didn't have anything else to say. But with Preston Tilford, even the entire deck wouldn't be enough. "Thanks for your time, sir. I can find my way out."

"Nice to meet you, young lady." Mr. Tilford came around to her side of the desk, and to her surprise, he shook her hand. "It's good to know that my son has such fine friends."

"He does!" she exclaimed, and then she turned around and walked out.

All the way home in the car, Angie kept thinking about her meeting with Mr. Tilford. She hadn't really had great hopes of convincing him, but she'd thought at least that she could make a little headway for Pres. Walt's plan about living with the Manners seemed awfully half baked to her, but maybe that was because she was the kind of girl for whom family was family, and there were no intermediate steps on the way to being close with them. Other people weren't like her — she knew that — but she was certainly glad there weren't a lot of other people like Preston Tilford II, either.

CHAPTER

 12

Pres hated Tuesday nights because on Tuesdays, Kerry babysat for the lady across the street who went to some adult education class. As far as Pres was concerned, adults had had all the education they needed — and they were still grossly lacking in any basic intelligence.

So on Tuesdays, Kerry had to be home for dinner early, and that meant that Pres had virtually no time alone with her. Tonight he was sitting glumly in front of the fire, wondering what to do next.

The only good thing that had happened lately was that James had been home for five days straight, long enough for him and A.J. to really get on each other's nerves. A.J. finally agreed to go back to school because he was bored out of his mind in Tarenton. Pres never mentioned the incident with Vanessa — he didn't have to. A.J. spoiled everything for himself just by sticking his big foot in his big mouth.

It got him thinking, though, about himself and his own father. Of course, the situation was entirely different: A.J. had wanted to come home, and Pres wanted to stay away from home. But did he? For all the aggravation, for all the cold looks and closed doors and the stupid fights that never went anywhere, he kind of missed the house on Fable Point. He missed his room and his old routine, and the good meals. Maybe, just possibly, he missed his parents, too. Not that he really liked them or believed that stuff about absence making the heart grow fonder. (*What heart?* he'd have said about his father.) But still and all, he got something out of that home of his. Maybe he liked the fact that being with Felicia and Preston Tilford II made him aware of how different he was from them.

He was so engrossed in his fog, he scarcely heard the sound of a car pulling up in front of James's house. Then another. He jumped up and went to the window.

Walt and Olivia led the way, and Mary Ellen came next, followed by Angie, Nancy, and that new guy, Josh. What were they doing here? He wasn't sure he wanted the new guy on the team in his house, but he couldn't very well tell him not to come in. He opened the door for them and they filed in slowly.

"Hey, guys, how's it going?" he asked cheerily. He couldn't help but notice that everyone looked extremely serious.

"Pres, we've come for a summit conference," Olivia told him grimly.

"We want you to listen and keep your trap

shut — if that's possible," Walt continued. "So sit down."

"Hey, what is all this?" Pres demanded, sitting cross-legged on the floor. The others sprawled out around him.

"Well, I guess it's mainly my fault," Josh said sheepishly. "I got everyone on the alert because I let them know I was going out for track again in the spring, which meant the squad would be one man short again. So after they decided they wouldn't murder me, and after Nancy reluctantly agreed to keep going out with me — even though I was a loathesome specimen of the human race — everyone figured we better come see you."

Nancy gave Josh a disparaging look, but when he put his arm around her, she sighed and relaxed into it. She couldn't stay mad at him.

"Where do things stand on your moving back home, Pres?" Mary Ellen asked quietly.

"Things stand just where they've been for the past month — in limbo," Pres shrugged.

"Not necessarily," Angie said.

"Hey, for me, nothing's changed. I'm sitting tight."

Walt took a deep breath and started talking in his low rumble, very slowly and carefully, so Pres wouldn't miss a word. "Look, how about we try this?" Walt offered. "My folks' place could be a safe house for a delinquent like you. If they take you in, you'll have a Tarenton parent looking over your shoulder. Not your parent, but close enough. Get it?"

502

"Walt, it's cool of you to ask. But I might as well just stick it out where I am. I mean, a house is a house, right?"

"No, it's not," Nancy pointed out. "This is a legitimate way to get you back on the team. We're not thinking of you — this is a pretty selfish move on our parts. And since Josh won't cooperate," she gave her boyfriend a despairing glance, "*you're* it. You have to go along with our plan. And that's that."

Pres looked at the floor, then into the bright crimson glow of the fire. "I'll think about it. I mean, I'd kill to get back on the team, but I can't see that moving in with somebody else's parents is the solution."

"There *is* another solution," Angie reminded him.

He was about to answer her when the sound of another car purring to a halt made them all look up. Pres got to his feet. He was such a motor-head, he *knew* the sound of that engine. It was his father's Mercedes, without a doubt.

"Oh boy, I can't believe this!" he muttered.

"Hey gang, time to split." Angie was with him at the window, nearly jumping up and down in her gleeful anticipation of the moment that was about to be. "See you at practice tomorrow, kid," she sang out, punching Pres playfully on the shoulder.

The others looked very confused as she led them out onto the path, steering clear of the rather determined man who was stalking up the path as if he was being pushed by a stiff wind. Angie offered a "Good-night, Mr. Tilford," as she

503

got into Josh's car after Nancy and Mary Ellen, but he didn't hear her. His mind was elsewhere.

Pres swallowed hard, then rubbed his hands on his chinos. Despite the chill air coming through the open door of the studio, he was sweating. "Hi, Dad," he said softly, looking at his father's lined face. God, he hadn't seen him in so long!

"Pres, how are you?" Mr. Tilford walked into the tiny studio, and it seemed to shrink in size as he took its measure. Funny, Pres thought, there could be seven kids in here at once and it didn't seem at all crowded. Now, however, there was scarcely room to move around.

His father stood in front of the fire for a minute, then sat on the couch, looking extremely uncomfortable. "I haven't been inside this place since just after James finished building it — what was it, ten years ago? It's not too bad, actually." He chuckled a little, but Pres could tell he was just making chit-chat for the sake of filling air space.

"How *is* James?" he asked, when his son just stood there.

"Oh, he's great. In and out a lot, you know, because he's doing so many shows these days. This is some of his stuff."

His father stared at the easel holding the painting of the green man and the blue and yellow woman in a clinch. He frowned for a second, then rolled his eyes to the ceiling. "I don't really understand modern art."

"Me, neither," Pres confessed. Well, at least they had *one* thing in common. They both thought that painting was weird.

"Pres, listen," his father began, sitting forward in his seat. "Your mother and I. . . ." He stopped, considering his words carefully. It seemed to be hard for him to get the right ones in combination, which kind of astounded Pres. He always thought of his father as right on the mark about everything.

"What I'm trying to say is," Mr. Tilford started again, "we'd like you to think about coming home. Will you?"

Pres bit his upper lip, turning away from his father. "Why should I?"

"Well, because it is your home, for one thing." Mr. Tilford heard himself beginning to sound angry, and stopped again. "And because, well, your mother misses you. And so do I," he added in a small voice.

Pres heard the words and tried to hear the meaning behind them. He couldn't let his father get away so easy. Anyhow, there had to be a catch to this. "We always fight — it's no good. And you're always jumping down my throat about every little thing I want to do. So maybe we're better off like this."

"Do you really think so? Because I don't." Mr. Tilford got up and walked over to his son, challenging him to look into those steely eyes. "I can be unreasonable, I'm aware of that. But you can be, too, you know. Like father, like son."

Pres looked at him curiously. Was that possible? Was he really just as pig-headed and stubborn as his father? "Look," he said, wanting to give a little, "I could come back for maybe a trial period, okay? But if it doesn't work out, that's it."

"I don't want any ultimatums from you," his father stated firmly. "If you're home, you're home. And we'll work things out next time."

"Like what? Like that job you were going to force me into?"

Mr. Tilford shook his head. "All right, that was a mistake. I'll admit it."

"And like my cheerleading? You think that's just about the pits, don't you?"

His father's mouth twisted as he searched for the right answer to Pres's question. "It's not what I'd choose for you, no. In my day, of course, it would have been unheard of for a young man with your potential to lead cheers at school games. But I can't deny that things have changed. And that team does seem to be made up of some nice boys and girls. Maybe cheerleading isn't the worst thing in the world, after all."

Pres's face lit up. "You mean that? I can go back on the squad?"

"If you like." His father's harsh face looked softer in the firelight, and as he started for the door, Pres had an urge to go after him. "I'll be waiting at home for you. I hope to see you within the next few hours."

But then, he felt Pres's hand on his arm and he stopped, turning to face him.

"Dad," Pres said, "I've been thinking about this for a long time. I don't really need to chew it over any more. I guess I was just waiting for you to tell me you still wanted me. Let's go home together, okay?"

The smile on his father's face was real and heartfelt. "It would be my pleasure."

"Right after we go say thanks to Uncle James for putting up with me for so long," Pres said, his own grin threatening to crack his cheeks. He knew this would be the ultimate test. His father hadn't talked to James in years, and probably had no intention of doing so now.

"Well, I. . . ." Mr. Tilford procrastinated.

"What about burying a few hatchets all at once?" Pres suggested softly.

His father hesitated for only a minute. Then he shrugged and said, "That might not be such a bad idea." Mr. Tilford laughed, knowing that his son had him where he wanted him. In his own way, Pres was just as clever a manipulator as he himself, and he was hooked. "Shall we?"

And together, matching stride for stride, they walked out of the little studio and up the path to James's house.

The away game at Wickfield was going to be tough. The Tarenton Wolves had won three straight football games, just squeaking by in the last game with a spectacular touchdown in the final seconds of play. As the crowd started filing through the gates early on that crisp Saturday afternoon, there was a feeling of expectation in the air. Would they or wouldn't they?

The Varsity team always came early so they could warm up, but today, by special arrangement with Ardith, they had done their preliminary practice in their own gym. The surprise they had in store was simply too good to spoil. So they arrived with everyone else, with little time to spare in the dressing rooms where they'd put on their uniforms and get ready to burst on the scene.

Nancy and Josh got there first, but Walt and Olivia pulled in right beside them moments after they'd picked a prime space in the Wickfield parking lot. Unfortunately, none of them saw that Vanessa had parked four cars over and was lying in wait.

"Oh, this is going to be super!" Olivia squealed, relishing the feeling of Walt's strong arms around her delicate waist.

"And what a day for it," Nancy said decisively. It was, too, with pillowlike clouds floating in a gigantic sea of azure, tinged with just a hint of rosy pink. The girls' faces were ruddy from the cold, but luckily, there was no wind at all.

"Hi, guys, are we late?" Mary Ellen and Angie piled out of Patrick's truck, and he walked them over to the group, an arm around each of them. Neither girl seemed to mind at all. Sharing was perfectly copacetic on a beautiful day like today.

"Right on time," Walt smiled, tugging Olivia forward. "But we better get moving and get changed. I can feel it in the air — we're gonna slaughter 'em today!"

"That's all very optomistic, isn't it?" they heard a husky voice say right behind them. "But as I understand it, you six will be rather down in the dumps before long. Not that I can predict the future or anything." Vanessa, dressed in her old raccoon coat with a fur cap set jauntily on her dark hair, positively gleamed with evil intent.

"Oh, do please look into your crystal ball and

tell us what's up, Vannie," Angie insisted, snuggling a little closer to Patrick.

"It's gotta be a beaut," Patrick chortled, "or you wouldn't look so darn smug about it."

"Well, word is out that they're going to put together a whole new cheerleading squad for the spring and summer meets and competitions. Since Pres is out and since rumor has it that Josh isn't sticking around, everybody just thought it might be better to start from scratch — maybe get all girls this time," she added pointedly.

"Oh, and who's this everybody, Vanessa?" Pres and Kerry walked up to the group, their hands linked. "Your father maybe?"

"Maybe, Pres." She gave her little catlike smile, her claws all ready to scratch.

"Oh, is that so!" Nancy sputtered. "Well, you know, Vanessa, sometimes it's better to watch and wait. Sometimes things work out."

"They certainly might for me." Vanessa tossed this statement off as lightly as she could. "I was next in line for a place on the squad, so I could very well be a shoo-in if they assembled a new one. All of you guys have had your chance anyway. You're old hat by now. The crowds are getting sick of you."

"Not as sick as we are of you, Van," Walt said disgustedly. Then he jerked his head toward the side gate of the stadium. "Let's get in there and get dressed, gang." They all marched away from the annoying presence and toward the back of the bleachers, united in their dislike of Vanessa. Then, at the doors to the dressing rooms, they split apart.

"Let's give that dumb kid a run for her money," Josh suggested.

"Right on," Patrick agreed.

"Be wonderful, all of you," Kerry told them with a special look in her eyes for Pres, who took his place with his team proudly.

"So tell me," Josh asked him, "what's it like living at home again?"

"Yeah," Angie chimed in. "Can you bear it?"

He looked around at the circle of friends who were his closest allies. "You know," he said slowly, "it's not as bad as I remembered. Maybe being with my folks isn't such a terrible idea — for another year, anyhow."

They all turned at the sound of Ardith, slightly out of her mind, who nearly screeched as she approached them. "Aren't you ready yet? The game's about to start, for heaven's sake!" They scattered fast, making tracks toward their respective dressing rooms.

The stands were filled and waiting when the Tarenton Varsity team raced onto the field. And then, an audible cheer went up as the crowd saw the team's lineup. It was Mary Ellen at the forefront, followed by Walt, Olivia, Angie, and Nancy. Pres Tilford brought up the rear! With a death-defying set of cartwheels and aerial spins, he sat every person in the bleachers on their ear. The girls did banana jumps around him, making way for his next tumbling feat, which was a triple back flip followed by a stag leap. He came out of the move to a standing ovation, and he knew he deserved it. All the energy that had been bottled in him for so long was spilling out now, all over the whole stadium. Even when the football players ran out, their names booming over the loudspeaker system, the crowd's eyes were still on him.

The music started and the cheerleaders took their places.

"What's the ticket to VICTORY?
It's power, skill, and ENERGY!
We're the best — now don't say no,
Give us a hand and let us GO!

"Down that field! Move it on down!
Start the game, let's go to town!
Tarenton's a winner, can't be beat!
Knock their socks right off their feet!

"Give it all you got!
Tarenton's hot!
Yeah, team! W-I-N!"

Patrick, Josh, and Kerry looked down from the stands, yelling themselves hoarse. They watched the scarlet and white uniforms flash, the high kicks and spins making both colors run together against the brilliant blue sky. Mary Ellen, Angie, Nancy, Walt, Olivia, and Pres had something indefinable, something so special it couldn't be tampered with. They were a team . . . for better or for worse. They knew what the better was, but they wondered if they'd seen the worse.